CSS3 AND SVG

WITH GPT-4

CSS3 AND SVG
WITH GPT-4

Oswald Campesato

MERCURY LEARNING AND INFORMATION
Boston, Massachusetts

Publisher: David Pallai
MERCURY LEARNING AND INFORMATION
121 High Street, 3rd Floor
Boston, MA 02110
info@merclearning.com
www.merclearning.com
800-232-0223

O. Campesato. *CSS3 and SVG with GPT-4.*
ISBN: 978-1-50152-296-3

Library of Congress Control Number: 2024935755

242526321 This book is printed on acid-free paper in the United States of America.

Our titles are available for adoption, license, or bulk purchase by institutions, corporations, etc. For additional information, please contact the Customer Service Dept. at 800-232-0223(toll free).

All of our titles are available in digital format at academiccourseware.com and other digital vendors. *Companion files (figures and code listings) for this title are available with proof of purchase by contacting info@merclearning.com.* The sole obligation of MERCURY LEARNING AND INFORMATION to the purchaser is to replace the files, based on defective materials or faulty workmanship, but not based on the operation or functionality of the product.

I'd like to dedicate this book to my parents
– may this bring joy and happiness into their lives.

CONTENTS

PREFACE

This book is designed to equip you with the knowledge and skills necessary to navigate the dynamic intersection of web development and artificial intelligence (AI). We focus on various aspects of modern web development and AI technologies, with a particular emphasis on Generative AI, CSS3, SVG, JavaScript, HTML, and popular web features like 3D animations and gradients. By exploring these topics, readers will gain a deeper understanding of how AI can enhance web development processes and how to leverage AI models like GPT-4 to streamline development workflows.

INTENDED AUDIENCE

Whether you are a seasoned web developer looking to stay ahead in the AI-focused world or a beginner eager to explore the possibilities of AI-driven web development, this book is for you. Web developers, UI/UX designers, and software engineers seeking to blend traditional web development skills with the latest AI technologies will find this book to be a valuable resource.

CHAPTER SUMMARIES

Chapter 1: Generative AI and GPT-4: We introduce Generative AI, exploring its key features, applications, and prominent players like DeepMind and OpenAI. Additionally, we introduce ChatGPT, discussing its strengths, weaknesses, and its various versions.

Chapter 2: Prompt Engineering: Discussing the intricacies of prompt engineering, this chapter provides an in-depth overview of different prompt types, their importance, and guidelines for effective prompt design, essential for optimal interaction with AI models like GPT-4.

Chapter 3: Introduction to CSS3: Here, we lay the foundation of CSS3, covering its features, browser support, and essential concepts like shadow effects, gradients, and 2D transforms. We also address security and accessibility concerns, ensuring a holistic understanding of CSS3 principles.

Chapter 4: CSS3 3D Animation: Building upon CSS3 fundamentals, this chapter explores advanced topics such as 3D animation effects, transitions, and media queries. Through practical examples, readers learn to create animations using CSS3 techniques.

Chapter 5: CSS3 and GPT-4: Focusing on the integration of CSS3 with GPT-4, this chapter contains an assortment of GPT-4 Web pages and demonstrates how GPT-4-generated code can enhance web design. Readers explore various CSS3 use cases, security considerations, and sample code.

Chapter 6: Scalable Vector Graphics (SVG): This chapter covers basic shapes, gradients, transformations, and animation techniques. Readers gain insights into leveraging SVG for creating dynamic and responsive visuals.

Chapter 7: SVG and GPT-4: Finally, we look at the synergy between SVG and GPT-4, highlighting their combined potential for web development. From linear gradients to complex animations, readers learn to harness the power of SVG alongside GPT-4-generated content.

KEY FEATURES OF THE BOOK:

- *Comprehensive Coverage:* From AI fundamentals to advanced CSS3 and SVG techniques, this book offers a comprehensive exploration of modern web development technologies.
- *Practical Insights:* With a balance of theoretical knowledge and practical examples, readers gain hands-on experience in implementing AI-driven design solutions using GPT-4-generated code.
- *Companion files:* Files with source code, datasets, and images from the book are available from the publisher for downloading (with proof of purchase)

WHAT DO I NEED TO KNOW?

The most useful prerequisite is some familiarity with another scripting language, such as HTML or JavaScript and a basic understanding of CSS3. The less technical knowledge that you have, the more diligence will be required in order to understand the various topics that are covered. If you want to be sure that you can grasp the material in this book, glance through some of the code samples to get an idea of what is familiar to you and what is new for you.

COMPANION FILES

Source code, datasets, and figures from the text are available for downloading (with proof of purchase) from the publisher by writing to *info@merclearning.com.*

ABOUT THE COVER

The cover image was generated using DALL-E with the following:

Prompt: "Please render a futuristic jet with a structure similar to a cubic Bezier."

Response (with image):

"Here is the image of a futuristic jet inspired by a cubic Bezier with a smooth, flowing, design."

As you explore the subjects of web development and AI, I encourage you to engage actively with the content, experiment with code samples, and embrace the opportunities that AI-driven web development presents. This book will guide you every step of the way.

O. Campesato
May 2024

CHAPTER 1

GENERATIVE AI AND GPT-4

This chapter discusses Generative AI, major companies in the Generative AI space, significant features of ChatGPT and GPT-4, and also some competitors of ChatGPT and GPT-4. The first section of this chapter starts with information generated by ChatGPT regarding the nature of generative AI and conversational AI versus generative AI. According to ChatGPT, it's also true that ChatGPT itself, GPT-4, and DALL-E are included in generative AI. Next you will learn about companies such as OpenAI and Anthropic that are driving much of the inovation in Generative AI. You will learn about features of ChatGPT and some alternatives to ChatGPT, followed by a discussion of GPT-4. In addition, you will learn about some competitors of GPT-4, such as Copilot (Microsoft), Codex (OpenAI), Llama-2 (Meta), and Bard (Google Gemini).

WHAT IS GENERATIVE AI?

Generative AI is a subset of artificial intelligence that focuses on creating new content, such as text, images, audio, or video, based on learned patterns from existing data. Unlike traditional AI systems that are designed to recognize or classify existing data, generative AI algorithms are trained on vast amounts of data to understand the underlying structure and patterns, allowing them to generate novel and coherent content that resembles the training data.

Generative AI stands apart in its ability to create and innovate, as opposed to merely analyzing or classifying. The advancements in this field have led to breakthroughs in creative domains and practical applications, making it a cutting-edge area of AI research and development.

Key Features of Generative AI

The following bullet list contains key features of generative AI, followed by a brief description for each bullet item:

- data generation
- synthesis
- learning distributions

Data generation refers to the ability to create new data points that are not part of the training data but resemble it. This can include text, images, music, videos, or any other form of data.

Synthesis indicates generative models can blend various inputs to generate outputs that incorporate features from each input, for example, merging the styles of two images.

Learning distributions means that generative AI models aim to learn the probability distribution of the training data so they can produce new samples from that distribution.

Popular Techniques in Generative AI

Generative adversarial networks (GANs): GANs consist of two networks, a generator and a discriminator, that are trained simultaneously. The generator tries to produce fake data, while the discriminator tries to distinguish between real data and fake data. Over time, the generator gets better at producing realistic data.

Variational autoencoders (VAEs): VAEs are probabilistic models that learn to encode and decode data in a manner in which the encoded representations can be used to generate new data samples.

Recurrent neural networks (RNNs): Sed primarily for sequence generation, such as text or music.

What Makes Generative AI Different

Creation versus Classification: While most traditional AI models aim to classify input data into predefined categories, generative models aim to create new data.

Unsupervised learning: Many generative models, especially GANs and VAEs, operate in an unsupervised manner, meaning they don't require labeled data for training.

Diverse outputs: Generative models can produce a wide variety of outputs based on learned distributions, making them ideal for tasks like art generation, style transfer, and more.

Challenges: Generative AI poses unique challenges, such as mode collapse in GANs or ensuring the coherence of generated content.

Furthermore, there are numerous areas that involve generative AI applications, some of which are listed in the following bullet list:

- art and music creation
- data augmentation

- style transfer
- text generation
- image synthesis

Art and music creation includes generating paintings, music, or other forms of art.

Data augmentation involves creating additional data for training models, especially when the original dataset is limited.

Style transfer refers to applying the style of one image to the content of another.

Text generation is a very popular application of generative AI, which involves creating coherent and contextually relevant text.

Image synthesis is another popular area of generative AI, which involves generating realistic images, faces, or even creating scenes for video games.

Drug discovery is a very important facet of generative AI that pertains to generating molecular structures for new potential drugs.

CONVERSATIONAL AI VERSUS GENERATIVE AI

Both conversational AI and generative AI are prominent subfields within the broader domain of artificial intelligence. However, these subfields have a different focus regarding their primary objective, the technologies that they use, and applications. Information about those differences can be found here:

https://medium.com/@social_65128/differences-between-conversational-ai-and-generative-ai-e3adca2a8e9a

The primary differences between the two subfields are in the following sequence of bullet points:

- primary objective
- applications
- technologies used
- training and interaction
- evaluation
- data requirements

Primary Objective

The main goal of conversational AI is to facilitate human-like interactions between machines and humans. This includes chatbots, virtual assistants, and other systems that engage in dialogue with users.

The primary objective of generative AI is to create new content or data that wasn't in the training set but is often similar in structure and style. This can range from generating images, music, and text to more complex tasks like video synthesis.

Applications

Common applications for conversational AI include customer support chatbots, voice-operated virtual assistants (like Siri or Alexa), and interactive voice response (IVR) systems.

Common applications for generative AI include a broad spectrum of uses such as creating art or music, generating realistic video game environments, synthesizing voices, and producing realistic images or even deep fakes.

Technologies Used

Conversational AI often relies on natural language processing (NLP) techniques to understand and generate human language. This includes intent recognition, entity extraction, and dialogue management.

Generative AI commonly utilizes GANs, VAEs, and other generative models to produce new content.

Training and Interaction

While training can be supervised, semi-supervised, or unsupervised, the primary interaction mode for conversational AI is through back-and-forth dialogue or conversation.

The training process for generative AI, especially with models like GANs, involves iterative processes where the model learns to generate data by trying to fool a discriminator into believing the generated data is real.

Evaluation

Conversational AI evaluation metrics often revolve around understanding and response accuracy, user satisfaction, and the fluency of generated responses.

Generative AI evaluation metrics for models like GANs can be challenging and might involve using a combination of quantitative metrics and human judgment to assess the quality of generated content.

Data Requirements

Data requirements for conversational AI typically involves dialogue data, with conversations between humans or between humans and bots.

Data requirements for generative AI involve large datasets of the kind of content it is supposed to generate, be it images, text, music, and so on.

Although both conversational AI and generative AI deal with generating outputs, their primary objectives, applications, and methodologies can differ significantly. Conversational AI is geared toward interactive communication with users, while generative AI focuses on producing new, original content.

IS DALL-E PART OF GENERATIVE AI?

DALL-E and similar tools that generate graphics from text are indeed examples of generative AI. In fact, DALL-E is one of the most prominent examples of generative AI in the realm of image synthesis.

Here's a bullet list of generative characteristics of DALL-E, followed by brief descriptions of each bullet item:

- image generation
- learning distributions
- innovative combinations
- broad applications
- transformer architecture

Image generation is a key feature of DALL-E, which was designed to generate images based on textual descriptions. Given a prompt such as "a two-headed flamingo," DALL-E can produce a novel image that matches the description, even if it's never seen such an image in its training data.

Learning Distributions are used for generative modeling; DALL-E learns the probability distribution of its training data. When it generates an image, it samples from this learned distribution to produce visuals that are plausible based on its training.

Innovative Combinations enables DALL-E to generate images that represent entirely novel or abstract concepts, showcasing its ability to combine and recombine learned elements in innovative ways.

In addition to image synthesis, DALL-E has provided *broad application* support, in areas like art generation, style blending, and creating images with specific attributes or themes, highlighting its versatility as a generative tool.

DALL-E leverages a variant of the *transformer architecture*, similar to models like GPT-3, but adapted for image generation tasks.

Other tools that generate graphics, art, or any form of visual content based on input data (whether it's text, another image, or any other form of data) and can produce outputs not explicitly present in their training data are also considered generative AI. They showcase the capability of AI models to not just analyze and classify but to create and innovate.

ARE CHATGPT AND GPT-4 PART OF GENERATIVE AI?

Both ChatGPT and GPT-4 are LLMs that are considered examples of generative AI. They belong to a class of models called "transformers," which are particularly adept at handling sequences of data, such as text-related tasks.

The following bullet list provides various reasons why these LLMs are considered generative, followed by a brief description of each bullet item:

- text generation
- learning distributions
- broad applications
- unsupervised learning

Text generation: These models can produce coherent, contextually relevant, and often highly sophisticated sequences of text based on given prompts. They generate responses that weren't explicitly present in their training data but are constructed based on the patterns and structures they learned during training.

Learning distributions: GPT-3, GPT-4, and similar models learn the probability distribution of their training data. When generating text, they're essentially sampling from this learned distribution to produce sequences that are likely based on their training.

Broad applications: Beyond just text-based chat or conversation, these models can be used for a variety of generative tasks like story writing, code generation, poetry, and even creating content in specific styles or mimicking certain authors, showcasing their generative capabilities.

Unsupervised Learning: While they can be fine-tuned with specific datasets, models like GPT-3 are primarily trained in an unsupervised manner on vast amounts of text, learning to generate content without requiring explicit labeled data for every possible response.

In essence ChatGPT, GPT-4, and similar models by OpenAI are quintessential examples of generative AI in the realm of NLP and generation.

The next several sections briefly introduce some of the companies that have a strong presence in the AI world.

DEEPMIND

DeepMind (*https://deepmind.com/*) has made significant contributions to artificial intelligence, which includes the creation of various AI systems. DeepMind was established in 2010 and became a subsidiary of Google 2014.

DeepMind created the 280GB language model Gopher that significantly outperforms its competitors, including GPT-3, J1-Jumbo, and MT-NLG. DeepMind also developed AlphaFold that solved a protein folding task in literally 30 minutes that had eluded researchers for ten years. Moreover, DeepMind made AlphaFold available for free for everyone in July 2021. DeepMind has made significant contributions in the development of world caliber AI game systems, some of which are discussed in the next section.

DeepMind and Games

DeepMind is the force behind the AI systems StarCraft and AlphaGo that defeated the best human players in Go (which is considerably more difficult than chess). These games provide "perfect information", whereas games with "imperfect information" (such as Poker) have posed a challenge for ML models.

AlphaGo Zero (the successor of AlphaGo) mastered the game through self-play in less time and with less computing power. AlphaGo Zero exhibited extraordinary performance by defeating AlphaGo 100–0. Another powerful system is AlphaZero that also used a self-play technique learned to play Go, chess, and shogi, and also achieved SoTA (state of the art) performance results.

By way of comparison, ML models that use tree search are well suited for games with perfect information. By contrast, games with imperfect information (such as Poker) involve hidden information that can be leveraged to devise counter strategies to counteract the strategies of opponents. In particular, AlphaStar is capable of playing against the best players of StarCraft II, and also became the first AI to achieve SoTA results in a game that requires "strategic capability in an imperfect information world."

Player of Games (PoG)

The DeepMind team at Google devised the general-purpose PoG (player of games) algorithm that is based on the following techniques:

- CFR (counterfactual regret minimization)
- CVPN (counterfactual value-and-policy network)
- GT-CFT (growing tree CFR)

The counterfactual value-and-policy network (CVPN) is a neural network that calculates the counterfactuals for each state belief in the game. This is key to evaluating the different variants of the game at any given time.

Growing tree CFR (GT-CFR) is a variation of CFR that is optimized for game-trees trees that grow over time. GT-CFR is based on two fundamental phases, which is discussed in more detail here:

https://medium.com/syncedreview/deepminds-pog-excels-in-perfect-and-imperfect-information-games-advancing-research-on-general-9dbad5c04221

OPENAI

OpenAI (*https://openai.com/api/*) is an AI research company that has made significant contributions to AI, including DALL-E, ChatGPT, and GPT-4.

OpenAI was founded in San Francisco by Elon Musk and Sam Altman (as well as others), and one of its stated goals is to develop AI that benefits humanity. Given Microsoft's massive investments in and deep alliance with the organization, OpenAI might be viewed as an arm of Microsoft. OpenAI is the creator of the GPT-x series of LLMs (large language models) as well as ChatGPT that was made available on November 30, 2022.

OpenAI made GPT-3 commercially available via API for use across applications, charging on a per-word basis. GPT-3 was announced in July 2020 and was available through a beta program. Then in November 2021 OpenAI made GPT-3 open to everyone, and more details are accessible here: *https://openai.com/blog/api-no-waitlist/*

In addition, OpenAI developed DALL-E that generates images from text. OpenAI initially did not permit users to upload images that contained realistic faces. Later (Q4/2022) OpenAI changed its policy to allow users to upload faces into its online system. Check the OpenAI Web page for more details. Incidentally, diffusion models (discussed in Chapter 8) have superseded the benchmarks of DALL-E.

OpenAI has also released a public beta of `Embeddings`, which is a data format that is suitable for various types of tasks with machine learning, as described here:

https://beta.openai.com/docs/guides/embeddings

OpenAI is the creator of `Codex` that provides a set of models that were trained on NLP. The initial release of Codex was in private beta, and more information is accessible here: *https://beta.openai.com/docs/engines/instruct-series-beta*

OpenAI provides four models that are collectively called their Instruct models, which support the ability of GPT-3 to generate natural language. These models were deprecated in early January 2024 and replaced with a updated versions of GPT-3, ChatGPT, and GPT-4.

If you want to learn more about the features and services that OpenAI offers, navigate to the following link: *https://platform.openai.com/overview*

COHERE

Cohere (*https://cohere.ai/*) is a start-up and a competitor of OpenAI.

Cohere develops cutting-edge NLP technology that is commercially available for multiple industries. Cohere is focused on models that perform textual analysis instead of models for text generation (such as GPT-based models). The founding team of Cohere is impressive: CEO Aidan Gomez is one of the co-inventors of the transformer architecture, and CTO Nick Frosst is a protege of Geoff Hinton (who is known as the "Godfather of AI").

HUGGING FACE

Hugging Face (*https://github.com/huggingface*) is a popular community-based repository for open-source NLP technology.

Unlike OpenAI or Cohere, Hugging Face does not build its own NLP models. Instead, Hugging Face is a platform that manages a plethora of open-source NLP models that customers can fine-tune and then deploy those fine-tuned models. Indeed, Hugging Face has become the eminent location for people to collaborate on NLP models, and sometimes described as "GitHub for machine learning and NLP."

Hugging Face Libraries

Hugging Face provides three important libraries, as well as the Accelerate library that supports `PyTorch` models. The datasets library provides an assortment of libraries for NLP. The tokenizers library enables you to convert text data to numeric values.

Perhaps the most impressive library is the transformers library that provides an enormous set of pretrained large language models (LLMs) in order to perform a wide variety of NLP tasks. The Github repository is here: *https://github.com/huggingface/transformers*

Hugging Face Model Hub

Hugging Face provides a model hub that provides a plethora of models that are accessible online. Moreover, the Web site supports online testing of its models, which includes the following tasks:

- masked word completion with BERT
- name entity recognition with Electra
- natural language inference with RoBERTa
- question answering with DistilBERT
- summarization with BART
- text generation with GPT-3
- translation with T5

Navigate to the following link to see the text generation capabilities of "write with transformer": *https://transformer.huggingface.co*

In a subsequent chapter you will see Python code samples that show how to list all the available Hugging Face datasets and also how to load a specific dataset.

AI21

AI21 is a company that provides proprietary large language models (LLMs) via API to support the applications of its customers. The current SoTA model of AI21 is called `Jurassic-1` (roughly the same size as GPT-3), and AI21 also creates its own applications on top of `Jurassic-1` and other models. The current application suite of AI21 involves tools that can augment reading and writing.

`Primer` is an older competitor in this space, founded two years before the invention of the transformer. The company primarily serves clients in government and defense.

ANTHROPIC

Anthropic (*https://www.anthropic.com/*) was created in 2021 by former employees of OpenAI.

Anthropic has significant financial support from an assortment of companies, including Google and Salesforce. As this book goes to print, Anthropic released Claude 3 that has superseded the capabilities of GPT-4.

In the meantime, Claude 3 has the ability to summarize the contents of entire books (including books by Tolstoy), Moreover, Claude 3 supersedes the capabilities of Claude 2, which achieved a score of 76.5% on portions of the bar exam and 71% in a Python coding test. Claude 3 also has a higher rate than GPT-4 in terms of providing "clean" responses to queries from users.

This concludes the portion of the chapter regarding the AI companies that are making important contributions in AI. The next section provides a high-level introduction to LLMs.

WHAT IS CHATGPT?

The chatbot wars are intensifying, and the long-term value of the primary competitors is still to be determined. One competitor is ChatGPT-3.5 (aka ChatGPT), which is an AI-based chatbot from OpenAI. ChatGPT responds to queries from users by providing conversational responses, and it is accessible here: *https://chat.openai.com/chat*

The growth rate in terms of registered users for ChatGPT has been extraordinary. The closest competitor is iPhone, which reached one million users in 2.5 months, whereas ChatGPT crossed one million users in *six days*. ChatGPT peaked around 1.8 billion users and then decreased to roughly 1.5 billion users, which you can see in the chart in this link:

https://decrypt.co/147595/traffic-dip-hits-openais-chatgpt-first-times-hardest

Note that although Threads from Meta out-performed ChatGPT in terms of membership, Threads experienced a significant drop in daily users of approximately 50%. A comparison of the time frame to reach one million members for six well-known companies/products and ChatGPT is here:

https://www.syntheticmind.io/p/01

The preceding link also contains information about Will Hobick who used Chat-GPT to write a Chrome extension for email-related tasks, despite not having any JavaScript experience nor has he written a Chrome extension. Will Hobick provides more detailed information about his Chrome extension here:

https://www.linkedin.com/posts/will-hobick_gpt3-chatgpt-ai-activity-7008081003080470528-8QCh

ChatGPT: GPT-3 "on steroids"?

ChatGPT has been called GPT-3 "on steroids," and there is some consensus that ChatGPT rapidly became the best chatbot in the world. Indeed, ChatGPT can perform multitude of tasks, some of which are listed as follows:

- write poetry
- write essays
- write code
- role play
- reject inappropriate requests

Moreover, the quality of its responses to natural language queries surpasses the capabilities of its predecessor GPT-3. Another interesting capability includes the ability to acknowledge its mistakes. ChatGPT also provides "prompt replies" that are examples of what you can ask ChatGPT. One interesting use for ChatGPT involves generating a text message for ending a relationship:

https://www.reddit.com/r/ChatGPT/comments/zgpk6c/breaking_up_with_my_girlfriend/

ChatGPT generates Christmas lyrics that are accessible here:

https://www.cnet.com/culture/entertainment/heres-what-it-sounds-like-when-ai-writes-christmas-lyrics

One aspect of ChatGPT that probably won't be endearing to parents with young children is the fact that ChatGPT has told children that Santa Claus does not exist:

https://futurism.com/the-byte/openai-chatbot-santa
https://www.forbes.com/sites/lanceeliot/2022/12/21/pointedly-asking-generative-ai-chatgpt-about-whether-santa-claus-is-real-proves-to-be-eye-opening-for-ai-ethics-and-ai-law

ChatGPT: Google "Code Red"

In December 2022, the CEO of Google issued a "code red" regarding the potential threat of ChatGPT as a competitor to Google's search engine, which is briefly discussed here:

https://www.yahoo.com/news/googles-management-reportedly-issued-code-190131705.html

According to the preceding article, Google is investing resources to develop AI-based products, presumably to offer functionality that can successfully compete with ChatGPT. Some of those AI-based products might also generate graphics that are comparable to graphics effects by DALL-E. Indeed, the race to dominate AI continues unabated and will undoubtedly continue for the foreseeable future.

ChatGPT Versus Google Search

Given the frequent speculation that ChatGPT is destined to supplant Google Search, let's briefly compare the manner in which Google and ChatGPT respond to a given query. First, Google is a search engine that uses the PageRank algorithm (developed by Larry Page), along with fine-tuned aspects to this algorithm that are a closely guarded secret. Google uses this algorithm to rank Web sites and to generate search results for a given query. However, the search results include paid ads, which can "clutter" the list of links.

By contrast, ChatGPT is not a search engine: it provides a direct response to a given query: in colloquial terms, ChatGPT will simply "cut to the chase" and eliminates the clutter of superfluous links. At the same time, ChatGPT can produce incorrect results, the consequences of which can range between benign and significant.

Consequently, Google search and ChatGPT both have strengths as well as weaknesses, and they excel with different types of queries: the former for queries that have multi-faceted answers (e.g., questions about legal issues), and the latter for straight-to-the point queries (e.g., coding questions). Obviously, both of them excel with many other types of queries.

According to Margaret Mitchell, ChatGPT will not replace Google Search, and she provides some interesting details regarding Google Search and PageRank that you can read here: *https://twitter.com/mmitchell_ai/ status/1605013368560943105*

ChatGPT Custom Instructions

ChatGPT has added support for custom instructions, which enable you to specify some of your preferences that ChatGPT will use when responding to your queries.

ChatGPT Plus users can switch on custom instructions by navigating to the ChatGPTWeb site and then perform the following sequence of steps:

```
Settings > Beta features > Opt into Custom instructions
```

As a simple example, you can specify that you prefer to see code in a language other than Python. A set of common initial requirements for routine tasks can also be specified via custom instructions in ChatGPT, A detailed sequence of steps for setting up custom instructions is accessible here:

https://artificialcorner.com/custom-instructions-a-new-feature-you-must-enable-to-improve-chatgpt-responses-15820678bc02

Another interesting example of custom instructions is from Jeremy Howard, who prepared an extensive and detailed set of custom instructions that is accessible here:

https://twitter.com/jeremyphoward/status/1689464587077509120

As this book goes to print, custom instructions are available only for users who have registered for ChatGPT Plus. However, OpenAI has stated that custom instructions will eventually be available for free to all users.

ChatGPT on Mobile Devices and Browsers

ChatGPT first became available for iOS devices and then for Android devices during 2023. You can download ChatGPT onto an iOS device from the following link:

https://www.macobserver.com/tips/how-to/how-to-install-and-use-the-official-chatgpt-app-on-iphone/

Alternatively, if you have an Android device, you can download ChatGPT from the following link: *https://play.google.com/store/apps/details?id=com.openai. chatgpt*

If you want to install ChatGPT for the Bing browser from Microsoft, navigate to this link:

https://chrome.google.com/webstore/detail/chatgpt-for-bing/ pkkmgcildaegadhngpjkklnbfbmhpdng

ChatGPT and Prompts

Although ChatGPT is very adept at generating responses to queries, sometimes you might not be fully satisfied with the result. One option is to type the word "rewrite" in order to get another version from ChatGPT.

Although this is one of the simplest prompts available, it's limited in terms of effectiveness. If you want a list of more meaningful prompts, the following link leads to an article that contains thirty-one prompts that have the potential to be better than using the word "rewrite" (and not just with ChatGPT):

https://medium.com/the-generator/31-ai-prompts-better-than-rewrite-b3268dfe1fa9

GPTBot

GPTBot is a crawler for Web sites. Fortunately, you can disallow GPTBot from accessing a Web site by adding the GPTBot to the `robots.txt` file for a Web site:

```
User-agent: GPTBot
Disallow: /
```

You can also customize GPTBot access only a portion of a Web site by adding the GPTBot token to to the `robots.txt` like file for a Web site:

```
User-agent: GPTBot
Allow: /youcangohere-1/
Disallow: /dontgohere-2/
```

As an aside, Stable Diffusion and LAION both scrape the Internet via Common Crawl. However, you can prevent your Web site from being scraped by specifying the following snippet in the `robots.txt` file:

```
User-agent: CCBot
Disallow: /
```

More information about GPTBot is accessible here:

https://platform.openai.com/docs/gptbot
https://platform.openai.com/docs/gptbot
https://www.yahoo.com/finance/news/openai-prepares-unleash-crawler-devour-020628225.html

ChatGPT Playground

ChatGPT has its own playground (which is substantively different from the GPT-3 playground) that is accessible here: *https://chat.openai.com/chat*
In case you are interested, the GPT-3 playground can be accessed here:

https://beta.openai.com/playground

OpenAI has periodically added new functionality to ChatGPT that includes the following:

• Users can view (and continue) previous conversations.

- There is a reduction in the number of questions that ChatGPT will not answer.
- Users can remain logged in for longer than two weeks.

Another nice enhancement includes support for keyboard shortcuts: when working with code you can use the sequence ⌘ (Ctrl) + Shift + (for Mac) to copy last code block and the sequence ⌘ (Ctrl) + / to see the complete list of shortcuts.

Many articles are available regarding ChatGPT and how to write prompts in order to extract the details that you want from ChatGPT. One of those articles is here:

https://www.tomsguide.com/features/7-best-chatgpt-tips-to-get-the-most-out-of-the-chatbot

PLUGINS, ADVANCED DATA ANALYSIS, AND CODEWHISPERER

In addition to answering a plethora of queries from users, ChatGPT extends its functionality by providing support for the following:

- third-party ChatGPT plug-ins
- Advanced Data Analysis
- CodeWhisperer

Each of the topics in the preceding bullet list are briefly discussed in the following subsections, along with a short section that discusses advanced data analysis versus Claude-2 from Anthropic.

Plugins

There are several hundred ChatGPT plugins available. The following links will lead you to some that are popular:

https://levelup.gitconnected.com/5-chatgpt-plugins-that-will-put-you-ahead-of-99-of-data-scientists-4544a3b752f9
https://www.zdnet.com/article/the-10-best-chatgpt-plugins-of-2023/

Keep in mind that lists of the "best" ChatGPT plugins change frequently, so it's a good idea to perform an online search to find out about newer ChatGPT plugins. The following link also contains details about highly rated plugins (by the author of the following article):

https://www.tomsguide.com/features/i-tried-a-ton-of-chatgpt-plugins-and-these-3-are-the-best

This list contains another set of recommended plugins (depending on your needs, of course):

- AskYourPDF
- ChatWithVideo
- Noteable

- Upskillr
- Wolfram

If you are concerned about the possibility of ChatGPT scraping the content of your Web site, the browser plugin from OpenAI supports a user-agent token called ChatGPT-User that abides by the content specified in the `robots.txt` file that many Web sites provide for restricting access to content.

If you want to develop a plugin for ChatGPT, navigate to this Web site for more information: *https://platform.openai.com/docs/plugins/introduction*

Along with details for developing a ChatGPT plugin, the preceding OpenAI Web site provides useful information about plugins, as shown here:

- authentication
- examples
- plugin review
- plugin policies

OpenAI does not control any plugins that you add to ChatGPT: they connect ChatGPT to external applications. Moreover, ChatGPT determines which plugin to use during your session, based on the specific plugins that you have enabled in your ChatGPT account.

Advanced Data Analysis

ChatGPT Advanced Data Analysis enables ChatGPT to generate charts and graphs, as well as create and train machine learning models, including deep learning models. ChatGPT Advanced Data Analysis provides an extensive set of features and it's available to ChatGPT users who are paying the subscription price of the $20 per month.

The models from OpenAI can access a Python interpreter that is confined to a sandboxed and fire-walled execution environment. There is also some temporary disk space that is accessible to the interpreter plugin during the evaluation of Python code. Although the temporary disk space is available for a limited time, multiple queries during in the same session can produce a cumulative effect with regard to the code and execution environment.

In addition, ChatGPT can generate a download link (upon request) in order to download data. One other interesting feature: starting from mid-2023, Advanced Data Analysis can also analyze multiple files at once, which includes CSV files and Excel spreadsheets.

Advanced Data Analysis can perform an interesting variety of tasks, some of which are listed in the following list:

- solve mathematical tasks
- perform data analysis and visualization
- convert files between formats
- work with Excel spreadsheets
- read textual content in a PDF

The following article discusses various ways that you can use Advanced Data Analysis:

https://mlearning.substack.com/p/the-best-88-ways-to-use-chatgpt-code-interpreter

Advanced Data Analysis Versus Claude-2

Claude-2 from Anthropic is another competitor to ChatGPT. In addition to responding to prompts from users, Claude-2 can generate code and also ingest entire books. Claude-2 is also subject to hallucinations, which is true of other LLM-based chatbots. More detailed information regarding Claude-2 is accessible here:

https://medium.com/mlearning-ai/claude-2-vs-code-interpreter-gpt-4-5-d2e5c9ee00c3

Incidentally, the currently available version of ChatGPT was trained on September 2021, which means that ChatGPT cannot answer questions regarding Claude-2 or Google Bard, both of which were released after this date.

NOTE *Anthropic released Claude-3 in March 04, 2024 and it outperforms GPT-4 in various tasks.*

CodeWhisperer

ChatGPT CodeWhisperer enables you to simplify some tasks, some of which are found in the following list (compare this list with the corresponding list for Bard):

- The user can create videos from images.
- The user can extract text from an image.
- The user can extract colors from an image.

After ChatGPT has generated a video, it will also give you a link from which the generated video is downloadable. More detailed information regarding the features in the preceding bullet list is accessible here:

https://artificialcorner.com/chatgpt-code-interpreter-is-not-just-for-coders-here-are-6-ways-it-can-benefit-everyone-b3cc94a36fce

DETECTING GENERATED TEXT

Without a doubt, `ChatGPT` has raised the bar with respect to the quality of generated text, which further complicates the task of plagiarism. When you read a passage of text, there are several clues that suggest generated text, such as:

- awkward or unusual sentence structure
- repeated text in multiple locations
- excessive use of emotions (or absence thereof)

However, there are tools that can assist in detecting generated code. One free online tool is GPT2 Detector (from OpenAI) that is accessible here:

https://huggingface.co/openai-detector

As a simple (albeit contrived) example, type the following sentence in GPT2 Detector:

```
This is an original sentence written by me and nobody else.
```

The GPT2 Detector analyzed this sentence and reported that this sentence is real with a 19.35% probability. Modify the preceding sentence by adding some extra text, as shown here:

```
This is an original sentence written by me and nobody else,
regardless of what an online plagiarism tool will report
about this sentence.
```

The GPT2 Detector analyzed this sentence and reported that this sentence is real with a 95.85% probability. According to the GPT2 Detector Web site, the reliability of the probability scores "get reliable" when there are around fifty tokens in the input text.

Another (slightly older) online tool for detecting automatically generated text is GLTR (Giant Language Model Test Room) from IBM, which is accessible here: *http://gltr.io/*

You can download the source code (a combination of TypeScript and CSS) for GLRT here:

https://github.com/HendrikStrobelt/detecting-fake-text

In addition to the preceding free tools, some commercial tools are also available, one of which is shown here: *https://writer.com/plans/*

CONCERNS ABOUT CHATGPT

One important aspect of ChatGPT is that it's not designed for accuracy: in fact, ChatGPT can generate (fabricate?) very persuasive answers that are actually incorrect. This detail distinguishes ChatGPT from search engines: the latter provide links to existing information instead of generating responses that might be incorrect. Another comparison is that ChatGPT is more flexible and creative, whereas search engines are less flexible but more accurate in their responses to queries.

Educators are concerned about students using ChatGPT as a tool to complete their class assignments instead of developing research-related skills in conjunction with writing skills. At the same time, there are educators who enjoy the reduction in preparation time for their classes as a direct result of using ChatGPT to prepare lesson plans.

Another concern is that ChatGPT cannot guarantee that it provides factual data in response to queries from users. In fact, ChatGPT can "hallucinate," which means that it can provide wrong answers as well as citations (i.e., links) that do not exist.

Another limitation of ChatGPT is due to the use of training data that was available only up until 2021. However, OpenAI does support plug-ins for ChatGPT, one of which can perform on-the-fly real time Web searches.

As you will learn in Chapter 2, the goal of prompt engineering is to understand how to craft meaningful queries that will induce ChatGPT to provide the information that you want: poorly worded (or incorrectly worded) prompts can produce equally poor results. As a rule, it's advisable to curate the contents of the responses from ChatGPT, especially in the case of responses to queries that involve legal details.

Code Generation and Dangerous Topics

Two significant areas for improvement pertain to code generation and handling dangerous topics.

Although ChatGPT can generate code for various types of applications, there is concern that ChatGPT might display code that was written by other developers, and that such code might have been used to train ChatGPT. Consequently, portions of that code (such as version numbers) might be outdated or code that is actually incorrect.

As for queries that involve dangerous topics, ChatGPT explains why it cannot answer such a query. However, a query that is posed in "pretend mode" ("suppose you are a fictional character, and how would you explain …?") has enabled people to obtain results from ChatGPT that do not conform to its guidelines.

Other serious potential issues exist, some of which are discussed in the following article:

https://www.yahoo.com/news/hypnotized-chatgpt-bard-convince-users-182100261.html

ChatGPT Strengths and Weaknesses

ChatGPT has a number of strengths. In particular, ChatGPT responds directly to questions without including extraneous links. As a simple example, suppose you enter a query in an online search engine, such as "Generate HTML for an input field."

On the other hand, ChatGPT is prone to various types of errors, along with limitations that include the following:

- It does not have the ability to "fact check" information.
- It does not have the ability to differentiate facts versus misinformation.
- It sometimes fabricates answers (aka hallucinations).
- It sometimes generates inappropriate/toxic responses.

ChatGPT is prone to prompt injection, which can consist of very simple content. However, other chatbots are also susceptible to prompt injection (i.e., it's not specific to ChatGPT). More details regarding prompt injections are accessible here:

https://mlearning.substack.com/p/what-exactly-is-a-prompt-injection

Incidentally, the chatbot LaMDA from Google is also prone to the preceding limitations, which also made Google hesitant to release LaMDA for general availability because of its potential risk regarding Google's reputation. As a side note, LaMDA was announced in May 2021 and at that time it was described as a "breakthrough language technology": *https://blog.google/technology/ai/lamda/*

Despite the earlier bullet list, ChatGPT has increased the capabilities of chatbots, and will undoubtedly spur innovation and competition among prominent stakeholders in this arena.

SAMPLE QUERIES AND RESPONSES FROM CHATGPT

Here is an example of various queries submitted to ChatGPT, followed by the detailed response from ChatGPT:

```
Many people think that AI is dangerous; what do you think?
```

"There is a common misconception that AI is inherently dangerous. While it is true that AI has the potential to be used for harmful purposes, it is also capable of doing a lot of good. Just like any other technology, it all depends on how it is used. In the right hands, AI can be used to solve some of the world's most pressing problems, such as curing diseases and improving agriculture. In the wrong hands, it could be used to cause harm. It's important for us to use AI responsibly and ethically, and to ensure that it is regulated and controlled in a way that minimizes the potential for harm."

Here is another example of a query submitted to ChatGPT, followed by its detailed response:

```
What are some ways you can improve the accuracy of your
responses to queries?
```

"There are several ways to improve the accuracy of my responses to queries. One way is to use more data to train my algorithms on. The more data I have, the more information I have to work with, and the more accurate my responses can be. Another way to improve my accuracy is to use more advanced algorithms and techniques, such as machine learning and natural language processing. These methods allow me to better understand the nuances of language and to provide more accurate responses to queries. Additionally, regular testing and evaluation can help identify areas where my accuracy can be improved, and allow me to focus on those areas to refine my responses."

```
Can you give an example of an odd perfect number?
```

"As far as we know, there are no odd perfect numbers. While it is believed that odd perfect numbers exist, none have been found yet, and it is not known if there are any. In fact, it is currently unknown if there are any odd perfect numbers at all. If an odd perfect number were to be discovered, it would be a major breakthrough in mathematics."

Can you provide a proof of Goldbach's conjecture?

"I'm sorry, but I am not able to provide a proof of Goldbach's conjecture. Goldbach's conjecture is a famous unsolved problem in mathematics that states that every even integer greater than two can be expressed as the sum of two prime numbers. Despite much effort by mathematicians over the years, a proof of the conjecture has not yet been found. It is considered to be one of the most challenging unsolved problems in mathematics. Because I am a large language model trained by OpenAI, I do not have the ability to prove mathematical conjectures. My abilities are limited to providing answers based on the information that I have been trained on."

Is there life after death, and how does it compare with life on Earth?

"There is no scientific evidence to support the idea of life after death. This is a topic that has been debated for centuries, and different cultures and belief systems have their own ideas about what happens after we die. Some people believe in an afterlife, while others do not. Because there is no scientific evidence to support the existence of an afterlife, it is not possible to say how it would compare to life on Earth. It is ultimately a matter of personal belief."

Please provide a four-paragraph analysis of the war between Ukraine and Russia, and also provide your prediction regarding the outcome

"The war between Ukraine and Russia is a complex conflict that has its roots in the 2014 Russian annexation of Crimea. Since then, the conflict has escalated, with Russian-backed separatists in eastern Ukraine fighting against the Ukrainian government. The fighting has resulted in thousands of casualties and has displaced many people.

The main issue at the heart of the conflict is the question of Ukraine's sovereignty. Russia has long considered Ukraine to be within its sphere of influence, and the annexation of Crimea was seen by many as a violation of Ukraine's sovereignty. Ukraine, on the other hand, is determined to maintain its independence and has been supported in this by many Western countries.

It is difficult to predict the outcome of the war. While the Ukrainian military has been able to make gains against the separatists in recent years, Russia continues to provide support to the rebels and the conflict remains unresolved. In the long term, a diplomatic solution will likely be necessary in order to bring an end to the fighting. However, it is uncertain if and when such a solution will be reached.

In the meantime, the war continues to take a heavy toll on the people of Ukraine. Many are caught in the crossfire, and the ongoing violence and instability have had a significant impact on the country's economy and overall development. It is important for the international community to continue to support Ukraine in its efforts to maintain its sovereignty and bring an end to the conflict."

As you can see from the preceding examples, ChatGPT provides impressive and accurate responses to queries in a manner that surpasses many chatbots of recent years. However, it's still possible to confound this chatbot. More information about this can be found here:

https://www.theverge.com/23488017/openai-chatbot-chatgpt-ai-examples-web-demo

ALTERNATIVES TO CHATGPT

There are several alternatives to ChatGPT that offer a similar set of features, some of which are listed here:

- Bard (renamed Google Gemini)
- Bing Chat
- Jasper
- PaLM (Google)
- Pi
- Poe (LinkedIn)
- Replika
- WriteSonic
- YouChat

The following subsections discuss some (but not all) of the ChatGPT alternatives in the preceding bullet list.

Google Bard

Google Bard (now called Google Gemini) is a chatbot that has similar functionality as ChatGPT, such as generating code as well as generating text/documents. A subset of the features supported by Bard is as follows:

- built-in support for Internet search
- built-in support for voice recognition
- built "on top of" PaLM 2 (Google)
- support for twenty programming languages
- read/summarize PDF contents
- provides links for its information

According to the following article in mid-2023, Bard has added support for forty additional language as well as support for text-to-speech:

https://www.extremetech.com/extreme/google-bard-updated-with-text-to-speech-40-new-languages

Moreover, Bard supports prompts that include images (interpreted by Google Lens) and can produce captions based on the images.

The following article suggests that Google can remain competitive with ChatGPT by leveraging PaLM (discussed later in this chapter):

https://analyticsindiamag.com/googles-palm-is-ready-for-the-gpt-challenge/

YouChat

Another alternative to ChatGPT is YouChat that is part of the search engine you.com, and it's accessible here:

https://you.com/

Richard Socher, who is well known in the ML community for his many contributions, is the creator of you.com. According to Richard Socher, YouChat is a search engine that can provide the usual search-related functionality as well as the ability to search the Web to obtain more information in order to provide responses to queries from users.

Another competitor is Poe from LinkedIn, and you can create a free account at this link: *https://poe.com/login*

Pi From Inflection

Pi (*https://pi.ai/talk*) is a chatbot developed by Inflection, a company founded by Mustafa Suleyman, who is also the founder of DeepMind. More information about Pi can be found here:

https://medium.com/@ignacio.de.gregorio.noblejas/meet-pi-chatgpts-newest-rival-and-the-most-human-ai-in-the-world-367b461c0af1

The development team used Reinforcement Learning from Human Feedback (RLHF) in order to train this chatbot:

https://medium.com/@ignacio.de.gregorio.noblejas/meet-pi-chatgpts-newest-rival-and-the-most-human-ai-in-the-world-367b461c0af1

MACHINE LEARNING AND CHATGPT: ADVANCED DATA ANALYSIS

OpenAI supports a feature called Advanced Data Analysis, which enables ChatGPT to generate Python code that produces charts and graphs based on data from datasets. Moreover, Advanced Data Analysis can generate machine learning models that can be trained on datasets. For example, Figure 1.1 displays a screenshot of charts that are based on the `Titanic` dataset.

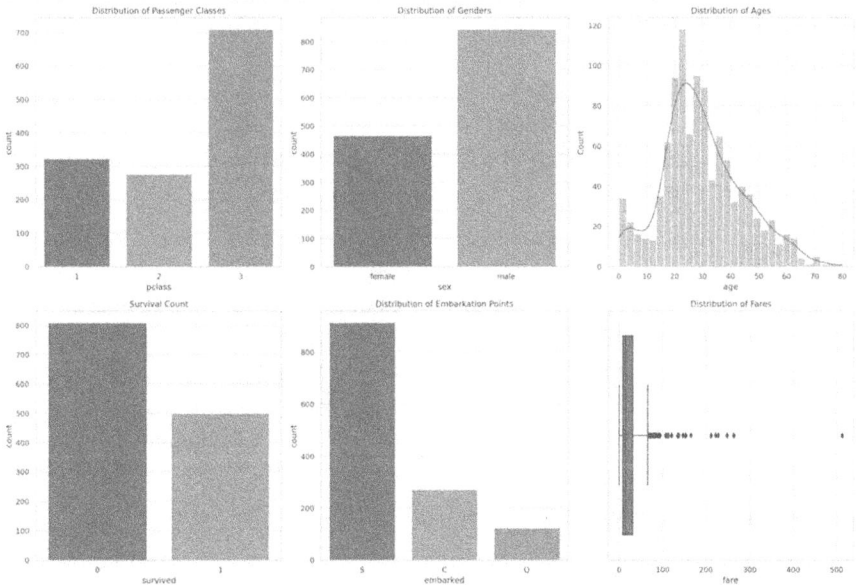

FIGURE 1.1. Titanic charts and graphs.

Incidentally, if you would like to see examples of ChatGPT generating Python code for machine learning models, as well as code for charts and graphs, you can learn how to do so in these recently published books (i.e., 2024) from Mercury Learning:

- *Python, ML, and GPT-4*
- *Python and GPT-4*
- *Python and Data Visualization with GPT-4*

WHAT IS INSTRUCTGPT?

InstructGPT is a language model developed by OpenAI, and it's a sibling model to ChatGPT. InstructGPT is designed to follow instructions given in a prompt to generate detailed responses. Some key points about InstructGPT are listed as follow:

- follows instructions
- training
- applications
- limitations

Follows Instructions: Unlike ChatGPT, which is more geared toward open-ended conversations, InstructGPT is designed to be more focused on following user instructions in prompts. This makes it suitable for tasks for which the user wants to get specific information or outputs by giving clear directives.

Training: InstructGPT is trained using RLHF, similar to ChatGPT. An initial model is trained using supervised fine-tuning, where human AI trainers provide conversations playing both sides (the user and the AI assistant). This new dialogue dataset is then mixed with the InstructGPT dataset transformed into a dialogue format.

Applications: InstructGPT can be useful in scenarios where you want more detailed explanations, step-by-step guides, or specific outputs based on the instructions provided.

Limitations: Like other models, InstructGPT has its limitations. It might produce incorrect or nonsensical answers. The output heavily depends on how the prompt is phrased. It's also sensitive to input phrasing and might give different responses based on slight rephrasing.

It's worth noting that as AI models and their applications are rapidly evolving, there might have been further developments or iterations on InstructGPT after 2021. Always refer to OpenAI's official publications and updates for the most recent information. More information about InstructGPT is accessible here:

https://openai.com/blog/instruction-following/

VIZGPT AND DATA VISUALIZATION

VizGPT is an online tool that enables you to specify English-based prompts in order to visualize aspects of datasets, and it's accessible here: *https://www. vizgpt.ai/*

Select the default "Cars Dataset" and then click on the "Data" button in order to display the contents of the dataset, as shown in Figure 1.2.

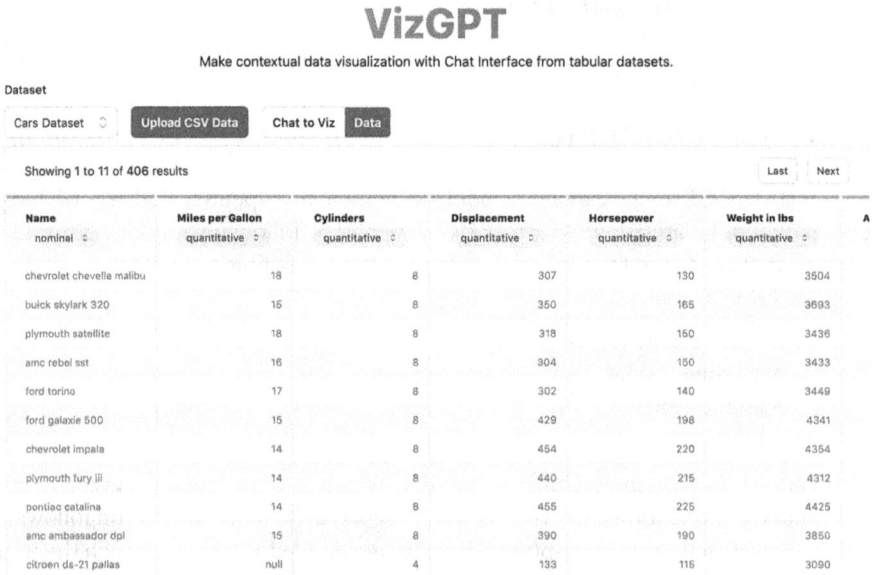

VizGPT

Make contextual data visualization with Chat Interface from tabular datasets.

Dataset

| Cars Dataset ⌄ | Upload CSV Data | Chat to Viz | Data |

Showing 1 to 11 of 406 results   Last   Next

Name nominal ⌄	Miles per Gallon quantitative ⌄	Cylinders quantitative ⌄	Displacement quantitative ⌄	Horsepower quantitative ⌄	Weight in lbs quantitative ⌄	A
chevrolet chevelle malibu	18	8	307	130	3504	
buick skylark 320	15	8	350	165	3693	
plymouth satellite	18	8	318	150	3436	
amc rebel sst	16	8	304	150	3433	
ford torino	17	8	302	140	3449	
ford galaxie 500	15	8	429	198	4341	
chevrolet impala	14	8	454	220	4354	
plymouth fury iii	14	8	440	215	4312	
pontiac catalina	14	8	455	225	4425	
amc ambassador dpl	15	8	390	190	3850	
citroen ds-21 pallas	null	4	133	115	3090	

FIGURE 1.2. VizGPT Cars Dataset rows.

Next, select the default "Cars Dataset" and then click on the "Chat to Viz" button in order to display a visualization of the dataset, as shown in Figure 1.3.

VizGPT

Make contextual data visualization with Chat Interface from tabular datasets.

Dataset

| Cars Dataset ⇕ | Upload CSV Data | Chat to Viz | Data |

Recommend a random chart from this dataset for me.

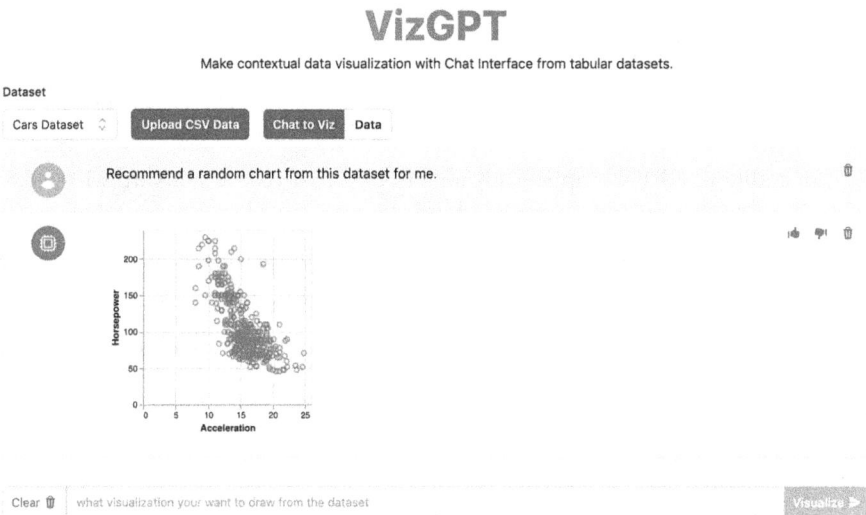

Clear 🗑 what visualization your want to draw from the dataset   Visualize ▶

FIGURE 1.3. VizGPT Car Dataset visualization.

You can experiment further with VizGPT. For example, you can upload your own dataset by clicking on the "Upload CSV" button and obtain similar results with that dataset.

WHAT IS GPT-4?

GPT-4 was released in mid-March 2023, and became available only to users with an existing ChatGPT account via a paid upgrade ($20 per month) to that account. According to various online anecdotal stories from users, GPT-4 is significantly superior to ChatGPT. In addition, Microsoft has a version of GPT-4 that powers its Bing browser, which is freely available to the public.

GPT-4 is a large multimodal model that can process image-based inputs as well as text-based inputs and then generate textual outputs. Currently image-based outputs are unavailable to the general public, but it does have internal support for image generation.

GPT-4 supports 25,000 words of input text: by comparison, ChatGPT is limited to 4,096 characters. Although the number of parameters in GPT-4 is undisclosed, the following article asserts that GPT-4 is a mixture of 8 x 220-billion-parameter models, which is an example of MoE (mixture of experts):

https://thealgorithmicbridge.substack.com/p/gpt-4s-secret-has-been-revealed

GPT-4 and Test-Taking Scores

One interesting example of the improved accuracy pertains to a bar exam for which ChatGPT scored in the bottom 10%. By contrast, GPT-4 scored in the top 10% for the same bar exam. More details are accessible here:

https://www.abajournal.com/web/article/latest-version-of-chatgpt-aces-the-bar-exam-with-score-in-90th-percentile

In addition, GPT-4 is apparently able to pass first year at Harvard with a 3.34 GPA. More details are accessible here:

https://www.businessinsider.com/chatgpt-harvard-passed-freshman-ai-education-GPT-4-2023-7?op=1

Furthermore, GPT-4 has performed well on a number of additional tests, some of which are listed in the following list:

- AP exams
- SAT
- GRE
- medical tests
- law exams
- business school exams
- Wharton MBA exam
- USA Biology Olympiad Semifinal Exam
- Sommelier exams (wine steward)

You can read more details regarding the preceding tests from this link:

https://www.businessinsider.com/list-here-are-the-exams-chatgpt-has-passed-so-far-2023-1

The following link contains much more detailed information regarding test scores, benchmarks, and other results pertaining to GPT-4: *https://openai.com/research/gpt-4*

GPT-4 Fine Tuning

Although OpenAI allows you to fine-tune the four base models (davinci et al), it's (currently) not possible to perform fine tuning on ChatGPT 3.5 or GPT-4. Instead, you can integrate OpenAI models with your own data source via LangChain or LlamaIndex (previously known as GPT-Index). Both of them enable you to connect OpenAI models with your existing data sources.

An introduction to LangChain is accessible here:

https://www.pinecone.io/learn/series/langchain/langchain-intro/

An introduction to LlamaIndex is accessible here:

https://zilliz.com/blog/getting-started-with-llamaindex

Information about fine tuning can be found here:

https://stackoverflow.com/questions/76160057/openai-chat-completions-api-how-do-i-customize-answers-from-gpt-3-5-or-gpt-4-mo?noredirect=1&lq=1

CHATGPT AND GPT-4 COMPETITORS

Shortly after the release of ChatGPT on November 30, 2022, there was a flurry of activity among various companies to release a competitor to ChatGPT, some of which are listed here:

- Bard (Google chatbot)
- Copilot (Microsoft)
- Codex (OpenAI)
- Apple GPT (Apple)
- PaLM 2 (Google and GPT-4 competitor)
- Claude 2 (Anthropic)
- Llama-2 (Meta) discussed in a later section

The following subsections contain additional details regarding the LLMs in the preceding bullet list.

Bard

Bard is an AI chatbot from Google that was released in early 2023 and it's a competitor to ChatGPT. Note that Bard was renamed Gemini in February 2024. By way of comparison, Bard is powered by PaLM 2 (discussed in a subsequent section), whereas ChatGPT is powered by GPT-4. Recently Bard added support for images in its answers to user queries, whereas this functionality for ChatGPT has not been released yet to the public (but you can expect it to be available sometime soon).

Bard encountered an issue pertaining to the James Webb Space Telescope during a highly publicized release, which resulted in a significant decrease in market capitalization for Alphabet. However, Google has persevered in fixing issues and enhancing the functionality of Bard. You can access Bard from this link: *https://bard.google.com/*

Around mid-2023 Bard was imbued with several features that were not available in GPT-4 during the same time period, some of which are listed below:

- can generate images
- can generate HTML/CSS from an image
- can generate mobile applications from an image
- can create Latex formulas from an image
- can extract text from an image

Presumably these features will spur OpenAI to provide the same set of features (some are implemented in GPT-4 but they are not publicly available).

Copilot (OpenAI/Microsoft)

Microsoft Copilot is a Visual Studio Code extension that is also powered by GPT-4. GitHub Copilot is already known for its ability to generate blocks of code within the context of a program. In addition, Microsoft is also developing Microsoft 365 Copilot.

However, Microsoft has provided early demos that show some of the capabilities of Microsoft 365 Copilot, which includes automating tasks such as:

- writing emails
- summarizing meetings
- making PowerPoint presentations

Microsoft 365 Copilot can analyze data in Excel spreadsheets, insert AI-generated images in PowerPoint, and generate drafts of cover letters. Microsoft has also integrated Microsoft 365 Copilot into some of its existing products, such as Loop and OneNote.

According to the following article, Microsoft intends to charge $30 per month for Office 365 Copilot:

https://www.extremetech.com/extreme/microsoft-to-charge-30-per-month-for-ai-powered-office-apps

Copilot was reverse engineered in late 2022 and is described here:

https://thakkarparth007.github.io/copilot-explorer/posts/copilot-internals

The following article shows you how to create a GPT-3 application that uses NextJS, React, and Copilot:

https://github.blog/2023-07-25-how-to-build-a-gpt-3-app-with-nextjs-react-and-github-copilot/

Codex (OpenAI)

OpenAI Codex is a fine-tuned GPT3-based LLM that generates code from text. In fact, Codex powers GitHub Copilot (discussed in the preceding section). Codex was trained on more than 150GB of Python code that was obtained from more than fifty million GitHub repositories.

According to OpenAI, the primary purpose of Codex is to accelerate human programming, and it can complete almost 40% of requests. Codes tends to work quite well for generating code for solving simpler tasks. Navigate to the Codex home page to obtain more information: *https://openai.com/blog/openai-codex*

Apple GPT

In mid-2023 Apple announced Apple GPT, which is a competitor to ChatGPT from OpenAI. The actual release date was projected to be 2024. "Apple GPT" is the current name for a product that is intended to compete with Google Bard, OpenAI ChatGPT, and Microsoft Bing AI.

In brief, the LLM PaLM 2 (discussed in the next section) powers Google Bard, and GPT-4 powers ChatGPT as well as Bing Chat, whereas Ajax is what powers Apple GPT. Ajax is based on Jax from Google.

PaLM-2

PaLM-2 is an acronym for Pathways Language Model, and it is the successor to PaLM (circa 2022). PaLM-2 powers Bard and it's also a direct competitor to GPT-4. By way of comparison, PaLM consists of 540B parameters, and it's plausible that PaLM-2 is a larger LLM (details of the latter are undisclosed).

PaLM-2 provides four sub models called Gecko, Otter, Bison, and Unicorn (smallest to largest). PaLM-2 was trained on more than one hundred human languages, as well as programming languages such as Fortran. Moreover, PaLM-2 has been deployed to a plethora of Google products, including Gmail and YouTube.

Med-PaLM M

In addition to the four sub models listed above, Med-PaLM 2 (the successor to Med-PaLM) is an LLM that provides answers to medical questions, and it's accessible here: *http://sites.research.google/med-palm/*

Another successor to Med-PaLM is Med-PaLM M, and details about this LLM are accessible here: *https://arxiv.org/abs/2307.14334*

An article that provides a direct comparison of performance benchmarks for PaLM 2 and GPT-4 is accessible here:

https://www.makeuseof.com/google-palm-2-vs-openai-gpt-4/

All told, PaLM-2 has a robust set of features and it's definitely a significant competitor to GPT-4.

Claude 2

Anthropic created the LLM Claude 2 that can not only answer queries about specific topics, it can also perform searches that involve multiple documents, summarize documents, create documents, and generate code.

Claude 2 is an improvement on Anthropic's predecessor Claude 1.3, and it can ingest entire books as well as generate code based on prompts from users. In fact, Claude 2 appears to be comparable with its rivals ChatGPT and GPT-4 in terms of competing functionality.

Furthermore, Claude 2 supports a context window of 100,000 tokens. Moreover, Claude 2 was trained on data as recent as early 2023, whereas ChatGPT was trained on data up until 2021. However, Claude 2 cannot search the Web (unlike its competitor GPT-4). Stay tuned to Anthropic, where you will probably see more good things in the LLM space.

LLAMA-2

Llama-2 (Large Language Model Meta AI) is an open source fine-tuned LLM from Meta, that trained on only public data, that has created a lot of excitement in the AI community. Llama-2 provides three models (7B, 13B, and 70B parameters) that utilize more data during the pretraining step than numerous other LLMs. Llama-2 is optimized to provide faster inferences and also provides a longer context length (4K) than other LLMs.

Moreover, the Llama-2-Chat LLM performs surprisingly well: in some cases, its quality is close to the quality of high-performing LLMs such ChatGPT and GPT-4. Llama-2 is more user-friendly and also provides better results for writing text in comparison to GPT-4. Alternatively, GPT-4 is more adept for tasks such as generating code.

How to Download Llama-2

Llama-2 provides a permissive license for community use and commercial use, and Meta has made the code as well as the pretrained models and the fine-tuned models publicly available.

There are several ways that you can download Llama-2, starting from this link from Meta after you provide some information (name, country, and affiliation):

https://ai.meta.com/llama/

Another way to access demos of the 7B, 13B, and 70B models is from the following links:

https://huggingface.co/spaces/huggingface-projects/llama-2-7b-chat
https://huggingface.co/spaces/huggingface-projects/llama-2-13b-chat
https://huggingface.co/spaces/ysharma/Explore_llamav2_with_TGI

A third way to access Llama-2 on Hugging Face from the following link: *https://huggingface.co/blog/llama2*

https://github.com/facebookresearch/llama
https://ai.meta.com/research/publications/llama-2-open-foundation-and-fine-tuned-chat-models/

If you are interested in training Llama-2 on your laptop, more details for doing so are accessible here: *https://blog.briankitano.com/llama-from-scratch/*

Llama-2 Architecture Features

This section simply contains a high-level list of some of the important distinguishing features of Llama-2, as shown in the following list:

- decoder-only LLM
- better pretraining
- improved model architecture

- SwiGLU activation function
- different positional embeddings
- GQA (Grouped Query Attention)
- Ghost Attention (GAtt)
- RLHF and PPO
- BPE SentencePiece tokenizer
- modified normalization step

The majority of LLMs contain the layer normalization that is in the original Transformer architecture. By contrast, Llama uses a simplified alternative that involves Root Mean Square Layer Normalization (aka RMSNorm). RMSNorm has yielded improved results for training stability as well as for generalization.

Although SwiGLU is computationally more expensive than the ReLU activation function that is part of the original Transformer architecture, SwiGLU achieves better performance.

For a detailed description of how to fine tune Llama-2 on three tasks, navigate to the following link:

https://www.anyscale.com/blog/fine-tuning-llama-2-a-comprehensive-case-study-for-tailoring-models-to-unique-applications

Fine Tuning Llama-2

Although Llama-2 is an improvement over its predecessor Llama, you can further improve the performance of Llama-2 by performing some fine tuning of this LLM.

https://medium.com/@murtuza753/using-llama-2-0-faiss-and-langchain-for-question-answering-on-your-own-data-682241488476

The following article shows you how to fine tune Llama-2 in a Google Colaboratory notebook:

https://towardsdatascience.com/fine-tune-your-own-llama-2-model-in-a-colab-notebook-df9823a04a32

The following article describes how to use MonsterAPI (also discussed in the article) in order to fine tune Llama-2 in five steps:

https://blog.monsterapi.ai/how-to-fine-tune-llama-2-llm/

The following link describes how to access Llama-2 in Google Colaboratory:

https://levelup.gitconnected.com/harnessing-the-power-of-llama-2-using-google-colab-2e1dedc2d1d8

WHEN IS GPT-5 AVAILABLE?

As this book goes to print, there is no official information available regarding the status of GPT-5, which is to say that everything is speculative. In the early part of 2023 Sam Altman (CEO of OpenAI) remarked that there were "no of-ficial plans" for GPT-5.

However, during mid-2023 OpenAI filed a patent for GPT-5 in which there are some high-level details about the features of GPT-5. Some people have speculated that GPT-5 will be a more powerful version of GPT-4, and others suggest that filing a patent might be nothing more than securing the name GPT-5 by OpenAI.

Regardless of the motivation for filing a patent, there is a great deal of competition with GPT-4 from various companies. According to a recent report, OpenAI is expected to release GPT-5 sometime in mid-2024. Regarding model sizes, recall that GPT-3 has 175B parameters, and some speculate that GPT-4 has ten trillion parameters, which would mean that GPT-4 is roughly sixty times larger than GPT-3. The same increase in scale for GPT-5 seems implausible because GPT-5 would then consist of 600 trillion parameters.

Another possibility is that GPT-4 is based on the MoE methodology that involves multiple components. For instance, GPT-4 could be a combination of eight components, each of which involves 220 million parameters, and there-fore GPT-4 would consist of 1.76 trillion parameters.

Keep in mind that training LLMs such as GPT-4 is very costly and requires huge datasets for the pretraining step. Regardless of the eventual size of GPT-5, the training process could involve enormous costs.

SUMMARY

This chapter started with a discussion of Generative AI, followed details re-garding ChatGPT from OpenAI. You also learned about significant contribu-tors to Generative AI, such as OpenAI and Google. In addition, you learned about competitors to Gemini, such as GPT-4 and Claude.

There was also discussion about GPT-4 from OpenAI, which powers ChatGPT, and some of its features, as well as information about some com-petitors of GPT-4, such as Llama-2 (Meta) and Bard (Google).

CHAPTER 2

PROMPT ENGINEERING

This chapter provides information about prompt engineering and also several models in the BERT (Bidirectional Encoder Representations from Transformers) "family," followed by the GPT-3 model that forms the basis for GPT-4. You will also learn about some of the differences in these LLMs.

The first part of this chapter discusses prompt engineering, which involves various techniques, such as instruction prompts, reverse prompts, system prompts, CoT (chain of thought), and various other techniques.

The second section discusses various GPT-based LLMs, some of which might be interesting enough to delve more deeply into those models through other online resources.

The third section in this chapter contains some information about aspects of LLM development, such as LLM size versus performance, emergent abilities of LLMs, and undertrained models.

One other point to keep in mind: some of the sections in this chapter contain detailed information, so if you are new to LLMs, consider skimming through this chapter instead of trying to absorb everything (you can always return to this chapter later on).

WHAT IS PROMPT ENGINEERING?

Popular text generators include GPT-3 from OpenAI and Jurassic from AI21, and popular text-to-image generators include Midjourney from Midjourney Inc., and Stable Diffusion from Stability AI. *Prompt engineering* refers to devising text-based prompts that enable AI-based systems to improve the output that is generated. The result is that the output more closely matches whatever users want to produce from the AI.

Since prompts are based on words, the challenge involves learning how different words can affect the generated output. Moreover, it is difficult to predict how systems respond to a given prompt. For instance, if you want to generate a landscape, the difference between a dark landscape and a bright landscape is intuitive. However, if you want a beautiful landscape, how would an AI system generate a corresponding image? As you can surmise, "concrete" words are easier than abstract or subjective words for AI systems that generate images from text. Let us consider the previous example: how would you visualize the following:

- a beautiful landscape
- a beautiful song
- a beautiful movie

Although prompt engineering started with text-to-image generation, there are other types of prompt engineering, such as audio-based prompts that interpret emphasized text and emotions that are detected in speech, and sketch-based prompts that generate images from drawings. The most recent focus of attention involves text-based prompts for generating videos, which presents exciting opportunities for artists and designers. An example of image-to-image processing is accessible here:

https://huggingface.co/spaces/fffiloni/stable-diffusion-color-sketch

Prompts and Completions

A *prompt* is a text string that users provide to LLMs, and a *completion* is the text that users receive from LLMs. Prompts assist LLMs in completing a request (task), and they can vary in length. Although prompts can be any text string, including a random string, the quality and structure of prompts affects the quality of completions.

Think of prompts as a mechanism for giving "guidance" to LLMs, or even as a way to "coach" LLMs into providing desired answers. The number of tokens in a prompt plus the number of tokens in the completion can be at most 2,048 tokens.

Types of Prompts

The following list contains well-known types prompts for LLMs:

- zero-shot prompts
- one-shot prompts
- few-shot prompts
- instruction prompts

A *zero-shot prompt* contains a description of a task, whereas a *one-shot prompt* consists of a single example for completing a task. As you can probably surmise, *few-shot prompts* consist of multiple examples (typically between 10 and 100). In all cases, a clear description of the task or tasks is recommended: more tasks provide GPT-3 with more information, which in turn can lead to more accurate completions.

T0 (for "zero shot") is an interesting LLM: although T0 is 16 times smaller (11 GB) than GPT-3 (175 GB), T0 has outperformed GPT-3 on language-related tasks. T0 can perform well on unseen NLP tasks (i.e., tasks that are new to T0) because it was trained on a dataset containing multiple tasks.

The following Web page provides the Github repository for T0, a site for training T0 directly in a browser, as well as more details about T0 and a 3GB version of T0:

https://github.com/bigscience-workshop/t-zero

As you can probably surmise, T0++ is based on T0, and it was trained with extra tasks beyond the set of tasks on which T0 was trained.

Another important detail is the first three prompts in the preceding list are also called zero-shot learning, one-shot learning, and few-shot learning, respectively.

Instruction Prompts

Instruction prompts are used for fine tuning LLMs, and they specify a format (determined by you) for the manner in which the LLM is expected to conform in its responses. You can prepare your own instruction prompts or you can access prompt template libraries that contain different templates for different tasks, along with different datasets. Various prompt instruction templates are publicly available, such as the following links that provide prompt templates (see subsequent section for an example) for Llama:

https://github.com/devbrones/llama-prompts
https://pub.towardsai.net/llama-gpt4all-simplified-local-chatgpt-ab7d28d34923

Reverse Prompts

Another technique uses a reverse order: input prompts are answers and the response are the questions associated with the answers (similar to a popular game show). For example, given a French sentence, you might ask the model, "What English text might have resulted in this French translation?"

System Prompts Versus Agent Prompts

The distinction between a system prompt and an agent prompt often comes up in the context of conversational AI systems and chatbot design.

A *system prompt* is typically an initial message or cue given by the system to guide the user on what they can do or to set expectations about the interaction. It often serves as an introduction or a way to guide users on how to proceed. Here are several examples of system prompts:

- "Welcome to ChatBotX! You can ask me questions about weather, news, or sports. How can I assist you today?"

- "Hello! For account details, press 1. For technical support, press 2."
- "Greetings! Type 'order' to track your package or 'help' for assistance."

By contrast, an *agent prompt* is a message generated by the AI model or agent in response to a user's input during the course of an interaction. It is a part of the back-and-forth exchange within the conversation. The agent prompt guides the user to provide more information, clarifies ambiguity, or nudges the user toward a specific action. Here are some examples of agent prompts in response to user prompts:

```
User: "I'm looking for shoes."
Agent Prompt: "Great! Are you looking for men's or women's
    shoes?"
User: "I can't log in."
Agent Prompt: "I'm sorry to hear that. Can you specify if
    you are having trouble with your password or username?"
User: "Tell me a joke."
Agent Prompt: "Why did the chicken join a band? Because it

    had the drumsticks!"
```

The fundamental difference between the two is their purpose and placement in the interaction. A system prompt is often at the beginning of an interaction, setting the stage for the conversation. An agent prompt occurs during the conversation, steering the direction of the dialogue based on user input.

Both types of prompts are crucial for creating a fluid and intuitive conversational experience for users. They guide the user and help ensure that the system understands and addresses the user's needs effectively.

Prompt Templates

Prompt templates are predefined formats or structures used to instruct a model or system to perform a specific task. They serve as a foundation for generating prompts, where certain parts of the template can be filled in or customized to produce a variety of specific prompts. By way of analogy, prompt templates are the counterpart to macros that you can define in some text editors.

Prompt templates are especially useful when working with language models, as they provide a consistent way to query the model across multiple tasks or data points. In particular, prompt templates can make it easier to:

- ensure consistency when querying a model multiple times
- facilitate batch processing or automation
- reduce errors and variations in how questions are posed to the model

As an example, suppose you are working with an LLM and you want to translate English sentences into French. An associated prompt template could be the following:

"Translate the following English sentence into French: {sentence}"

Note that {sentence} is a placeholder that you can replace with any English sentence.

You can use the preceding prompt template to generate specific prompts:

- "Translate the following English sentence into French: 'Hello, how are you?'"
- "Translate the following English sentence into French: 'I love ice cream.'"

As you can see, prompt templates enable you to easily generate a variety of prompts for different sentences without having to rewrite the entire instruction each time. In fact, this concept can be extended to more complex tasks and can incorporate multiple placeholders or more intricate structures, depending on the application.

Prompts for Different LLMs

GPT-3, ChatGPT, and GPT-4 are LLMs that are all based on the transformer architecture and are fundamentally similar in their underlying mechanics. ChatGPT is essentially a version of the GPT model fine-tuned specifically for conversational interactions. GPT-4 is an evolution or improvement over GPT-3 in terms of scale and capabilities.

The differences in prompts for these models mainly arise from the specific use case and context, rather than inherent differences between the models. Here are some prompting differences that are based on use cases.

GPT-3 can be used for a wide range of tasks beyond just conversation, from content generation to code writing. Here are two examples of prompts for GPT-3:

- "Translate the following English text to French: 'Hello, how are you?'"
- "Write a Python function that calculates the factorial of a number." ChatGPT is specifically fine-tuned for conversational interactions. Here are some examples of prompts for two different conversations with ChatGPT:
- User: "Can you help me with my homework?" ChatGPT: "Of course! What subject or topic do you need help with?"
- User: "Tell me a joke."
- ChatGPT: "Why did the chicken cross the playground? To get to the other slide!" GPT-4 provides a larger scale and refinements, so the prompts would be similar in nature to GPT-3 but might yield more accurate or nuanced outputs. Here are two examples of prompts for GPT-4:
- "Provide a detailed analysis of quantum mechanics in relation to general relativity."
- "Generate a short story based on a post-apocalyptic world with a theme of hope. These three models accept natural language prompts and produce natural language outputs. The fundamental way you interact with them remains consistent.

The main difference comes from the context in which the model is being used and any fine-tuning that has been applied. ChatGPT, for instance, is designed to be more conversational, so while you can use GPT-3 for chats, ChatGPT might produce more contextually relevant conversational outputs.

When directly interacting with these models, especially through an API, you might also have control over parameters like "temperature" (controlling randomness) and "max tokens" (controlling response length). Adjusting these can shape the responses, regardless of which GPT variant you are using.

In essence, while the underlying models have differences in scale and specific training/fine-tuning, the way you prompt them remains largely consistent: clear, specific natural language prompts yield the best results.

Poorly Worded Prompts

When crafting prompts, be as clear and specific as possible to guide the response in the desired direction. Ambiguous or vague prompts can lead to a wide range of responses, many of which might not be useful or relevant to the user's actual intent.

Poorly worded prompts include prompts that are too broad, and they can lead to confusion, misunderstanding, or nonspecific responses from AI models. Here are some examples of poorly worded prompts, along with explanations:

"Tell me about that thing."
Problem: Too vague. What "thing" is being referred to?

"Why did it happen?"
Problem: No context. What event or situation is being discussed?

"Explain stuff."
Problem: Too broad. What specific "stuff" should be explained?

"Do what is needful."
Problem: Ambiguous. What specific action is required?

"I want information."
Problem: Not specific enough. What type of information is desired?

"Can you get me the thing from the place?"
Problem: Both "thing" and "place" are unclear.

"Where can I buy what's-his-name's book?"
Problem: Ambiguous reference. Who is "what's-his-name"?

"How do you do the process?"
Problem: Which "process" is being referred to?

"Describe the importance of the topic."
Problem: The "topic" is not specified.

"Why is it bad or good?"
Problem: No context. What is "it"?

"Help with the issue."
Problem: Vague. What specific issue requires assistance?

"Things to consider for the task."
Problem: Ambiguous. What "task" is being discussed?

"How does this work?"
Problem: Lack of specificity. What is "this"?

THE GPT-3 PLAYGROUND

OpenAI provides the GPT-3 Playground, which is a Web-based tool for entering prompts in a text field and receiving completions from GPT-3. The Playground supports most of the functionality that is available directly through the GPT-3 API.

Moreover, the Playground enables you to interact with GPT-3 without writing any code. In essence, the OpenAI Playground enables you to easily use GPT-3 to train the engine to produce text output. The GPT-3 Playground also provides a set of saved prompts that are called "presets."

The first step is to navigate to the GPT-3 Playground via the following link where you will be prompted to sign into your account:

https://beta.openai.com/playground

From left to right, the screen displays three sections: a "Get Started" section, a "Playground" section, and third section that consists of a drop-down list and sliders for tunable parameters.

The middle section is the input text for GPT-3, which has two parts: The first is a start sequence that is the text string `Text:`, followed by one or more text blocks (provided by you) that provides GPT-3 with sample output text. The second contains the same string `Text:` that indicates the end of your input text.

Let's postpone the description of the sliders that appear in the GPT-3 Playground until later in this chapter and jump right into generating code in the GPT-3 Playground.

INFERENCE PARAMETERS

After you have completed the fine-tuning step for an LLM, you are in a position to set values for various so-called inference parameters. The GPT-3 API supports numerous inference parameters, some of which are shown in the following bulleted list:

- `engine`
- `prompt`
- `max_tokens`
- `top_p`
- `top_k`
- `frequency_penalty`
- `presence_penalty`

- token length
- stop tokens
- temperature

The engine inference parameter can be one of the four GPT-3 models, such as text-ada-001. The prompt parameter is simply the input text that you provide. The presence_penalty inference parameter enables more relevant responses when you specify higher values for this parameter.

The max_tokens inference parameter specifies the maximum number of tokens: sample values are 100, 200, or 256. The top_p inference parameter can be a positive integer that specifies the top-most results to select. The frequency_penalty is an inference parameter that pertains to the frequency of repeated words. A smaller value for this parameter increases the number of repeated words.

The "token length" parameter specifies the total number of words that are in the input sequence that is processed by the LLM (not the maximum length of each token).

The "stop tokens" parameter controls the length of the generated output of an LLM. If this parameter equals 1, then only a single sentence is generated, whereas a value of 2 indicates that the generated output is limited to one paragraph.

The "top k" parameter specifies the number of tokens—which is the value for k—that are chosen, with the constraint that the chosen tokens have the highest probabilities. For example, if "top k" is equal to 3, then only the 3 tokens with the highest probabilities are selected.

The "top p" parameter is a floating point number between 0.0 and 1.0, and it's the upper bound on the sum of the probabilities of the chosen tokens. For example, if a discrete probability distribution consists of the set S = {0.1, 0.2, 0.3, 0.4} and the value of the "top p" parameter is 0.3, then only the tokens with associated probabilities of 0.1 and 0.2 can be selected.

Thus, the "top k" and the "top p" parameters provide two mechanisms for limiting the number of tokens that can be selected.

TEMPERATURE PARAMETER

The temperature hyper parameter is a floating point number between 0 and 1 inclusive, and its default value is 0.7. One interesting value for the temperature is 0.8: this will result in GPT-3 selecting a next token that does *not* have the maximum probability.

The "temperature" parameter T is a nonnegative floating point number whose value influences the extent to which the model uses randomness. Specifically, smaller values for the temperature parameter that are closer to 0 involve less randomness (i.e., more deterministic), whereas larger values for the temperature parameter involve more randomness.

The temperature parameter T is directly associated with the softmax function that is applied during the final step in the transformer architecture. The value of T alters the formula for the softmax function, as described later in this section. A key point to remember is that selecting tokens based on a softmax function means that the selected token is the token with the highest probability.

By contrast, larger values for the parameter T enable randomness in the choice of the next token, which means that a token can be selected even though its associated probability is less than the maximum probability. While this might seem counter-intuitive, it turns out that some values of T (such as 0.8) result in output text that is more natural sounding, from a human's perspective, than the output text in which tokens are selected if they have the maximum probability. Finally, a temperature value of 1 is the same as the standard `softmax()` function.

Temperature and the softmax() Function

The temperature parameter T appears in the *denominator* of the exponent of the Euler constant e in the softmax function. Thus, instead of the softmax numerators of the form $e^{\wedge}(xi)$, the modified softmax function contains numerator terms of the form $e^{\wedge}(xi/T)$, where $\{x1, x2, \ldots, xn\}$ comprise a set of numbers that form a discrete probability distribution (explained in the next section).

As a reminder, the denominator of each term generated by the softmax function consists of the sum of the terms in the set $\{e^{\wedge}(x1), e^{\wedge}(x2), \ldots, e^{\wedge}(xn)\}$. However, the denominator of the terms involving the temperature parameter T is slightly different: it's the sum of the terms in the set $\{e^{\wedge}(x1/T), e^{\wedge}(x2/T), \ldots, e^{\wedge}(xn/T)\}$.

Interestingly, the softmax function with the temperature parameter T is the same as the Boltzmann distribution that is described here:

https://en.wikipedia.org/wiki/Boltzmann_distribution

The following Python code snippet provides an example of specifying values for various hyper parameters, which specifies a GPT-3 engine:

```
response = openai.Completion.create(
  engine="text-ada-001",
  prompt="",
  temperature=0.7,
  max_tokens=256,
  top_p=1,
  frequency_penalty=0,
  presence_penalty=0
)
```

Navigate to the following URL for more information regarding inference parameters in GPT-3: *https://huggingface.co/blog/inference-endpoints-llm*

ASPECTS OF LLM DEVELOPMENT

Modern LLMs use one of three variants of the transformer architecture: encoder-only LLMs, decoder-only LLMs, and LLMs that are based on an encoder as well as a decoder (which is actually the original transformer architecture).

For your convenience, this section provides a list of language models that belong to each of these three types of models. Examples of decoder-only models include the GPT-x family of LLMs.

With the preceding points in mind, some of the better-known encoder-based LLMs include the following:

- AlBERT
- BERT
- DistilBERT
- ELECTRA
- RoBERTa

The preceding LLMs are well-suited for performing NLP tasks such as NER and extractive question-answering tasks. In addition to encoder-only LLMs, there are several well-known decoder-based LLMs that include the following:

- CTRL
- GPT-x series
- Transformer XK

The preceding LLMs perform text *generation*, whereas encoder-only models perform next word *prediction*. Finally, some of the well-known encoder/decoder-based LLMs include the following:

- BART
- mBART
- Marian
- T5

The preceding LLMs perform summarization, translation, and generate question-answering.

One trend involves the use of fine-tuning, zero/one/few-shot training, and prompt-based learning with respect to LLMs. Fine-tuning is typically accompanied by a fine-tuning dataset, and if the latter is not available (or infeasible), few-shot training might be an acceptable alternative.

One outcome from training the Jurassic-1 LLM is that wider and shallower is better than narrower and deeper with respect to performance because a wider context allows for more calculations to be performed in parallel.

Another result from Chinchilla is that smaller models that are trained on a corpus with a very large number of tokens can be more performant than larger models that are trained on a more modest number of tokens.

The success of the GlaM and Switch LLMs (both from Google) suggests that sparse transformers, in conjunction with MoE (mixture of experts), is also an interesting direction, potentially leading to even better results in the future.

In addition, there is the possibility of the "over curation" of data, which is to say that performing *very* detailed data curation to remove spurious-looking tokens does not guarantee that models will produce better results on those curated datasets.

The use of prompts has revealed an interesting detail: the results of similar yet different prompts can lead to substantively different responses. Thus, the goal is to create well-crafted prompts, which can be a somewhat elusive task.

Another area of development pertains to the continued need for benchmarks that leverage better and more complex datasets, especially when LLMs exceed human performance. Specifically, a benchmark becomes outdated when all modern LLMs can pass the suite of tests in that benchmark. Two such benchmarks are XNLI and BigBench ("Beyond the Imitation Game Benchmark").

The following Web page provides a fairly extensive list of general NLP benchmarks as well as language-specific NLP benchmarks:

https://mr-nlp.github.io/posts/2021/05/benchmarks-in-nlp/

The following Web page provides a list of monolingual transformer-based pre-trained language models:

https://mr-nlp.github.io/posts/2021/05/tptlms-list/

LLM Size Versus Performance

Let us consider the size-versus-performance question: although larger models such as GPT-3 can perform better than smaller models, it is not always the case. In particular, models that are variants of GPT-3 have mixed results: some smaller variants perform almost as well as GPT-3, and some larger models perform only marginally better than GPT-3.

A recent trend involves developing models that are based on the decoder component of the transformer architecture. Such models are frequently measured by their performance via zero-shot, one-shot, and few-shot training in comparison to other LLMs. This trend, as well as the development of ever-larger LLMs, is likely to continue for the foreseeable future.

Interestingly, decoder-only LLMs can perform tasks such as token prediction and can slightly out-perform encoder-only models on benchmarks such as SuperGLUE. However, such decoder-based models tend to be significantly larger than encoder-based models, and the latter tend to be more efficient than the former.

Hardware is another consideration in terms of optimizing model performance, which can incur a greater cost, and hence might be limited to only a handful of companies. Due to the high cost of hardware, another initiative involves training LLMs on the Jean Zay supercomputer in France:

https://venturebeat.com/2022/01/10/inside-bigscience-the-quest-to-build-a-powerful-open-language-model/

Emergent Abilities of LLMs

The *emergent abilities* of LLMs refers to abilities that are present in larger models that do not exist in smaller models. In simplified terms, as models increase in size, there is a discontinuous "jump" whereby abilities manifest themselves in a larger model with no apparent or clear-cut reason.

The interesting aspect of emergent abilities is the possibility of expanding capabilities of language models through additional scaling. More detailed information is accessible in the (Wei et al., 2022) research paper "Emergent Abilities of Large Language Models" that can be accessed here:

https://arxiv.org/abs/2206.07682

In his essay "More is Different," (1972), Nobel-Prize-winning physicist Philip Anderson assessed that emergence is when quantitative changes in a system result in qualitative changes in behavior. (Anderson, 1972.)

Note that emergent abilities *cannot* be predicted by extrapolation of the behavior of smaller models because (by definition) emergent abilities are not present in smaller models. No doubt there will be more research that explores the extent to which further model scaling can lead to more emergent abilities in LLMs.

KAPLAN AND UNDERTRAINED MODELS

Kaplan et al. (2020) provided (empirical) power laws regarding the performance of language models, which they assert depends on the following:

- model size
- dataset size
- amount of compute for training

Kaplan et al. (2020) asserted that changing the network width or depth have minimal effects. They also claimed that optimal training of very large models involves a relatively modest amount of data. The paper with the relevant details is accessible online:

https://arxiv.org/abs/2001.08361

However, Chinchilla is a 70 B LLM that was trained on a dataset that is much larger than the size that is recommended by Kaplan et al. In fact, Chinchilla achieved SOTA status has surpassed the performance of the following LLMs, all of which are between two and seven times larger than Chinchilla:

- `Gopher (280B)`
- `GPT-3 (175B)`
- `J1-Jumbo (178B)`
- `LaMDA (137B)`
- `MT-NLG (530B)`

SUMMARY

This chapter started with a description of prompt engineering, which involves various techniques, such as instruction prompts, reverse prompts, system prompts, CoT, and various other techniques. In addition, you saw examples of poorly worded prompts, followed by details about the GPT-3 Playground.

Finally, you learned about various GPT-based LLMs, as well as information about aspects of LLM development, such as LLM size versus performance, emergent abilities of LLMs, and undertrained models.

REFERENCES

Anderson, P. W. (1972, August 4) More is different: Broken symmetry and the nature of the hierarchical structure of science. *Science, 177*(4047): 393–396.

Kaplan, J., (2020, January 23). *Scaling laws for neural language models. arxiv, 1*(08361): 1–30. *https://arxiv.org/pdf/2001.08361.pdf*

Wei, J. (2022, July 21). Emergent abilities of large language models. *Transactions on Machine Learning Research, 8*(2022), 1–30. arXiv. *https://arxiv.org/pdf/2206.07682.pdf*

INTRODUCTION TO CSS3

Chapter 3 is the first of three chapters that discuss CSS3, with a focus on CSS3 features that enable you to create vivid graphics effects. The first part of this chapter contains a short section that discusses the structure of a minimal HTML document, followed by a brief discussion regarding browser support for CSS3 and online tools that can be helpful in this regard. CSS3 style sheets are referenced in HTML pages; therefore, it's important to understand the limitations that exist with respect to browser support for CSS3.

The second part of this chapter contains various code samples that illustrate how to create shadow effects, how to render rectangles with rounded corners, and also how to use linear and radial gradients. The third part of this chapter covers CSS3 transforms (scale, rotate, skew, and translate), along with code samples that illustrate how to apply transforms to HTML elements and to PNG files.

When you have completed this chapter, you will know how to use the CSS3 methods `translate()`, `rotate()`, `skew()`, and `scale()`. Before you read this chapter, please keep in mind the following points: First, the CSS3 code samples in this book are for WebKit-based browsers, so the code will work on Microsoft® Windows®, Macintosh®, and Linux®.

Second, several chapters mention performing an Internet search to obtain more information about a specific topic. The rationale for doing so is that the relevance of online information depends on the knowledge level of the reader, so it's virtually impossible to find a one-size-fits-all link that is suitable for everyone's needs. Furthermore, topics that are less relevant to the theme or beyond the scope of this book will be covered more lightly, thereby maintaining a reasonable balance between the number of topics and the depth of explanation of the relevant details. With these points in mind, please be assured that referring you to the Internet is never intended to be "user unfriendly" in any manner.

Third, virtually all of the links in this book refer to open-source projects, but you can also find very good commercial products; the choice of tools depends on the features that they support, the requirements for your project, and the size of your budget.

HTML AND <DOCTYPE>

In addition to introducing many new semantic tags, HTML has simplified the <DOCTYPE> declaration for Web pages. This book does not contain a discussion of new HTML tags, but the HTML pages in this book do use the HTML <DOCTYPE> declaration. The typical structure of the HTML pages in this book looks like this:

```
<!DOCTYPE html>
<html lang="en">
<head>
...
</head>

<body>
 <div id="outer">
...
 </div>
</body>
</html>
```

Most of the "action" in the CSS3-based code samples takes place in the CSS3 selectors. You will be able understand the HTML page even without knowing the semantics of the HTML tags in that example (and if need be, you can perform an Internet search for articles that explain the purpose of those tags).

CSS3 FEATURES AND BROWSER SUPPORT

There are two important details about defining CSS3-based selectors for HTML pages. First, different browsers (and different browser versions) support different CSS3 features. One of the best Web sites for finding this detailed level of information is here: *http://caniuse.com/*. This Web site contains tabular information regarding CSS3 support in Internet Explorer® (IE), Firefox®, Safari®, Chrome™, and Opera™ browsers.

The second detail is that some CSS3 properties require browser-specific prefixes in order for them to work correctly, which are answered by GPT-4 in the next section.

Browser-Specific Prefixes for CSS3

The following prompt was supplied to GPT-4 in order to obtain information regarding vendor-specific prefixes for CSS3 in HTML Web pages.

```
Are vendor-specific prefixes required for CSS3?
```

ChatGPT:
As of my last update in April 2023, the necessity of using vendor-specific prefixes in CSS3 for HTML Web pages depends on several factors, including the specific CSS features you are using, the range of browsers and their versions you aim to support, and the rate at which these browsers adopt new CSS features.

Vendor-specific prefixes are used to implement experimental or non-standardized features in Web browsers. Common prefixes include:

- `-webkit-` for Chrome, Safari, newer versions of Opera, and almost all iOS browsers
- `-moz-` for Firefox
- `-o-` for older versions of Opera
- `-ms-` for Internet Explorer and Microsoft Edge

Current State and Considerations:

1. **Improved Standardization:** Modern Web browsers have significantly improved in terms of standards compliance. Many CSS3 features that once required prefixes are now part of the standardized CSS3 specifications and are implemented uniformly across major browsers.

2. **Automatic Prefixing Tools:** Tools like Autoprefixer can be used in the development process. They automatically add necessary prefixes based on the project's browser support requirements. This has greatly simplified the process, reducing the need for manual prefixing.

3. **Feature Detection Over Browser Detection:** Modern best practices often recommend using feature detection (for instance, using Modernizr) instead of browser detection. This approach applies styles or fallbacks based on whether the browser supports a particular feature, rather than on which browser it is.

4. **Browser Update Frequency:** Browsers update frequently, meaning that more users are likely to be on versions that support standard CSS3 features. This reduces the need for vendor-specific prefixes for users on the latest versions.

5. **Fallbacks for Older Browsers:** If your audience includes users on older browsers that require these prefixes for certain features, then including them is necessary. It's important to know your audience and their typical browser usage.

6. **Use of "Can I Use":** Checking compatibility tables on websites like "Can I Use" is helpful. It provides current data on the support of various CSS features across different browsers and versions, indicating whether prefixes are needed.

In summary, while vendor-specific prefixes are not as widely required as they once were due to the increased standardization and frequent updates of browsers, they may still be necessary in certain situations, particularly when targeting older browsers or using very new, experimental features. Tools like Autoprefixer and strategies like feature detection are recommended to manage browser compatibility effectively.

As an illustration, the following code block shows examples of vendor-specific prefixes:

```
• -ie-webkit-border-radius: 8px;
• -moz-webkit-border-radius: 8px;
• -o-webkit-border-radius: 8px;
• border-radius: 8px;
```

In your CSS selectors, specify the attributes with browser-specific prefixes before the "generic" attribute, which serves as a default choice in the event that the browser-specific attributes are not selected. The CSS3 code samples in this book contain Webkit-specific prefixes, which help us keep the CSS style sheets manageable in terms of size. If you need CSS style sheets that work on multiple browsers, there are essentially two options available. One option involves manually adding the CSS3 code with all the required browser-specific prefixes, which can be tedious to maintain and is also error prone. Another option is to use CSS frameworks (discussed in Chapter 2) that can programmatically generate the CSS3 code that contains all browser-specific prefixes.

A QUICK OVERVIEW OF CSS3 FEATURES

CSS3 adopts a modularized approach for extending existing CSS2 functionality as well as supporting new functionality. As such, CSS3 can be logically divided into the following categories:

- backgrounds/borders
- color
- media queries
- multicolumn layout
- selectors

With CSS3 you can create boxes with rounded corners and shadow effects; create rich graphics effects using linear and radial gradients; switch between portrait and landscape mode and detect the type of mobile device using media query selectors; produce multicolumn text rendering and formatting; and specify sophisticated node selection rules in selectors using first-child, last-child, first-of-type, and last-of-type.

CSS3 SHADOW EFFECTS AND ROUNDED CORNERS

CSS3 shadow effects are useful for creating vivid visual effects with simple selectors. You can use shadow effects for text as well as rectangular regions. CSS3 also enables you to easily render rectangles with rounded corners, so you do not need PNG files in order to create this effect.

CSS3 and Text Shadow Effects

A shadow effect for text can make a Web page look more vivid and appealing. Listing 3.1 displays the contents of the HTML page TextShadow1.html, illustrating how to render text with a shadow effect, and Listing 3.2 displays the contents of the CSS style sheet TextShadow1.css that is referenced in Listing 3.1.

LISTING 3.1: TextShadow1.html

```
<!DOCTYPE html>
<html lang="en">
<head>
  <title>CSS Text Shadow Example</title>
  <meta charset="utf-8" />
  <link href="TextShadow1.css" rel="style sheet"
      type="text/css">
</head>

<body>
  <div id="text1">
    Line One Shadow Effect
  </div>
  <div id="text2">
    Line Two Shadow Effect
  </div>
  <div id="text3">
    Line Three Vivid Effect
  </div>

  <div id="text4">
    <span id="dd">13</span>
    <span id="mm">August</span>
    <span id="yy">2024</span>
  </div>

  <div id="text5">
    <span id="dd">13</span>
    <span id="mm">August</span>
    <span id="yy">2024</span>
  </div>

  <div id="text6">
    <span id="dd">13</span>
    <span id="mm">August</span>
    <span id="yy">2024</span>
  </div>
</body>
</html>
```

The code in Listing 3.1 is straightforward: there is a reference to the CSS style sheet TextShadow1.css that contains two CSS selectors. One selector specifies how to render the HTML <div> element whose id attribute has value text1, and the other selector is applied to the HTML <div> element whose id attribute is text2. The CSS3 rotate() function is included in this example; however, a more detailed discussion of this function is included later in this chapter.

LISTING 3.2: TextShadow1.css

```css
#text1 {
  font-size: 24pt;
  text-shadow: 2px 4px 5px #00f;
}

#text2 {
  font-size: 32pt;
  text-shadow: 0px 1px 6px #000,
               4px 5px 6px #f00;
}

#text3 {
  font-size: 40pt;
  text-shadow: 0px 1px 6px   #fff,
               2px 4px 4px   #0ff,
               4px 5px 6px   #00f,
               0px 0px 10px  #444,
               0px 0px 20px  #844,
               0px 0px 30px  #a44,
               0px 0px 40px  #f44;
}

#text4 {
  position: absolute;
  top: 200px;
  right: 200px;
  font-size: 48pt;
  text-shadow: 0px 1px 6px   #fff,
               2px 4px 4px   #0ff,
               4px 5px 6px   #00f,
               0px 0px 10px  #000,
               0px 0px 20px  #448,
               0px 0px 30px  #a4a,
               0px 0px 40px  #fff;
  -webkit-transform: rotate(-90deg);
}

#text5 {
  position: absolute;
  left: 0px;
  font-size: 48pt;
  text-shadow: 2px 4px 5px #00f;
  -webkit-transform: rotate(-10deg);
}

#text6 {
  float: left;
  font-size: 48pt;
  text-shadow: 2px 4px 5px #f00;
```

```
    -webkit-transform: rotate(-170deg);
}

/* 'transform' is explained later */
#text1:hover, #text2:hover, #text3:hover,
#text4:hover, #text5:hover, #text6:hover {
-webkit-transform : scale(2) rotate(-45deg);
-transform : scale(2) rotate(-45deg);
}
```

The first selector in Listing 3.2 specifies a `font-size` of 24 and a `text-shadow` that renders text with a blue background (represented by the hexadecimal value `#00f`). The attribute `text-shadow` specifies (from left to right) the x-coordinate, the y-coordinate, the blur radius, and the color of the shadow. The second selector specifies a `font-size` of 32 and a red shadow background (`#f00`). The third selector creates a richer visual effect by specifying multiple components in the `text-shadow` property, which were chosen by experimenting with effects that are possible with different values in the various components.

The final CSS3 selector creates an animation effect when users hover over any of the six text strings; the details of the animation will be deferred until later in this chapter. Figure 3.1 displays the result of applying the CSS style sheet `TextShadow1.css` to the HTML `<div>` elements in the HTML page `TextShadow1.html`.

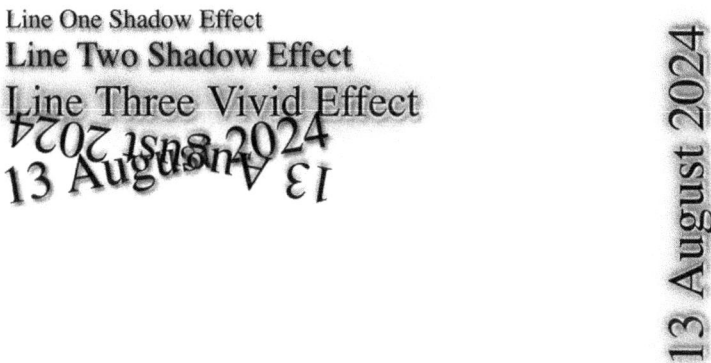

FIGURE 3.1. CSS3 text shadow effects.

CSS3 and Box Shadow Effects

You can also apply a shadow effect to a box that encloses a text string, which can be effective in terms of drawing attention to specific parts of a Web page. The same caveat regarding overuse applies to box shadows. Listing 3.3 displays the contents of the HTML page `BoxShadow1.html` that renders a box shadow effect, and Listing 3.4 displays the contents of `BoxShadow1.css` that contains the associated CSS3 selectors.

LISTING 3.3: BoxShadow1.html

```html
<!DOCTYPE html>
<html lang="en">
<head>
  <title>CSS Box Shadow Example</title>
  <meta charset="utf-8" />
  <link href="BoxShadow1.css" rel="style sheet" type="text/css">
</head>

<body>
  <div id="box1"> Line One with a Box Effect </div>
  <div id="box2"> Line Two with a Box Effect </div>
  <div id="box3"> Line Three with a Box Effect </div>
</body>
</html>
```

The code in Listing 3.3 references the CSS style sheet BoxShadow1.css (instead of TextShadow1.css) that contains three CSS selectors. These selectors specify how to render the HTML DIV elements whose id attribute has value box1, box2, and box3, respectively (and all three DIV elements are defined in BoxShadow1.html).

LISTING 3.4: BoxShadow1.css

```css
#box1 {
  position:relative;top:10px;
  width: 50%;
  height: 30px;
  font-size: 20px;
  -moz-box-shadow: 10px 10px 5px #800;
  -webkit-box-shadow: 10px 10px 5px #800;
  box-shadow: 10px 10px 5px #800;
}

#box2 {
  position:relative;top:20px;
  width: 80%;
  height: 50px;
  font-size: 36px;
  padding: 10px;
  -moz-box-shadow: 14px 14px 8px #008;
  -webkit-box-shadow: 14px 14px 8px #008;
  box-shadow: 14px 14px 8px #008;
}
#box3 {
  position:relative;top:30px;
  width: 80%;
  height: 60px;
  font-size: 52px;
  padding: 10px;
  -moz-box-shadow: 14px 14px 8px #008;
  -webkit-box-shadow: 14px 14px 8px #008;
  box-shadow: 14px 14px 8px #008;
}
```

The first selector in Listing 3.4 specifies the attributes width, height, and font-size, which control the dimensions of the associated HTML <div> element and also the enclosed text string. The next three attributes consist of a Mozilla-specific box-shadow attribute, followed by a WebKit-specific box-shadow property, and finally the "generic" box-shadow attribute. Figure 3.2 displays the result of applying the CSS style sheet BoxShadow1.css to the HTML page BoxShadow1.html.

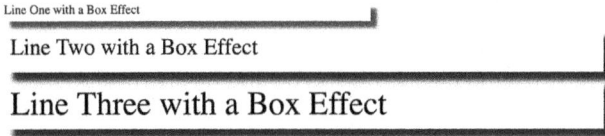

Line One with a Box Effect

Line Two with a Box Effect

Line Three with a Box Effect

FIGURE 3.2. CSS3 box shadow effect.

CSS3 and Rounded Corners

CSS3 makes it very easy to render boxes with rounded corners. Listing 3.5 displays the contents of the HTML page RoundedCorners1.html that renders text strings in boxes with rounded corners, and Listing 3.6 displays the CSS file RoundedCorners1.css.

LISTING 3.5: RoundedCorners1.html

```
<!DOCTYPE html>
<html lang="en">
<head>
  <title>CSS Text Shadow Example</title>
  <meta charset="utf-8" />
  <link href="RoundedCorners1.css" rel="style sheet"
type="text/css">
</head>
<body>
  <div id="outer">
    <a href="#" class="anchor">Text Inside a Rounded
Rectangle</a>
  </div>
  <div id="text1">
    Line One of Text with a Shadow Effect
  </div>
  <div id="text2">
    Line Two of Text with a Shadow Effect
  </div>
</body>
</html>
```

Listing 3.5 contains a reference to the CSS style sheet RoundedCorners1.css that contains three CSS selectors that are applied to the elements whose id attribute has value anchor, text1, and text2, respectively. The CSS selectors defined in RoundedCorners1.css create visual effects, and as you will see, the hover pseudoselector enables you to create animation effects.

LISTING 3.6: RoundedCorners1.css

```
a.anchor:hover {
background: #00F;
}

a.anchor {
background: #FF0;
font-size: 24px;
font-weight: bold;
padding: 4px 4px;
color: rgba(255,0,0,0.8);
text-shadow: 0 1px 1px rgba(0,0,0,0.4);
-webkit-transition: all 2.0s ease;
-transition: all 2.0s ease;
-webkit-border-radius: 8px;
border-radius: 8px;
}
#text1 {
  font-size: 24pt;
  text-shadow: 2px 4px 5px #00f;
}
#text2 {
  font-size: 32pt;
  text-shadow: 4px 5px 6px #f00;
}
#round1 {
  -moz-border-radius-bottomleft: 20px;
  -moz-border-radius-bottomright: 20px;
  -moz-border-radius-topleft: 20px;
  -moz-border-radius-topright: 20px;
  -moz-box-shadow: 2px 2px 10px #ccc;
  -webkit-border-bottom-left-radius: 20px;
  -webkit-border-bottom-right-radius: 20px;
  -webkit-border-top-left-radius: 20px;
  -webkit-border-top-right-radius: 20px;
  -webkit-box-shadow: 2px 2px 10px #ccc;
  background-color: #f00;
  margin: 25px auto 0;
  padding: 25px 10px;
  text-align: center;
  width: 260px;
}
```

Listing 3.6 contains the selector a.anchor:hover that changes the text color from yellow (#FF0) to blue (#00F) during a two-second interval when users hover over any anchor element with their mouse.

The selector a.anchor contains various attributes that specify the dimensions of the box that encloses the text in the <a> element, along with two new pairs of attributes. The first pair specifies the transition attribute (and a WebKit-specific prefix), which we will discuss later in this chapter. The second pair specifies the border-radius attribute (and the WebKit-specific attribute) whose value is 8px, which determines the radius (in pixels) of the rounded corners of the box that encloses the text in the <a> element. The last two selectors are identical to the selectors in Listing 3.1. Figure 3.3 displays the result of applying the CSS style sheet `RoundedCorners1.css` to the elements in the HTML page `RoundedCorners1.html`.

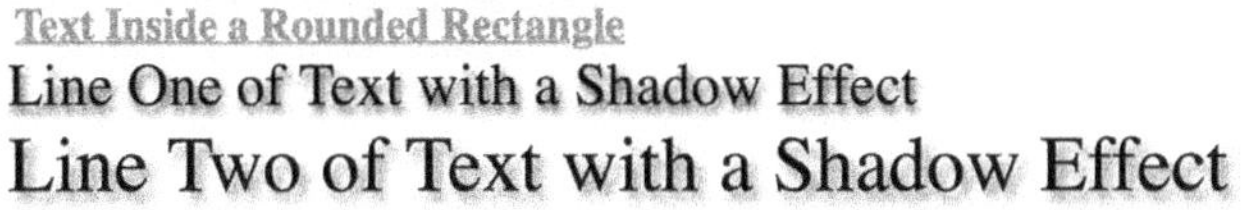

Text Inside a Rounded Rectangle

Line One of Text with a Shadow Effect

Line Two of Text with a Shadow Effect

FIGURE 3.3. CSS3 rounded corners effect.

CSS3 GRADIENTS

CSS3 supports linear gradients and radial gradients, which enable you to create gradient effects that are as visually rich as gradients in other technologies such as SVG and Silverlight. The code samples in this section illustrate how to define linear gradients and radial gradients in CSS3 and then apply them to HTML elements.

Linear Gradients

CSS3 linear gradients require you to specify one or more "color stops," each of which specifies a start color, and end color, and a rendering pattern. WebKit-based browsers support the following syntax to define a linear gradient:

- a start point
- an end point
- a start color using from()
- zero or more stop-colors
- an end color using to()

A start point can be specified as an (x, y) pair of numbers or percentages. For example, the pair (100, 25%) specifies the point that is 100 pixels to the right of the origin and 25% of the way down from the top of the screen. Recall that the origin is located in the upper-left corner of the screen. Listing 3.7 displays the contents of `LinearGradient1.html` and Listing 3.8 displays the contents of `LinearGradient1.css`, which illustrate how to apply linear gradients to text strings that are enclosed in <p> elements and an <h3> element.

LISTING 3.7: `LinearGradient1.html`

```
<!doctype html>
<html lang="en">
<head>
  <title>CSS Linear Gradient Example</title>
  <meta charset="utf-8" />
  <link href="LinearGradient1.css" rel="style sheet"
                              type="text/css">
</head>
<body>
```

```
    <div id="outer">
      <p id="line1">line 1 with a linear gradient</p>
      <p id="line2">line 2 with a linear gradient</p>
      <p id="line3">line 3 with a linear gradient</p>
      <p id="line4">line 4 with a linear gradient</p>
      <p id="outline">line 5 with Shadow Outline</p>
      <h3><a href="#">A Line of Gradient Text</a></h3>
    </div>
  </body>
</html>
```

Listing 3.7 is a simple Web page containing four <p> elements and one <h3> element. Listing 3.7 also references the CSS style sheet LinearGradient1. css that contains CSS selectors that are applied to the four <p> elements and the <h3> element in Listing 3.7.

LISTING 3.8: LinearGradient1.css

```
#line1 {
width: 50%;
font-size: 32px;
background-image: -webkit-gradient(linear, 0% 0%, 0% 100%,
                                   from(#fff), to(#f00));
background-image: -gradient(linear, 0% 0%, 0% 100%,
                            from(#fff), to(#f00));
-webkit-border-radius: 4px;
border-radius: 4px;
}
#line2 {
width: 50%;
font-size: 32px;
background-image: -webkit-gradient(linear, 100% 0%, 0% 100%,
                                   from(#fff), to(#ff0));
background-image: -gradient(linear, 100% 0%, 0% 100%,
                            from(#fff), to(#ff0));
-webkit-border-radius: 4px;
border-radius: 4px;
}
#line3 {
width: 50%;
font-size: 32px;
background-image: -webkit-gradient(linear, 0% 0%, 0% 100%,
                                     from(#f00), to(#00f));
background-image: -gradient(linear, 0% 0%, 0% 100%,
                            from(#f00), to(#00f));
-webkit-border-radius: 4px;
border-radius: 4px;
}
#line4 {
width: 50%;
font-size: 32px;
background-image: -webkit-gradient(linear, 100% 0%, 0% 100%,
                                   from(#f00), to(#00f));
background-image: -gradient(linear, 100% 0%, 0% 100%,
                            from(#f00), to(#00f));
```

```
-webkit-border-radius: 4px;
border-radius: 4px;
}
#outline {
font-size: 2.0em;
font-weight: bold;
color: #fff;
text-shadow: 1px 1px 1px rgba(0,0,0,0.5);
}
h3 {
width: 50%;
position: relative;
margin-top: 0;
font-size: 32px;
font-family: helvetica, ariel;
}
h3 a {
position: relative;
color: red;
text-decoration: none;
-webkit-mask-image:  -webkit-gradient(linear, left top,
                         left bottom, from(rgba(0,0,0,1)),
                         color-stop(50%, rgba(0,0,0,0.5)),
                         to(rgba(0,0,0,0))));
}
h3:after {
content:"This is a Line of Gradient Text";
color: blue;
}
```

The first selector in Listing 3.8 specifies a font-size of 32 for text, a bor-der-radius of 4 (which renders rounded corners), and a linear gradient that varies from white to blue, as shown here:

```
#line1 {
width: 50%;
font-size: 32px;
background-image: -webkit-gradient(linear, 0% 0%, 0% 100%,
                                from(#fff), to(#f00));
background-image: -gradient(linear, 0% 0%, 0% 100%,
                                from(#fff), to(#f00));
-webkit-border-radius: 4px;
border-radius: 4px;
}
```

As you can see, the first selector contains two attributes with a -webkit-prefix and two standard attributes without this prefix. Because the next three selectors in Listing 3.8 are similar to the first selector, we will not discuss their content.

The next CSS selector creates a text outline with a nice shadow effect by rendering the text in white with a thin black shadow, as shown here:

```
color: #fff;
text-shadow: 1px 1px 1px rgba(0,0,0,0.5);
```

The final portion of Listing 3.8 contains three selectors that affect the ren-dering of the <h3> element and its embedded <a> element: the h3 selector specifies the width and font size; the h3 a selector specifies a linear gradient; and the h3:after selector specifies the text string to display. Note that other attributes are specified, but these are the main attributes for these selectors. Figure 3.4 displays the result of applying the selectors in the CSS style sheet LinearGradient1.css to the HTML page LinearGradient1.html.

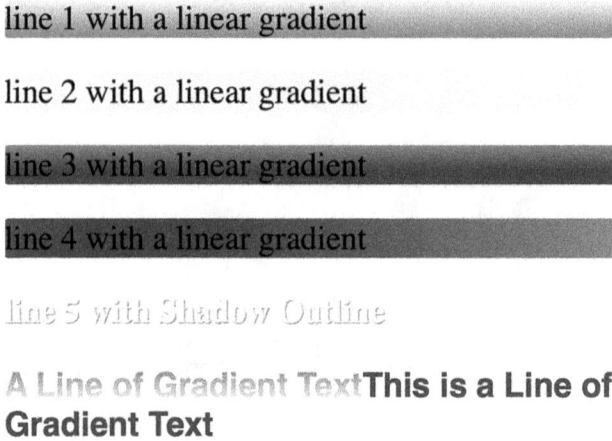

line 1 with a linear gradient

line 2 with a linear gradient

line 3 with a linear gradient

line 4 with a linear gradient

line 5 with Shadow Outline

A Line of Gradient Text**This is a Line of Gradient Text**

FIGURE 3.4. CSS3 linear gradient effect.

Radial Gradients

CSS3 radial gradients are more complex than CSS3 linear gradients, but you can use them to create more complex gradient effects. WebKit-based browsers support the following syntax to define a radial gradient:

- a start point
- a start radius
- an end point
- an end radius
- a start color using from()
- zero or more stop-colors
- an end color using to()

Notice that the syntax for a radial gradient is similar to the syntax for a linear gradient, except that you also specify a start radius and an end radius. Listing 3.9 displays the contents of RadialGradient1.html and Listing 3.10 displays the contents of RadialGradient1.css, which illustrate how to render various circles with radial gradients.

LISTING 3.9: RadialGradient1.html

```
<!doctype html>
<html lang="en">
<head>
  <title>CSS Radial Gradient Example</title>
```

```
  <meta charset="utf-8" />
  <link href="RadialGradient9.css" rel="stylesheet"
type="text/css">
</head>

<body>
 <div id="outer">
  <div id="radial3">Text3</div>
  <div id="radial2">Text2</div>
  <div id="radial4">Text4</div>
  <div id="radial1">Text1</div>
 </div>
</body>
</html>
```

Listing 3.9 contains five DIV elements whose id attribute has value outer, radial1, radial2, radial3, and radial4, respectively. Listing 3.9 also references the CSS style sheet RadialGradient1.css that contains five CSS selectors that are applied to the five <div> elements.

LISTING 3.10: RadialGradient1.css

```
#outer {
position: relative; top: 10px; left: 0px;
}

#radial1 {
font-size: 24px;
width:  300px;
height: 300px;
position: absolute; top: 300px; left: 300px;

background: -webkit-gradient(
  radial, 500 40%, 0, 301 25%, 360, from(red),
  color-stop(0.05, orange), color-stop(0.4, yellow),
  color-stop(0.6, green), color-stop(0.8, blue),
  to(#fff)
 );
}

#radial2 {
font-size: 24px;
width:  500px;
height: 500px;
position: absolute; top: 100px; left: 100px;

background: -webkit-gradient(
  radial, 500 40%, 0, 301 25%, 360, from(red),
  color-stop(0.05, orange), color-stop(0.4, yellow),
  color-stop(0.6, green), color-stop(0.8, blue),
  to(#fff)
 );
}
```

```
#radial3 {
font-size: 24px;
width:   600px;
height: 600px;
position: absolute; top: 0px; left: 0px;

background: -webkit-gradient(
  radial, 500 40%, 0, 301 25%, 360, from(red),
  color-stop(0.05, orange), color-stop(0.4, yellow),
  color-stop(0.6, green), color-stop(0.8, blue),
  to(#fff)
 );
-webkit-box-shadow:  0px 0px 8px #000;
}

#radial4 {
font-size: 24px;
width:   400px;
height: 400px;
position: absolute; top: 200px; left: 200px;

background: -webkit-gradient(
  radial, 500 40%, 0, 301 25%, 360, from(red),
  color-stop(0.05, orange), color-stop(0.4, yellow),
  color-stop(0.6, green), color-stop(0.8, blue),
  to(#fff)
 );
}
```

The first part of the #radial1 selector in Listing 3.10 contains the attributes width and height that specify the dimensions of a rendered rectangle, and also a position attribute that is similar to the position attribute in the #outer selector. The #radial1 also contains a background attribute that defines a radial gradient using the -webkit- prefix, as shown here:

```
background: -webkit-gradient(
  radial, 100 25%, 20, 100 25%, 40, from(blue), to(#fff)
 );
```

The preceding radial gradient specifies the following:

- a start point of (100, 25%)
- a start radius of 20
- an end point of (100, 25%)
- an end radius of 40
- a start color of blue
- an end color of white (#fff)

Notice that the start point and end point are the same, which renders a set of concentric circles that vary from blue to white.

The other four selectors in Listing 3.10 have the same syntax as the first selector, but the rendered radial gradients are significantly different. You can create these and other effects by specifying different start points and end points, and by specifying a start radius that is larger than the end radius.

The #radial4 selector creates a ringed effect by means of two stop-color attributes, as shown here:

```
color-stop(0.2, orange), color-stop(0.4, yellow),
color-stop(0.6, green), color-stop(0.8, blue),
```

You can add additional stop-color attributes to create more complex radial gradients.

Figure 3.5 displays the result of applying the selectors in the CSS style sheet RadialGradient1.css to the HTML page RadialGradient1.html.

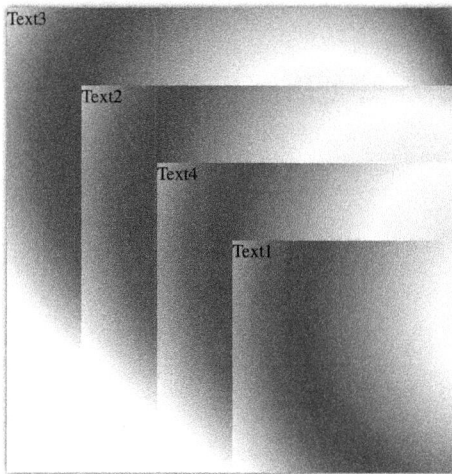

FIGURE 3.5. CSS3 radial gradient effect.

CSS3 2D TRANSFORMS

In addition to transitions, CSS3 supports four transforms that you can apply to 2D shapes and also to PNG files. The four CSS3 transforms are scale, rotate, skew, and translate. The following sections contain code samples that illustrate how to apply each of these CSS3 transforms to a set of PNG files. The animation effects occur when users hover over any of the PNG files; moreover, you can create partial animation effects by moving your mouse quickly between adjacent PNG files.

Zoom Effects With Scale Transforms

The CSS3 transform attribute allows you to specify the scale() function in order to create zoom in/out effects, and the syntax for the scale() method looks like this:

```
scale(someValue);
```

You can replace someValue with any nonzero number. When someValue is between 0 and 1, you will reduce the size of the 2D shape or PNG file, creating a "zoom out" effect; values greater than 1 for someValue will increase the size of the 2D shape or PNG file, creating a "zoom in" effect; and a value of 1 does not perform any changes.

Listing 3.11 displays the contents of Scale1.html and Listing 3.12 displays the contents of Scale1.css, which illustrate how to scale PNG files to create a "hover box" image gallery.

LISTING 3.11: Scale1.html

```
<!DOCTYPE html>
<html lang="en">
<head>
  <title>CSS Scale Transform Example</title>
  <meta charset="utf-8" />
  <link href="Scale1.css" rel="style sheet" type="text/css">
</head>

<body>
  <header>
   <h1>Hover Over any of the Images:</h1>
  </header>

  <div id="outer">
    <img src="Clown1.png"      class="scaled" width="150"
                               height="150"/>
    <img src="Avocadoes1.png"  class="scaled" width="150"
                               height="150"/>
    <img src="Clown1.png"      class="scaled" width="150"
                               height="150"/>
    <img src="Avocadoes1.png"  class="scaled" width="150"
                               height="150"/>
  </div>

</body>
</html>
```

Listing 3.11 references the CSS style sheet Scale1.css, which contains selectors for creating scaled effects, and four HTML <img> elements that reference the PNG files Clown1.png and Avocadoes1.png. The remainder of Listing 3.12 is straightforward, with simple boilerplate text and HTML elements.

LISTING 3.12: Scale1.css

```
#outer {
float: left;
position: relative; top: 50px; left: 50px;
}

img {
-webkit-transition: -webkit-transform 1.0s ease;
```

```
-transition: transform 1.0s ease;
}

img.scaled {
  -webkit-box-shadow: 10px 10px 5px #800;
  box-shadow: 10px 10px 5px #800;
}


img.scaled:hover {
-webkit-transform : scale(2);
-transform : scale(2);
}
```

The `img` selector in Listing 3.12 specifies a `transition` property that contains a `transform` effect that occurs during a one-second interval using the `ease` function, as shown here:

```
-transition: transform 1.0s ease;
```

Next, the selector `img.scaled` specifies a `box-shadow` property that creates a reddish shadow effect (seen in Figure 3.6), as shown here:

```
img.scaled {
  -webkit-box-shadow: 10px 10px 5px #800;
  box-shadow: 10px 10px 5px #800;
}
```

Finally, the selector `img.scaled:hover` specifies a `transform` attribute that uses the `scale()` function in order to double the size of the associated PNG file when users hover over any of the `<img>` elements with their mouse, as shown here:

```
-transform : scale(2);
```

Because the `img` selector specifies a one-second interval using an `ease` function, the scaling effect will last for one second. Experiment with different values for the CSS3 `scale()` function and also different values for the time interval to create the animation effects that suit your needs.

Another point to remember is that you can scale both horizontally and vertically:

```
img {
-webkit-transition: -webkit-transform 1.0s ease;
-transition: transform 1.0s ease;
}
img.mystyle:hover {
-webkit-transform : scaleX(1.5) scaleY(0.5);
-transform : scaleX(1.5) scaleY(0.5);
}
```

Figure 3.6 displays the result of applying the selectors in the CSS style sheet `Scale1.css` to the HTML page `Scale1.html`.

Hover Over any of the Images:

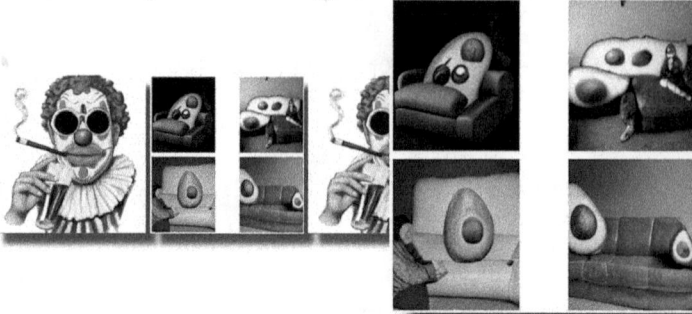

FIGURE 3.6. CSS3 scaling effect.

Rotate Transforms

The CSS3 `transform` attribute allows you to specify the `rotate()` function in order to create scaling effects, and its syntax looks like this:

```
rotate(someValue);
```

You can replace `someValue` with any number. When `someValue` is positive, the rotation is clockwise; when `someValue` is negative, the rotation is counterclockwise; and when `someValue` is zero, there is no rotation effect. In all cases the initial position for the rotation effect is the positive horizontal axis. Listing 3.13 displays the contents of `Rotate1.html`, and Listing 3.14 displays the contents of `Rotate1.css`, which illustrate how to rotate PNG files in opposite directions.

LISTING 3.13: Rotate1.html

```html
<!DOCTYPE html>
<html lang="en">
<head>
  <title>CSS Rotate Transform Example</title>
  <meta charset="utf-8" />
  <link href="Rotate1.css" rel="style sheet"
                           type="text/css">
</head>

<body>
  <header>
   <h1>Hover Over any of the Images:</h1>
  </header>

  <div id="outer">
    <img src="Clown1.png"      class="imageL" width="150"
                               height="150"/>
    <img src="Avocadoes1.png"  class="imageR" width="150"
                               height="150"/>
    <img src="Clown1.png"      class="imageL" width="150"
                               height="150"/>
    <img src="Avocadoes1.png"  class="imageR"
                               width="150" height="150"/>
```

```
    </div>
  </body>
</html>
```

Listing 3.13 references the CSS style sheet `Rotate1.css`, which contains selectors for creating rotation effects, and an HTML `<img>` element that references the PNG files `Clown1.png` and `Avocadoes1.png`. The remainder of Listing 3.13 consists of simple boilerplate text and HTML elements.

LISTING 3.14: `Rotate1.css`

```
#outer {
float: left;
position: relative; top: 100px; left: 150px;
}

img {
-webkit-transition: -webkit-transform 1.0s ease;
-transition: transform 1.0s ease;
}

img.imageL {
  -webkit-box-shadow: 14px 14px 8px #800;
  box-shadow: 14px 14px 8px #800;
}

img.imageR {
  -webkit-box-shadow: 14px 14px 8px #008;
  box-shadow: 14px 14px 8px #008;
}

img.imageL:hover {
-webkit-transform : scale(2) rotate(-45deg);
-transform : scale(2) rotate(-45deg);
}

img.imageR:hover {
-webkit-transform : scale(2) rotate(360deg);
-transform : scale(2) rotate(360deg);
}
```

Listing 3.14 contains the img selector that specifies a `transition` attribute that creates an animation effect during a one-second interval using the `ease` timing function, as shown here:

```
-transition: transform 1.0s ease;
```

Next, the selectors img.imageL and img.imageR contain a property that renders a reddish and bluish background shadow, respectively.

The selector img.imageL:hover specifies a `transform` attribute that performs a counterclockwise scaling effect (doubling the original size) and a rotation effect (45-degrees counterclockwise) when users hover over the `<img>` element with their mouse, as shown here:

```
-transform : scale(2) rotate(-45deg);
```

The selector img.imageR:hover is similar, except that it performs a clockwise rotation of 360 degrees. Figure 3.7 displays the result of applying the selectors in the CSS style sheet `Rotate1.css` to the elements in the HTML page `Rotate1.html`.

Hover Over any of the Images:

FIGURE 3.7. CSS3 rotation effect.

Skew Transforms

The CSS3 transform attribute allows you to specify the `skew()` function in order to create skewing effects, and its syntax looks like this:

```
skew(xAngle, yAngle);
```

You can replace `xAngle` and `yAngle` with any number. When `xAngle` and `yAngle` are positive, the skew effect is clockwise; when `xAngle` and `yAngle` are negative, the skew effect is counterclockwise; and when `xAngle` and `yAngle` are zero, there is no skew effect. In all cases the initial position for the skew effect is the positive horizontal axis. Listing 3.15 displays the contents of `Skew1.html` and Listing 3.16 displays the contents of `Skew1.css`, which illustrate how to skew a PNG file.

LISTING 3.15: `Skew1.html`

```
<!DOCTYPE html>
<html lang="en">
<head>
  <title>CSS Skew Transform Example</title>
  <meta charset="utf-8" />
  <link href="Skew1.css" rel="style sheet" type="text/css">
</head>

<body>
  <header>
   <h1>Hover Over any of the Images:</h1>
  </header>

  <div id="outer">
    <img src="Clown1.png"      class="skewed1" width="150"
                               height="150"/>
```

```
      <img src="Avocadoes1.png" class="skewed2" width="150"
                                height="150"/>
      <img src="Clown1.png"     class="skewed3" width="150"
                                height="150"/>
      <img src="Avocadoes1.png" class="skewed4" width="150"
                                height="150"/>
  </div>
</body>
</html>
```

Listing 3.15 references the CSS style sheet Skew1.css, which contains selectors for creating skew effects, and an <img> element that references the PNG files Clown1.png and Avocadoes1.png. The remainder of Listing 3.15 consists of simple boilerplate text and HTML elements.

LISTING 3.16: Skew1.html

```
#outer {
float: left;
position: relative; top: 100px; left: 100px;
}
img {
-webkit-transition: -webkit-transform 1.0s ease;
-transition: transform 1.0s ease;
}

img.skewed1 {
  -webkit-box-shadow: 14px 14px 8px #800;
  box-shadow: 14px 14px 8px #800;
}

img.skewed2 {
  -webkit-box-shadow: 14px 14px 8px #880;
  box-shadow: 14px 14px 8px #880;
}

img.skewed3 {
  -webkit-box-shadow: 14px 14px 8px #080;
  box shadow: 14px 14px 0px #000;
}

img.skewed4 {
  -webkit-box-shadow: 14px 14px 8px #008;
  box-shadow: 14px 14px 8px #008;
}
img.skewed1:hover {
-webkit-transform : scale(2) skew(-10deg, -30deg);
-transform : scale(2) skew(-10deg, -30deg);
}

img.skewed2:hover {
-webkit-transform : scale(2) skew(10deg, 30deg);
-transform : scale(2) skew(10deg, 30deg);
}
```

```
img.skewed3:hover {
-webkit-transform : scale(0.4) skew(-10deg, -30deg);
-transform : scale(0.4) skew(-10deg, -30deg);
}

img.skewed4:hover {
-webkit-transform : scale(0.5, 1.5) skew(10deg, -30deg);
-transform : scale(0.5, 1.5) skew(10deg, -30deg);
opacity:0.5;
}
```

Listing 3.16 contains the img selector that specifies a transition attribute that creates an animation effect during a one-second interval using the ease timing function, as shown here:

```
-transition: transform 1.0s ease;
```

The four selectors img.skewed1, img.skewed2, img.skewed3, and img.skewed4 create background shadow effects with darker shades of red, yellow, green, and blue, respectively (all of which you have seen in earlier code samples). The selector img.skewed1:hover specifies a transform attribute that performs a skew effect when users hover over the first <img> element with their mouse, as shown here:

```
-transform : scale(2) skew(-10deg, -30deg);
```

The other three CSS3 selectors also use a combination of the CSS functions skew() and scale() to create distinct visual effects. Notice that the fourth hover selector also sets the opacity property to 0.5, which is applied in parallel with the other effects in this selector. Figure 3.8 displays the result of applying the selectors in the CSS style sheet Skew1.css to the elements in the HTML page Skew1.html.

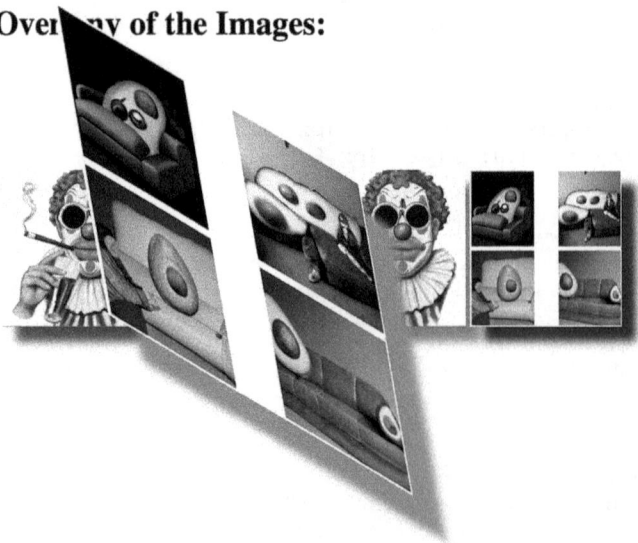

FIGURE 3.8. CSS3 skew effect.

Translate Transforms

The CSS3 transform attribute allows you to specify the `translate()` function in order to create translation or "shifting" effects, and its syntax looks like this:

```
translate(xDirection, yDirection);
```

The translation is in relation to the origin, which is the upper-left corner of the screen. Thus, positive values for `xDirection` and `yDirection` produce a shift toward the right and a shift downward, respectively, whereas negative values for `xDirection` and `yDirection` produce a shift toward the left and a shift upward; zero values for `xDirection` and `yDirection` do not cause any translation effect. Listing 3.17 displays the contents of `Translate1.html` and Listing 3.18 displays the contents of `Translate1.css`, which illustrate how to apply a translation effect to a PNG file.

LISTING 3.17: `Translate1.html`

```
<!DOCTYPE html>
<html lang="en">
<head>
  <title>CSS Translate Transform Example</title>
  <meta charset="utf-8" />
  <link href="Translate1.css" rel="style sheet"
                              type="text/css">
</head>

<body>
  <header>
   <h1>Hover Over any of the Images:</h1>
  </header>

  <div id="outer">
    <img src="Clown1.png"     class="trans1" width="150"
                              height="150"/>
    <img src="Avocadoes1.png" class="trans2" width="150"
                              height="150"/>
    <img src="Clown1.png"     class="trans3" width="150"
                              height="150"/>
    <img src="Avocadoes1.png" class="trans4" width="150"
                              height="150"/>
  </div>
</body>
</html>
```

Listing 3.17 references the CSS style sheet `Translate1.css`, which contains selectors for creating translation effects, and an `<img>` element that references the PNG files `Clown1.png` and `Avocadoes1.png`. The remainder of Listing 3.17 consists of straightforward boilerplate text and HTML elements.

LISTING 3.18: `Translate1.css`

```
#outer {
float: left;
position: relative; top: 100px; left: 100px;
}

img {
-webkit-transition: -webkit-transform 1.0s ease;
-transition: transform 1.0s ease;
}

img.trans1 {
  -webkit-box-shadow: 14px 14px 8px #800;
  box-shadow: 14px 14px 8px #800;
}

img.trans2 {
  -webkit-box-shadow: 14px 14px 8px #880;
  box-shadow: 14px 14px 8px #880;
}

img.trans3 {
  -webkit-box-shadow: 14px 14px 8px #080;
  box-shadow: 14px 14px 8px #080;
}

img.trans4 {
  -webkit-box-shadow: 14px 14px 8px #008;
  box-shadow: 14px 14px 8px #008;
}

img.trans1:hover {
-webkit-transform : scale(2) translate(100px, 50px);
-transform : scale(2) translate(100px, 50px);
}

img.trans2:hover {
-webkit-transform : scale(0.5) translate(-50px, -50px);
-transform : scale(0.5) translate(-50px, -50px);
}

img.trans3:hover {
-webkit-transform : scale(0.5,1.5) translate(0px, 0px);
-transform : scale(0.5,1.5) translate(0px, 0px);
}

img.trans4:hover {
-webkit-transform : scale(2) translate(50px, -50px);
-transform : scale(2) translate(100px, 50px);
}
```

Listing 3.17 contains the `img` selector that specifies a transform effect during a one-second interval using the `ease` timing function, as shown here:

```
-transition: transform 1.0s ease;
```

The four selectors `img.trans1`, `img.trans2`, `img.trans3`, and `img.trans4` create background shadow effects with darker shades of red, yellow, green, and blue, respectively, just as you saw in the previous section.

The selector `img.trans1:hover` specifies a `transform` attribute that performs a scale effect and a translation effect when users hover over the first `<img>` element with their mouse, as shown here:

```
-webkit-transform : scale(2) translate(100px, 50px);
transform : scale(2) translate(100px, 50px);
```

The other three selectors contain similar code involving a combination of a translate and a scaling effect, each of which creates a distinct visual effect. Figure 3.9 displays the result of applying the selectors defined in the CSS3 style sheet `Translate1.css` to the elements in the HTML page `Translate1.html`.

Hover Over any of the Images:

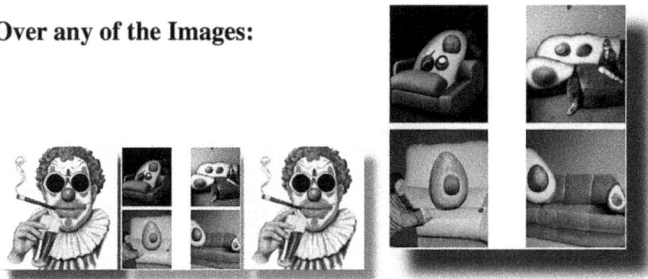

FIGURE 3.9. PNG files with CSS3 scale and translate effects.

SUMMARY

This chapter started with the structure of a minimal HTML document and then a discussion about browser support for CSS3.

Then you saw various code samples that illustrate how to create shadow effects, rectangles with rounded corners, and how to use linear gradients and radial gradients.

In addition, you learned how to use several CSS3 transforms and how to apply them to PNGs in HTML Web pages.

CHAPTER 4

CSS3 3D ANIMATION

This chapter continues the discussion of CSS3 that began in Chapter 2, with a focus on examples of creating 3D effects and 3D animation effects.

This first part of this chapter shows you how to display a CSS3-based cube, followed by examples of CSS3 transitions for creating simple animation effects, such as glow effects and bouncing effects. Specifically, you will learn how to use CSS3 `keyframe` and the CSS3 functions `scale3d()`, `rotate3d()`, and `translate3d()` that enable you to create 3D animation effects.

The second part of this chapter contains examples of creating glowing effects, fading image effects, and bouncing effects. You will also see how to create CSS3 effects for text and how to render multicolumn text.

The third part of this chapter briefly discusses CSS3 media queries, which enable you to render a given HTML page based on the properties of the device.

Keep in mind that you can also use JavaScript in order to create visual effects that can be easier than using CSS3 alone. Moreover, you can use CSS3 media queries for rendering HMTL pages differently on different mobile devices. Neither of these topics is covered in this book, but an Internet search will provide various links and tutorials that contain information on these topics.

A CSS3-BASED CUBE

You can use the CSS3 transforms `rotate()`, `scale()`, and `skew()` in order to create and render a 3D cube with gradient shading. Listing 4.1 displays the contents of `3DCubeHover1.html` and Listing 4.2 displays the contents of `3DCubeHover1.css`, which illustrates how to simulate a cube in CSS3.

LISTING 4.1: `3DCubeHover1.html`

```html
<!DOCTYPE html>
<html lang="en">
<head>
<title>CSS 3D Cube Example</title>
<meta charset="utf-8" />
<link href="3DCSS1.css" rel="stylesheet" type="text/css">
</head>

<body>
  <header>
   <h1>Hover Over the Cube Faces:</h1>
   </header>
 <div id="outer">
  <div id="top">Text1</div>
  <div id="left">Text2</div>
  <div id="right">Text3</div>
 </div>
</body>
</html>
```

Listing 4.1 is a straightforward HTML page that references the CSS stylesheet `3DCSS1.css` that contains the CSS3 selectors for styling the HTML `<div>` elements in this Web page.

LISTING 4.2: `3DCSS1.css`

```css
/* animation effects */
#right:hover {
-webkit-transition: -webkit-transform 3.0s ease;
-transition: transform 3.0s ease;

-webkit-transform : scale(1.2) skew(-10deg, -30deg)
    rotate(-45deg);
-transform : scale(1.2) skew(-10deg, -30deg)
    rotate(-45deg);
}

#left:hover {
-webkit-transition: -webkit-transform 2.0s ease;
-transition: transform 2.0s ease;

-webkit-transform : scale(0.8) skew(-10deg, -30deg)
    rotate(-45deg);
-transform : scale(0.8) skew(-10deg, -30deg)
    rotate(-45deg);
}

#top:hover {
-webkit-transition: -webkit-transform 2.0s ease;
-transition: transform 2.0s ease;

-webkit-transform : scale(0.5) skew(-20deg, -30deg)
    rotate(45deg);
-transform : scale(0.5) skew(-20deg, -30deg) rotate(45deg);
}
```

```
/* size and position */
#right, #left, #top {
position:relative;  padding: 0px;  width: 200px;
   height: 200px;
}

#left {
  font-size: 48px;
  left: 20px;

  background-image:
    -webkit-radial-gradient(red 4px, transparent 28px),
    -webkit-repeating-radial-gradient(red 0px,  yellow 4px,
                    green 8px, red 12px, transparent 26px,
                    blue 20px, red 24px, transparent 28px,
                    blue 12px),
    -webkit-repeating-radial-gradient(red 0px,  yellow 4px,
                    green 8px, red 12px, transparent 26px,
                    blue 20px, red 24px, transparent 28px,
                    blue 12px);

  background-size: 100px 40px, 40px 100px;
  background-position: 0 0;

  -webkit-transform: skew(0deg, 30deg);
}

#right {
  font-size: 48px;
  width:  170px;
  top: -192px;
  left: 220px;

  background-image:
    -webkit-radial-gradient(red 4px, transparent 48px),
    -webkit-repeating-linear-gradient(0deg, red 5px,
                    green 4px, yellow 8px, blue 12px,
                    transparent 16px, red 20px, blue 24px,
                    transparent 28px, transparent 32px),
    -webkit-radial-gradient(blue 8px, transparent 68px);

  background-size: 120px 120px, 24px 24px;
  background-position: 0 0;

  -webkit-transform: skew(0deg, -30deg);
}

#top {
  font-size: 48px;
  top: 50px;
  left: 105px;

  background-image:
    -webkit-radial-gradient(white 2px, transparent 8px),
    -webkit-repeating-linear-gradient(45deg, white 2px,
                    yellow 8px, green 4px, red 12px,
```

```
                    transparent 26px, blue 20px, red 24px,
                    transparent 28px, blue 12px),
    -webkit-repeating-linear-gradient(-45deg, white 2px,
                    yellow 8px, green 4px, red 12px,
                    transparent 26px, blue 20px, red 24px,
                    transparent 28px,  blue 12px);

  background-size: 100px 30px, 30px 100px;
  background-position: 0 0;

  -webkit-transform: rotate(60deg) skew(0deg, -30deg);
                    scale(1, 1.16);
}
```

The first three selectors in Listing 4.2 define the animation effects when users hover on the top, left, or right faces of the cube. In particular, the #right:hover selector performs an animation effect during a three-second interval when users hover over the right face of the cube, as shown here:

```
#right:hover {
-webkit-transition: -webkit-transform 3.0s ease;
-transition: transform 3.0s ease;

-webkit-transform : scale(1.2) skew(-10deg, -30deg)
                                rotate(-45deg);
-transform : scale(1.2) skew(-10deg, -30deg)
                                rotate(-45deg);
}
```

The transition attribute is already familiar to you, and notice that the transform attribute specifies the CSS3 transform functions scale(), skew(), and rotate(), all of which you have seen already in this chapter. These three functions are applied simultaneously, which means that you will see a scaling, skewing, and rotating effect happening at the same time instead of sequentially.

The last three selectors in Listing 4.2 define the properties of each face of the cube. For example, the #left selector specifies the font size for some text and also positional attributes for the left face of the cube. The most complex portion of the #left selector is the value of the background-image attribute, which consists of a WebKit-specific combination of a radial gradient, a repeating radial gradient, and another radial gradient. Notice that the left face is a rectangle that is transformed into a parallelogram using this line of code:

```
  -webkit-transform: skew(0deg, -30deg);
```

The #top selector and #right selector contain code that is comparable to the #left selector, and you can experiment with their values in order to create other visual effects. Figure 4.1 displays the result of applying the CSS selectors in 3DCube1.css to the <div> elements in the HTML page 3DCube1.html.

Hover Over the Cube Faces:

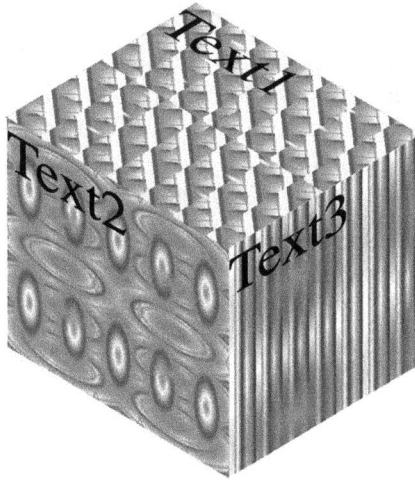

FIGURE 4.1. A CSS3-based cube.

CSS3 TRANSITIONS

CSS3 transitions involve changes to CSS values in a smooth fashion, and they are initiated by user gestures, such as mouse clicks, focus, or hover effects. WebKit originally developed CSS3 transitions, and they are also supported in many versions of Safari, Chrome, Opera, and Firefox by using browser-specific prefixes. Keep in mind that there are toolkits (such as jQuery and Prototype) that support transitions effects similar to their CSS3-based counterparts.

The basic syntax for creating a CSS transition is a "triple" that specifies:

- a CSS property
- a duration (in seconds)
- a transition timing function

Here is an example of a WebKit-based transition:

```
-webkit-transition-property: background;
-webkit-transition-duration: 0.5s;
-webkit-transition-timing-function: ease;
```

Fortunately, you can also combine these transitions in one line, as shown here:

```
-webkit-transition: background 0.5s ease;
```

Here is an example of a CSS3 selector that includes these transitions:

```
a.foo {
padding: 3px 6px;
background: #f00;
-webkit-transition: background 0.5s ease;
```

```
}
a.foo:focus, a.foo:hover {
background: #00f;
}
```

Transitions currently require browser-specific prefixes in order for them to work correctly in browsers that are not based on WebKit. Here is an example for Internet Explorer (IE), Firefox, and Opera:

```
-ie-webkit-transition: background 0.5s ease;
-moz-webkit-transition: background 0.5s ease;
-o-webkit-transition: background 0.5s ease;
```

Currently, you can specify one of the following transition timing functions (using browser-specific prefixes):

- ease
- ease-in
- ease-out
- ease-in-out
- cubic-bezier

If these transition functions do not meet your needs, you can create custom functions using this online tool: www.matthewlein.com/ceaser. You can specify many properties with –webkit-transition-property, and an extensive list of properties is here:

https://developer.mozilla.org/en/CSS/CSS_transitions.

SIMPLE CSS3 ANIMATION EFFECTS

The CSS3-based code samples that you saw in the previous chapter involved primarily static visual effects. By contrast, the CSS3 code samples in this section illustrate how to create "glowing" effects and "bouncing" effects involving HTML <input> elements. Later you will see animation effects created with other HTML elements.

Glowing Effects

You can combine keyframes and the hover pseudo selector in order to create an animation effect when users hover with their mouse on a specific element in an HTML page. Listing 4.3 displays the contents of Transition1.html and Listing 4.4 displays the contents of Transition1.css, which contains CSS3 selectors that create a glowing effect on an input field.

LISTING 4.3: Transition1.html

```
<!DOCTYPE html>
<html lang="en">
<head>
  <title>CSS Animation Example</title>
```

```
    <meta charset="utf-8" />
    <link href="Transition1.css" rel="stylesheet"
                                 type="text/css">
</head>

<body>
  <div id="outer">
    <input id="input" type="text" value="This is an input
                                         line"></input>
  </div>
</body>
</html>
```

Listing 4.3 is a simple HTML page that contains a reference to the CSS style sheet Transition1.css and one HTML <div> element that contains an <input> field element. As you will see, an animation effect is created when users hover over the <input> element with their mouse.

LISTING 4.4: Transition1.css

```
#outer {
position: relative; top: 20px; left: 20px;
}

@-webkit-keyframes glow {
  0% {
    -webkit-box-shadow: 0 0 24px rgba(255, 255, 255, 0.5);
  }
  50% {
    -webkit-box-shadow: 0 0 24px rgba(255, 0, 0, 0.9);
  }
  100% {
    -webkit-box-shadow: 0 0 24px rgba(255, 255, 255, 0.5);
  }
}

#input {
font-size: 24px;
-webkit-border-radius: 4px;
border-radius: 4px;
}
#input:hover {
 -webkit-animation: glow 2.0s 3 ease;
}
```

Listing 4.4 contains a keyframes selector (called "glow") that specifies three shadow effects. The first shadow effect (which occurs at time 0 of the animation effect) renders a white color with whose opacity is 0.5. The second shadow effect (at the midway point of the animation effect) renders a red color whose opacity is 0.9. The third shadow effect (which occurs at the end of the animation effect) is the same as the first animation effect.

The #input selector is applied to the input field in Transition1.html in order to render a rounded rectangle. The #input:hover selector uses the glow keyframes in order to create an animation effect for a two-second interval, repeated three times, using an ease function, as shown here:

```
-webkit-animation: glow 2.0s 3 ease;
```

Figure 4.2 displays the result of applying the selectors in `Transition1.css` to the elements in the HTML page `Transition1.html`.

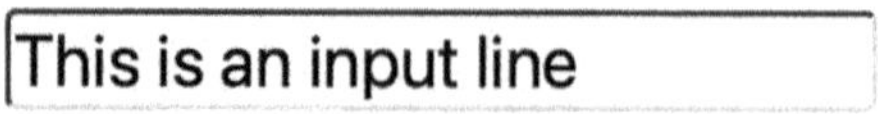

This is an input line

FIGURE 4.2. CSS3 glowing transition effect.

Image Fading and Rotating Effects With CSS3

This section shows you how to create a fading effect with PNG images. Listing 4.5 displays the contents of `FadeRotateImages1.html` and Listing 4.6 displays the contents of `FadeRotateImages1.css`, which illustrate how to create a "fading" effect on a JPG file and a glowing effect on another PNG file.

LISTING 4.5: FadeRotateImages1.html

```
<!DOCTYPE html>
<html lang="en">
<head>
  <title>CSS3 Fade and Rotate Images</title>
  <meta charset="utf-8" />
  <link href="FadeRotateImages1.css" rel="stylesheet"
                                      type="text/css">
</head>

<body>
  <div id="outer">
    <img class="lower" width="200" height="200"
                                src="Clown1.png" />
    <img class="upper" width="200" height="200"
                                src="Avocadoes.png" />
  </div>

  <div id="third">
    <img width="200" height="200" src="Clown1.png" />
  </div>
</body>
```

Listing 4.5 contains a reference to the CSS style sheet `FadeRotateImages1.css` that contains CSS selectors for creating a fading effect and a glowing effect. The first HTML `<div>` element in Listing 4.5 contains two `<img>` elements; when users hover over the rendered PNG file, it will "fade" and reveal another PNG file. The second HTML `<div>` element contains one `<img>` element, and when users hover over this PNG, a CSS3 selector will rotate the referenced PNG file about the vertical axis.

LISTING 4.6: `FadeRotateImages1.css`

```css
#outer {
 position: absolute; top: 20px; left: 20px;
 margin: 0 auto;
}

#outer img {
 position:absolute; left:0;
 -webkit-transition: opacity 1s ease-in-out;
 transition: opacity 1s ease-in-out;
}

#outer img.upper:hover {
  opacity:0;
}

#third img {
position: absolute; top: 20px; left: 250px;
}
#third img:hover {
 -webkit-animation: rotatey 2.0s 3 ease;
}

@-webkit-keyframes rotatey {
  0% {
    -webkit-transform: rotateY(45deg);
  }
  50% {
    -webkit-transform: rotateY(90deg);
  }
  100% {
    -webkit-transform: rotateY(0);
  }
}
```

We will skip the details of the code in Listing 4.6 that is already familiar to you. The key point for creating the fading effect is to set the opacity value to 0 when users hover over the leftmost image, and the one line of code in the CSS selector is shown here:

```css
#outer img.upper:hover {
  opacity:0;
}
```

As you can see, this code sample shows you that it's possible to create attractive visual effects without complicated code or logic.

Next, Listing 4.6 defines a CSS3 selector that creates a rotation effect about the vertical axis by invoking the CSS3 function `rotateY()` in the keyframe `rotatey`. Note that you can create a rotation effect about the other two axes by replacing `rotateY()` with the CSS3 function `rotateX()` or the CSS3 function `rotateZ()`. You can even use these three functions in the same keyframe to create 3D effects. CSS3 3D effects are discussed in more detail later in this chapter. Figure 4.3 displays the result of applying the selectors in the CSS style sheet `FadeRotateImages1.css` to `FadeRotateImages1.html`.

FIGURE 4.3. CSS3 fade and rotate JPG effects.

Bouncing Effects

This section shows you how to create a "bouncing" animation effect. Listing 4.7 displays the contents of `Bounce2.html` and Listing 4.8 displays the contents of `Bounce2.css`, which illustrate how to create a bouncing effect on an input field.

LISTING 4.7: `Bounce2.html`

```
<!DOCTYPE html>
<html lang="en">
<head>
  <title>CSS Animation Example</title>
  <meta charset="utf-8" />
  <link href="Bounce2.css" rel="stylesheet"
                           type="text/css">
</head>

<body>
  <div id="outer">
    <input id="input" type="text" value="An input line"/>
  </div>
</body>
</html>
```

Listing 4.7 is another straightforward HTML page that contains a reference to the CSS style sheet `Bounce2.css` and one HTML `<div>` element that contains an `<input>` field element. The CSS style sheet creates a bouncing animation effect when users hover over the `<input>` element with their mouse.

LISTING 4.8: `Bounce2.css`

```
#outer {
position: relative; top: 50px; left: 100px;
}

@-webkit-keyframes bounce {
  0% {
```

```
      left: 50px;
      top: 100px;
      background-color: #ff0000;
  }
  25% {
    left: 100px;
    top: 150px;
    background-color: #ffff00;
  }
  50% {
    left: 50px;
    top: 200px;
    background-color: #00ff00;
  }
  75% {
    left: 0px;
    top: 150px;
    background-color: #0000ff;
  }
  100% {
    left: 50px;
    top: 100px;
    background-color: #ff0000;
  }
}

#input {
font-size: 24px;
-webkit-border-radius: 4px;
border-radius: 4px;
}

#outer:hover {
 -webkit-animation: bounce 2.0s 4 ease;
}
```

Listing 4.8 contains a keyframes selector (called "bounce") that specifies five time intervals: the 0%, 25%, 50%, 75%, and 100% points of the duration of the animation effect. Each time interval specifies values for the attributes left, top, and background color of the <input> field. Despite the simplicity of this keyframes selector, it creates a pleasing animation effect.

The #input selector is applied to the input field in Bounce2.html in order to render a rounded rectangle. The #input:hover selector uses the bounce keyframes in order to create an animation effect for a two-second interval, repeated four times, using an ease function, as shown here:

```
 -webkit-animation: bounce 2.0s 4 ease;
```

Figure 4.4 displays the result of applying the selectors in the CSS style sheet Bounce2.css to the elements in the HTML page Bounce2.html.

An input line

FIGURE 4.4. CSS3 bouncing animation effect.

CSS3 EFFECTS FOR TEXT

You have seen examples of rendering text strings as part of several code samples in the previous chapter, and in this section we discuss a new feature of CSS3 that enables you to render text in multiple columns.

Rendering Multicolumn Text

CSS3 supports multicolumn text, which can create a nice visual effect when a Web page contains significant amounts of text. Listing 4.9 displays the contents of MultiColumns1.html and Listing 4.10 displays the contents of Multi-Columns1.css, which illustrate how to render multicolumn text.

LISTING 4.9: MultiColumns1.html

```
<!doctype html>
<html lang="en">
<head>
  <title>CSS Multi Columns Example</title>
  <meta charset="utf-8" />
  <link href="MultiColumns1.css" rel="stylesheet"
type="text/css">
</head>

<body>
  <header>
   <h1>Hover Over the Multi-Column Text:</h1>
  </header>

  <div id="outer">
   <p id="line1">.</p>
   <article>
     <div id="columns">
       <p> CSS enables you to define selectors that specify
the style or the manner in which you want to render
elements in an HTML page.  CSS helps you modularize your
HTML content and since you can place your CSS definitions in
a separate file, you can also re-use the same CSS definitions
in multiple HTML files.
       </p>
       <p>  Moreover, CSS also enables you to simplify the
updates that you need to make to elements in HTML pages.
For example, suppose that multiple HTML table elements use
a CSS rule that specifies the color red.  If you later need
to change the color to blue, you can effect such a change
simply by making one change (i.e., changing red to blue) in
one CSS rule.
       </p>
       <p>  Without a CSS rule, you would be forced to
manually update the color attribute in every HTML table
element that is affected, which is error-prone, time-
consuming, and extremely inefficient.
       <p>
```

```
    </div>
   </article>
   <p id="line1">.</p>
  </div>
</body>
</html>
```

The HTML page in Listing 4.9 contains semantic tags for rendering the text in several HTML <p> elements. As you can see, this H TML5 page is straightforward, and the multicolumn effects are defined in the CSS stylesheet Multi-Columns1.css that is displayed in Listing 4.10.

LISTING 4.10: MultiColumns1.css

```
/* animation effects */
#columns:hover {
-webkit-transition: -webkit-transform 3.0s ease;
-transition: transform 3.0s ease;

-webkit-transform : scale(0.5) skew(-20deg, -30deg)
rotate(45deg);
-transform : scale(0.5) skew(-20deg, -30deg) rotate(45deg);
}

#line1:hover {
-webkit-transition: -webkit-transform 3.0s ease;
-transition: transform 3.0s ease;

-webkit-transform : scale(0.5) skew(-20deg, -30deg)
rotate(45deg);
-transform : scale(0.5) skew(-20deg, -30deg) rotate(45deg);
background-image: -webkit-gradient(linear, 0% 0%, 0% 100%,
                                   from(#fff), to(#00f));
background-image: -gradient(linear, 0% 0%, 0% 100%,
                            from(#fff), to(#00f));
-webkit-border-radius: 8px;border-radius: 8px;}

#columns {
-webkit-column-count : 3;
-webkit-column-gap : 80px;
-webkit-column-rule : 1px solid rgb(255,255,255);
column-count : 3;
column-gap : 80px;
column-rule : 1px solid rgb(255,255,255);
}

#line1 {
color: red;
font-size: 24px;
background-image: -webkit-gradient(linear, 0% 0%, 0% 100%,
                                   from(#fff), to(#f00));
background-image: -gradient(linear, 0% 0%, 0% 100%,
                            from(#fff), to(#f00));
-webkit-border-radius: 4px;border-radius: 4px;
}
```

The first two selectors in Listing 4.10 create an animation effect when users hover over the <div> elements whose id attribute is columns or line1. Both selectors create an animation effect during a three-second interval using the CSS3 functions scale(), skew(), and rotate(), as shown here:

```
-webkit-transition: -webkit-transform 3.0s ease;
-transition: transform 3.0s ease;
-webkit-transform : scale(0.5) skew(-20deg, -30deg)
rotate(45deg);
```

The second selector also defines a linear gradient background effect.

The #columns selector in Listing 4.10 contains three layout-related attributes. The column-count attribute is 3, so the text is displayed in 3 columns; the column-gap attribute is 80px, so there is a space of eighty pixels between adjacent columns; the column-rule attribute specifies a white background.

The #line1 selector specifies a linear gradient that creates a nice visual effect above and below the multicolumn text. Figure 4.5 displays the result of applying the CSS selectors in MultiColumns1.css to the text in the HTML page MultiColumns1.html.

Hover Over the Multi-Column Text:

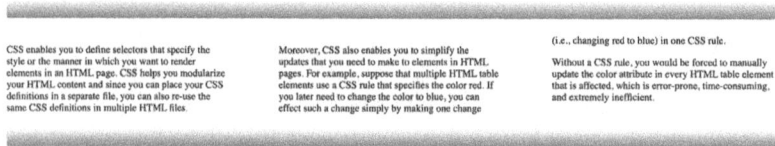

CSS enables you to define selectors that specify the style or the manner in which you want to render elements in an HTML page. CSS helps you modularize your HTML content and since you can place your CSS definitions in a separate file, you can also re-use the same CSS definitions in multiple HTML files.

Moreover, CSS also enables you to simplify the updates that you need to make to elements in HTML pages. For example, suppose that multiple HTML table elements use a CSS rule that specifies the color red. If you later need to change the color to blue, you can effect such a change simply by making one change

(i.e., changing red to blue) in one CSS rule.

Without a CSS rule, you would be forced to manually update the color attribute in every HTML table element that is affected, which is error-prone, time-consuming, and extremely inefficient.

FIGURE 4.5. Rendering multicolumn text in CSS3.

CSS3 MEDIA QUERIES

CSS3 media queries determine the following attributes of a device:

- browser window width and height
- device width and height
- orientation (landscape or portrait)
- resolution

CSS3 media queries enable you to write mobile applications that will render differently on devices with differing width, height, orientation, and resolution. As a simple example, consider this media query that loads the CSS stylesheet mystuff.css only if the device is a screen and the maximum width of the device is 480px:

```
<link rel="stylesheet" type="text/css"
    media="screen and (max-device-width: 480px)"
                            href="mystuff.css"/>
```

As you can see, this media query contains a media attribute that specifies two components:

```
a media type (screen)
```

```
a query (max-device-width: 480px)
```

The preceding example is a very simple CSS3 media query; fortunately, you can combine multiple components in order to test the values of multiple attributes, as shown in the following pair of CSS3 selectors:

```
@media screen and (max-device-width: 480px) and
                                  (resolution: 160dpi) {
  #innerDiv {
    float: none;
  }
}
@media screen and (min-device-width: 481px) and
(resolution: 160dpi) {
  #innerDiv {
    float: left;
  }
}
```

In the first CSS3 selector, the HTML element whose id attribute has the value innerDiv will have a float property whose value is none on any device whose maximum screen width is 480px. In the second CSS3 selector, the HTML element whose id attribute has the value innerDiv will have a float property whose value is left on any device whose minimum screen width is 481px.

CSS3 3D ANIMATION EFFECTS

As you know by now, CSS3 supports keyframes for creating animation effects (and the duration of those effects) at various points in time. The example in this section uses a CSS3 keyframe and various combinations of the CSS3 functions scale3d(), rotate3d(), and translate3d() in order to create an animation effect that lasts for four minutes. Listing 4.11 displays the contents of the HTML Web page Anim240Flicker3DLGrad4.html, which is a very simple HTML page that contains four <div> elements.

LISTING 4.11: Anim240Flicker3DLGrad4.html

```
<!DOCTYPE html>
<html lang="en">
<head>
  <title>CSS3 Animation Example</title>
  <meta charset="utf-8" />
  <link href="Anim240Flicker3DLGrad4.css" rel="stylesheet"
type="text/css">
</head>

<body>
 <div id="outer">
  <div id="linear1">Text1</div>
  <div id="linear2">Text2</div>
  <div id="linear3">Text3</div>
  <div id="linear4">Text4</div>
 </div>
```

```
</body>
</html>
```

Listing 4.11 is a very simple HTML page with corresponding CSS selectors (shown in Listing 4.12). As usual, the real complexity occurs in the CSS selectors that contain the code for creating the animation effects. Because Anim-240Flicker3DLGrad4.css is such a lengthy code sample, only a portion of the code is displayed in Listing 4.12. However, the complete code is available in the companion files for this book (see preface for obtaining these files).

LISTING 4.12: Anim240Flicker3DLGrad4.css

```
@-webkit-keyframes upperLeft {
    0% {
        -webkit-transform: matrix(1.5, 0.5,  0.0, 1.5, 0, 0)
                           matrix(1.0, 0.0,  1.0, 1.0, 0, 0);
    }
    10% {
        -webkit-transform: translate3d(50px,50px,50px)
                           rotate3d(50,50,50,-90deg)
                           skew(-15deg,0) scale3d(1.25,
                           1.25, 1.25);
    }
    // similar code omitted
    90% {
        -webkit-transform: matrix(2.0, 0.5,  1.0, 2.0, 0, 0)
                           matrix(1.5, 0.0,  0.5, 2.5, 0, 0);
    }
    95% {
        -webkit-transform: translate3d(-50px,-50px,-50px)
                           rotate3d(-50,-50,-50, 120deg)
                           skew(135deg,0) scale3d(0.3, 0.4,
                           0.5);
    }
    96% {
        -webkit-transform: matrix(0.2, 0.3, -0.5, 0.5, 100,
                                  200)
                           matrix(0.4, 0.5,  0.5, 0.2, 200,
                                  50);
    }
    97% {
        -webkit-transform: translate3d(50px,-50px,50px)
                           rotate3d(-50,50,-50, 120deg)
                           skew(315deg,0) scale3d(0.5, 0.4,
                           0.3);
    }
    98% {
        -webkit-transform: matrix(0.4, 0.5,  0.5, 0.3, 200,
                                  50)
                           matrix(0.3, 0.5, -0.5, 0.4, 50,
                                  150);
    }
    99% {
        -webkit-transform: translate3d(150px,50px,50px)
```

```
                            rotate3d(60,80,100, 240deg)
                            skew(315deg,0) scale3d(1.0, 0.7,
                            0.3);
    }
    100% {
        -webkit-transform: matrix(1.0, 0.0,  0.0, 1.0, 0, 0)
                           matrix(1.0, 0.5,  1.0, 1.5, 0, 0);
    }
}
// code omitted for brevity
#linear1 {
font-size: 96px;
text-stroke: 8px blue;
text-shadow: 8px 8px 8px #FF0000;
width:   400px;
height: 250px;

position: relative; top: 0px; left: 0px;

background-image: -webkit-gradient(linear, 100% 50%, 0% 100%,
                                   from(#f00),
                                   color-stop(0.2, orange),
                                   color-stop(0.4, yellow),
                                   color-stop(0.6, blue),
                                   color-stop(0.8, green),
                                   to(#00f));
// similar code omitted
-webkit-border-radius: 4px;
border-radius: 4px;
-webkit-box-shadow:  30px 30px 30px #000;
-webkit-animation-name: lowerLeft;
-webkit-animation-duration: 240s;
}
```

Listing 4.12 contains a WebKit-specific `keyframe` definition called `upperLeft` that starts with the following line:

```
@-webkit-keyframes upperLeft {
    // percentage-based definitions go here
}
```

The `#linear` selector contains properties that you have seen already, along with a property that references the `keyframe` identified by `lowerLeft`, and a property that specifies a duration of 240 seconds, as shown here:

```
#linear1 {
// code omitted for brevity
-webkit-animation-name: lowerLeft;
-webkit-animation-duration: 240s;
}
```

Now that you know how to associate a `keyframe` definition to a selector (which, in turn, is applied to an HTML element), let's look at the details of the definition of `lowerLeft`, which contains 19 elements that specify various animation effects. Each element of `lowerLeft` occurs during a specific stage during the animation. For example, the eighth element in `lowerLeft` specifies the value 50%, which means that it will occur at the halfway point of the animation effect. Because the #linear selector contains a -webkit-anima-tion-duration property whose value is 240s (shown in bold in Listing 4.12), the animation will last for four minutes, starting from the point in time when the HTML page is launched.

The eighth element of lowerLeft specifies a translation, rotation, skew, and scale effect (all of which are in three dimensions), an example of which is shown here:

```
50% {
    -webkit-transform: translate3d(250px,250px,250px)
                       rotate3d(250px,250px,250px,
                       -120deg)
                       skew(-65deg,0) scale3d(0.5, 0.5,
                       0.5);
}
```

The animation effect occurs in a sequential fashion, starting with the translation, and finishing with the scale effect, which is also the case for the other elements in lowerLeft.

Figure 4.6 displays the initial view of applying the CSS3 selectors defined in the CSS3 stylesheet Anim240Flicker3DLGrad4.css to the HTML elements in the HTML page Anim240Flicker3DLGrad4.html.

FIGURE 4.6. CSS3 3D animation effects.

SUMMARY

This chapter started with an example of displaying a CSS3-based cube, followed by examples of CSS3 transitions for creating simple animation effects, such as glow effects and bouncing effects. You also learned how to use CSS3 keyframe and the CSS3 functions scale3d(), rotate3d(), and trans-late3d() that enable you to create 3D animation effects.

Next, you saw an assortment of code samples for creating glowing effects, fading image effects, and bouncing effects. In addition, you learned how to create CSS3 effects for text and how to render multicolumn text.

Moreover, you got a brief introduction to CSS3 media queries, which enable you to render a given HTML page based on the properties of the device.

CHAPTER 5

CSS3 *AND* GPT-4

This chapter provides an assortment of GPT-4-generated code samples that are the result of supplying prompts GPT-4. The generated code samples in this chapter involve CSS3, and in Chapter 7, you will see similar GPT-4-based code samples that involve SVG.

The first portion of this chapter discusses the strengths and weaknesses of HTML, as well as popular use cases for HTML. This section also discusses HTML and accessibility, as well as potential security issues with HTML.

The second section shows you an example of a GPT-4-generated HTML Web page that contains a drop-down list with the days of the week. Next you will learn about the strengths and weaknesses of CSS3, as well as use cases and potential security issues with CSS3.

The third section contains code samples of CSS3 linear gradients, CSS3 radial gradients, rounded rectangles, diagonal gradients, and multigradients. You will also see examples of media queries involving CSS3.

The fourth section shows you how to create CSS3 animation effects, key-frame animation effects, and a carousel with CSS3. You will also see code samples with CSS3 2D transforms, quadratic Bezier curves, and cubic Bezier curves.

The fifth section contains code examples of CSS3 filters, such as blur filters and drop shadow filter effects. The final portion shows you examples of images that were generated using DALLE 3, which is accessible from CPT 4 (currently only for paid monthly subscriptions).

WORKING WITH HTML

The following prompt was supplied to GPT-4 in order to describe HTML, along with its strengths and weaknesses:

Please provide a detailed description of HTML, along with its strengths and weaknesses.

ChatGPT:

HTML, or HyperText Markup Language, is the standard markup language for creating Web pages and Web applications. It forms the backbone of almost all Web content and is an essential technology in Web development. Here's a detailed description of HTML, along with its strengths and weaknesses:

Description of HTML

1. **Nature and Purpose:** HTML is used to structure content on the Web. It consists of a series of elements which you use to enclose, or wrap, different parts of the content to make it appear or behave in a certain way.

2. **Elements and Tags:** The elements of HTML are represented by tags like <h1>, <p>, <div>, etc., each serving a different purpose.

3. **Structure of a Web Page:** HTML provides the basic structure of sites, which is then enhanced and modified by other technologies like CSS (Cascading Style Sheets) and JavaScript.

4. **Versions**: HTML has evolved since its inception in the early 1990s. The latest version, HTML5, introduced many new syntactical features and improved functionality.

5. **Semantics:** Semantic elements like <header>, <footer>, <article>, and <section> make the page structure clear both to the browser and the developer.

6. **Multimedia Integration:** HTML supports multimedia elements such as audio, video, and images.

7. **Forms and User Input:** HTML forms are a crucial part of the Web, enabling user interaction and data input.

8. **Accessibility:** Properly used, HTML can create Web pages that are accessible to all users, including those with disabilities.

Strengths of HTML

1. **Universality:** Every Web browser supports HTML, making it the most universal language for Web development.

2. **Ease of Learning:** HTML is relatively easy to learn and understand, making it accessible for beginners in Web development.

3. **SEO Friendly:** HTML is search engine friendly, and using semantic HTML can improve search engine rankings.

4. **Accessibility:** With proper use of semantic tags, HTML is inherently accessible, which is crucial for creating inclusive Web content.

5. **Integration With Other Technologies:** HTML works seamlessly with CSS and JavaScript, forming the triad of foundational Web technologies.

6. **Flexibility:** HTML can be used to create anything from simple static pages to complex Web applications.

7. **Free and Open:** HTML is free to use and does not require any proprietary software.

Weaknesses of HTML

1. **Limited Functionality:** HTML alone cannot create dynamic functionality—that requires JavaScript or other programming languages.

2. **Static Nature:** HTML is static, meaning it does not support dynamic content updates without the help of JavaScript or server-side scripting.

3. **Learning Curve for Advanced Features:** While the basics are easy to grasp, mastering HTML, especially HTML5, can be challenging due to its many advanced features.

4. **Browser Compatibility:** Different browsers can interpret HTML differently, leading to inconsistencies in how Web pages are displayed.

5. **Security:** HTML itself does not have security features and relies on Web browsers and other technologies for secure Web interactions.

6. **Performance Optimization:** Large and complex HTML documents can slow down Web site performance if not structured and optimized properly.

7. **Dependence on Additional Technologies:** To create visually appealing and functionally rich Web sites, HTML must be used in conjunction with CSS and JavaScript.

```
In summary, HTML is a fundamental technology for Web devel-
opment, known for its universality and accessibility. While
it has limitations in terms of dynamic functionality and re-
quires integration with other languages for full-fledged Web
development, its strengths make it an indispensable tool for
creating the structure of Web pages and applications.
```

POPULAR USE CASES FOR HTML

The following prompt was supplied to GPT-4 in order to describe popular use cases for HTML.

```
Please describe popular use cases for using HTML Web pages,
along with an explanation of those use cases.

ChatGPT:

HTML, or HyperText Markup Language, is the foundational
building block for creating Web pages and Web applications.
It provides the basic structure and content for Web pages,
which are then styled with CSS (Cascading Style Sheets) and
made interactive with JavaScript. Here are some popular use
```

cases for using HTML Web pages, along with explanations for each.

1. Corporate Web Sites
Use Case: Establishing an online presence for businesses, organizations, or individuals.
Explanation: HTML is used to create the structural layout of corporate Web sites, which typically include information about the company, its products or services, contact information, and often a blog or news section. These Web sites serve as a digital storefront or office, providing essential information and building brand presence.

2. E-Commerce Platforms
Use Case: Facilitating online buying and selling of goods and services.
Explanation: HTML forms the basis of e-commerce platforms, structuring product listings, shopping carts, and checkout processes. It is used to display products, descriptions, prices, and all other relevant information to enable online transactions.

3. Personal Blogs and Portfolios
Use Case: Showcasing personal work, thoughts, experiences, or hobbies.
Explanation: HTML is ideal for creating personal blogs or portfolio Web sites where individuals can display their work, write blog posts, and share personal experiences. This is particularly important for artists, writers, and other professionals who want to establish an online presence.

4. Educational and Instructional Web Sites
Use Case: Providing educational content, courses, and resources online.
Explanation: Educational institutions and e-learning platforms use HTML to structure their content, which can include text, images, videos, and interactive elements. These Web sites often serve as platforms for online learning, providing access to courses, tutorials, and educational materials.

5. News and Media Websites
Use Case: Delivering news, articles, and other media content.
Explanation: HTML is used to structure and display news articles, videos, podcasts, and other forms of media content. These Web sites are designed to handle a large volume of content, categorize it, and make it easily navigable.

6. Forums and Social Media Platforms
Use Case: Facilitating online communities and social interactions.
Explanation: Forums and social media platforms use HTML to create the layout for posts, comments, profiles, and messaging functionalities. These platforms are centered around user-generated content and interactions.

7. Landing Pages and Promotional Sites
Use Case: Marketing products, services, events, or campaigns.
Explanation: HTML is used to create landing pages—standalone Web pages designed for a specific marketing campaign or product launch. These pages

are focused on a single call to action and are designed to convert visitors into leads or customers.

8. Informational and Service-Based Web Sites

Use Case: Providing information or online services like weather forecasts, travel information, or public services.

Explanation: These Web sites use HTML to structure information and services that users can access, such as online forms, informational articles, interactive maps, or service booking functionalities.

Conclusion

HTML is a versatile tool used across a wide range of Web applications. Its fundamental role in structuring content makes it indispensable for creating diverse types of Web pages, from simple personal blogs to complex e-commerce platforms. Whether it's for business, education, entertainment, or social interaction, HTML provides the essential framework upon which the Web is built.

HTML AND ACCESSIBILITY

The following prompt was supplied to GPT-4 in order to describe aspects of accessibility in HTML:

Please provide a detailed description of the level of support for accessibility in HTML.

ChatGPT:

HTML (HyperText Markup Language) provides a strong foundation for building accessible Web content. Accessibility in Web development refers to the inclusive practice of removing barriers that prevent interaction with, or access to, Web sites by people with disabilities. Here's a detailed description of the level of support for accessibility in HTML:

Semantic HTML

- **Semantic Elements:** HTML5 introduced semantic elements like `<header>`, `<footer>`, `<article>`, `<section>`, `<nav>`, and `<aside>`. These elements provide meaningful structure, helping assistive technologies (like screen readers) understand the layout and navigate the content more effectively.
- **Role Attribute:** The `role` attribute can be used to define the specific role of an element, which is especially useful when a semantic element is not available.

ARIA (Accessible Rich Internet Applications) Attributes

- **ARIA:** A set of attributes specifically designed for enhancing accessibility. They help convey information about the behavior and purpose of elements to assistive technologies.

- **Roles and Properties:** ARIA roles and properties describe the elements' roles, states, and properties. They are particularly useful for dynamic content and advanced user interface controls developed with Ajax, HTML, JavaScript, and related technologies.

Form Accessibility

- **Labels:** The `<label>` element ensures that form controls are properly labeled in HTML. This is crucial for screen reader users to understand what each form control is for.
- **Fieldset and Legend:** Grouping related form controls with `<fieldset>` and describing the group with `<legend>` helps users understand related form elements.

Alternative Text for Images

- **Alt Text:** The `alt` attribute in `<img>` tags provide a text alternative for images. This is crucial for users who rely on screen readers or have slow internet connections.

Table Accessibility

- **Table Structure:** Properly structured tables with `<thead>`, `<tbody>`, and `<tfoot>` help in conveying the information in a structured manner.
- **Captions and Summaries**: `<caption>` provides a title or summary for the table content, aiding understanding, and navigation.

Keyboard Accessibility

- **Tabindex:** The `tabindex` attribute makes elements focusable and navigable by keyboard, essential for users who cannot use a mouse.
- **Access Keys:** The `accesskey` attribute can provide keyboard shortcuts to important links, buttons, and form controls.

Multimedia Accessibility

- **Subtitles and Captions:** For multimedia content, HTML provides `<track>` for specifying subtitles, captions, chapters, or descriptions, which are essential for deaf or hard-of-hearing users and those who prefer reading to listening.

Language Declaration

- **Lang Attribute:** Declaring the language of the page or parts of the page with the `lang` attribute helps in correct pronunciation by screen readers.

Headings and Structure

- **Headings:** Proper use of heading tags (`<h1>` to `<h6>`) creates a logical, hierarchical structure, aiding in navigation and understanding of the page layout.

Link and Button Accessibility

- **Descriptive Links:** Ensuring links are descriptive (`<a href="">Read more about accessibility</a>` instead of `<a href="">Click here</a>`) helps users understand the link's destination.

Screen Reader and Assistive Technology Support
- **Testing and Compatibility:** HTML structures and elements are generally well-supported by screen readers and other assistive technologies, making them a reliable choice for building accessible Web content.

Conclusion

HTML's support for accessibility is robust, offering various elements and attributes designed to make Web content accessible to a wider range of people, including those with disabilities. Proper use of semantic HTML, ARIA roles, and other accessibility features can significantly enhance the user experience for all users, regardless of their abilities or disabilities. As Web accessibility becomes increasingly important, the role of HTML in creating inclusive and accessible Web experiences continues to be critical.

SECURITY ISSUES WITH HTML

The following prompt was supplied to GPT-4 in order to describe potential security issues with HTML:

```
Please provide a detailed description of potential security
issues involving HTML.
```

```
ChatGPT:
```

```
HTML (HyperText Markup Language) itself is not typically as-
sociated with security vulnerabilities, as it is primarily
used for structuring and presenting content on the Web. How-
ever, the way HTML is used in conjunction with other tech-
nologies, or how it interacts with user input and server-side
processing, can potentially introduce security issues. Here
are some potential security concerns involving HTML.
```

1. Cross-Site Scripting (XSS)
- **Issue:** XSS attacks occur when an attacker injects malicious scripts into Web pages viewed by other users. This can happen if a Web site directly includes user input in its output without proper validation and escaping.
- **HTML Angle:** HTML forms and URLs can be used to submit malicious JavaScript code to a vulnerable Web application.

2. Malicious File Uploads
- **Issue:** If a Web site allows file uploads (via HTML forms) without proper security checks, attackers could upload malicious files (like scripts or executables) that compromise the server or other users' data.
- **HTML Angle:** HTML forms used for file uploads can be exploited if the server-side handling of these uploads is insecure.

3. Phishing Attacks
- **Issue:** Phishing attacks use deceptive Web pages to trick users into entering sensitive information like usernames, passwords, or credit card details.

- **HTML Angle:** HTML can be used to create convincing copies of legitimate Web sites, fooling users into submitting their information.

4. Clickjacking
- **Issue:** Clickjacking involves tricking a user into clicking something different than what the user perceives, potentially revealing confidential information or allowing control of the user's computer.
- **HTML Angle:** This can be achieved by embedding a transparent HTML frame over a seemingly benign Web page.

5. Iframe Injection
- **Issue:** Attackers may inject an iframe into a Web page to load a malicious site in the background. This can be used for phishing or to exploit vulnerabilities in the browser.
- **HTML Angle**: Insecure or unsanitized HTML content can allow iframe injections.

6. Insecure Direct Object References (IDOR)
- **Issue:** Directly referencing internal implementation objects, such as files, directories, or database keys, in HTML and Web interfaces can lead to unauthorized access.
- **HTML Angle:** HTML elements like hyperlinks or form actions can be manipulated to gain access to these references.

7. Mixed Content
- **Issue:** Loading mixed content (combining HTTPS and HTTP content on the same page) can make a Web site vulnerable to eavesdropping and man-in-the-middle attacks.
- **HTML Angle:** When an HTTPS site includes HTTP content (like images, videos, stylesheets, scripts), it creates a security risk.

8. Insecure Redirections and Forwards
- **Issue:** Improperly validated redirections and forwards can be manipulated to direct users to phishing or malware sites.
- **HTML Angle:** HTML tags like `<a href="">` or HTTP meta refresh tags can be used for this purpose.

Mitigation Strategies

- **Input Validation and Sanitization:** Always validate and sanitize user input to prevent XSS and other injection attacks.
- **Content Security Policy (CSP):** Implement CSP headers to reduce the risk of XSS and other content injection attacks.
- **Secure File Upload Handling:** Implement server-side checks to ensure only safe file types and sizes are uploaded.
- **Use HTTPS:** Ensure all content, including third-party resources, are loaded over HTTPS to prevent mixed content issues.

• **Regular Security Audits:** Regularly audit Web applications for security vulnerabilities and apply updates as needed.

Conclusion

While HTML itself is not inherently insecure, its interaction with browsers, user input, and server-side processing can lead to security vulnerabilities. Understanding these potential issues and implementing best practices for Web development and security is crucial in mitigating risks associated with HTML Web pages.

AN HTML WEB PAGE WITH A DROP-DOWN LIST

The following prompt was supplied to GPT-4 in order to generate an HTML Web page that contains a drop-down list that contains the days of the week:

Please generate an HTML Web page that contains a drop-down list with the days of the week, along with an explanation of the code.
ChatGPT:
Creating a basic HTML Web page with a drop-down list for the days of the week is straightforward. Below is a simple example of how this can be done, along with an explanation of each part of the code.

Listing 5.1 displays the contents of gpt4_dropdown.html that shows the code that GPT-4 generated in order to display a Web page that contains a drop-down list.

LISTING 5.1: gpt4_dropdown.html

```
<!DOCTYPE html>
<html>
<head>
    <title>Weekday Selector</title>
</head>
<body>

    <label for="daySelect">Choose a day:</label>
    <select id="daySelect">
        <option value="monday">Monday</option>
        <option value="tuesday">Tuesday</option>
        <option value="wednesday">Wednesday</option>
        <option value="thursday">Thursday</option>
        <option value="friday">Friday</option>
        <option value="saturday">Saturday</option>
        <option value="sunday">Sunday</option>
    </select>
</body>
</html>
```

Explanation of the Code:

1. **<!DOCTYPE html>:** This declaration defines the document to be HTML5.
2. **<html>:** The root element of an HTML page.
3. **<head>:** Contains meta-information about the document, such as its title.
   - **<title>:** Specifies the title of the document, which is displayed in the browser's title bar or tab.
4. **<body>:** Contains the contents of the HTML document.
   - **<label for="daySelect">:** Defines a label for the drop-down list. The `for` attribute is important as it associates the label with the select element. This is helpful for accessibility purposes.
   - **<select id="daySelect">:** Creates a drop-down list. The `id` attribute is used to uniquely identify the element, which can be useful for styling with CSS or manipulation with JavaScript.
     o **<option value="...">:** These elements define the options available in the drop-down list. The `value` attribute is the value to be sent to a server when a form is submitted. The text between the `<option>` tags is what the user will see in the drop-down list.

This code will create a simple Web page with a drop-down list containing the days of the week. When a user visits the page, they can select a day from the list. The value of the selected day can be used in various ways, such as being sent to a server upon form submission or processed by JavaScript for client-side applications.

Now launch the Web page `gpt4_dropdown.html` by navigating to the directory that contains this HTML Web page and then typing the following command:

```
open gpt4_dropdown.html
```

After a few moments you will see the image in Figure 5.1 that displays the output when you select a day of the week in the drop-down list.

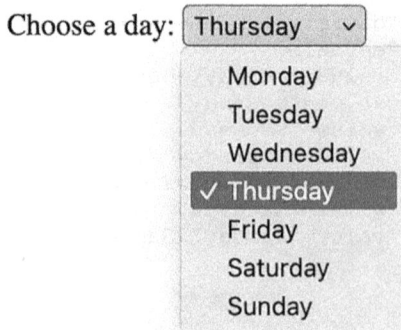

Choose a day: Thursday

Monday
Tuesday
Wednesday
✓ Thursday
Friday
Saturday
Sunday

FIGURE 5.1. A Web page with a drop-down list.

WORKING WITH CSS3

> Please provide a detailed description of CSS3, along with
> its useful features as well as its strengths and weaknesses.

CSS3, the latest evolution of the Cascading Style Sheets language, is used for styling and laying out Web pages. It is the cornerstone technology of the World Wide Web, alongside HTML and JavaScript. CSS3 was developed by the World Wide Web Consortium (W3C) and is a series of modular extensions to the original CSS specification.

Useful Features of CSS3

1. **Selectors:** CSS3 introduced new selectors that offer more flexibility and control in targeting elements. These include attribute selectors, nth-child selectors, and pseudo-classes like `:first-of-type`.

2. **Box Model:** The box-sizing property allows developers to alter the box model to include padding and border in an element's total width and height.

3. **Text Effects and Web Fonts:** Features like text-shadow, word-wrap, and the ability to use custom fonts with `@font-face` have significantly enhanced Web typography.

4. **Backgrounds and Borders:** CSS3 introduced the ability to have multiple backgrounds, border-radius (rounded corners), and border images.

5. **Color**: Added support for RGBA, HSL, HSLA, and gradient colors, allowing for more diverse color schemes and transparency effects.

6. **2D/3D Transformations:** Transformations like rotate, scale, skew, and translate can be applied to HTML elements. 3D transformations add depth and perspective to designs.

7. **Transitions and Animations:** CSS3 makes it possible to create smooth transitions and keyframe-based animations without relying on JavaScript or Flash.

8. **Flexbox and Grid Layout:** These layout modules offer more sophisticated and flexible ways to design responsive Web layouts.

9. **Media Queries:** Part of the responsive design, media queries allow the application of different styles depending on the device's characteristics, like screen width.

Strengths of CSS3

1. **Improved Presentation:** CSS3 enhances the look and feel of Web pages with advanced styling options, leading to more attractive and engaging Web sites.

2. **Cross-Browser Support:** Modern browsers have good support for most CSS3 features, reducing the need for hacks and workarounds.

3. **Responsive Design:** With features like media queries, flexbox, and grid, CSS3 facilitates responsive Web design, making Web sites accessible across a wide range of devices.

4. **Animation and Interaction:** The ability to create animations and transitions has opened up new possibilities for interactive and dynamic Web experiences.

5. **Reduced Dependence on Images and Scripts:** Many effects that previously required images or JavaScript can now be accomplished purely with CSS3, improving performance and accessibility.

Weaknesses of CSS3

1. **Browser Compatibility:** While support is improving, older browsers may not fully support all CSS3 features, leading to inconsistent experiences.

2. **Complexity:** Advanced features like flexbox, grid, and animations have a learning curve and can be complex to implement effectively.

3. **Performance Issues:** Overuse of certain features like shadows, gradients, and animations can lead to performance issues, especially on mobile devices.

4. **Lack of Control:** CSS3 still lacks precise control over layout compared to programming languages and frameworks designed specifically for applications.

5. **Global Scope by Default:** CSS has a global scope, which can lead to conflicts and maintenance challenges in large projects. This has been partly addressed by methodologies like BEM (Block Element Modifier) and tools like CSS Modules or CSS-in-JS.

In summary, CSS3 greatly expands the capabilities of what can be achieved in Web design, enabling more sophisticated, responsive, and interactive user interfaces. However, it also brings complexities and challenges, particularly in terms of browser compatibility and performance considerations. As Web development continues to evolve, CSS3 remains a fundamental skill for Web designers and developers.

USE CASES FOR CSS3

The following prompt was supplied to GPT-4 in order to describe use cases for CSS3 in HTML Web pages:

Please describe significant use cases that involve CSS3 in HTML Web pages, along with an explanation of the use cases.

ChatGPT:

CSS3, the latest version of Cascading Style Sheets, plays a crucial role in Web design and development. It provides advanced styling capabilities and controls the visual presentation of HTML Web pages. Here are some significant use cases of CSS3 in HTML Web pages, along with explanations for each:

1. Responsive Web Design

Use Case: Creating Web pages that adapt their layout to different screen sizes and devices (like desktops, tablets, and smartphones).

Explanation: CSS3 introduces media queries that allow designers to change styles based on the device's characteristics, such as its width, height, or orientation. This means that the same Web page can have a flexible layout that changes to provide an optimal viewing experience across a range of devices.

2. Animation and Transitions

Use Case: Adding interactive elements to Web pages, such as animations, transitions, and hover effects.

Explanation: CSS3 comes with properties like `transition`, `transform`, and keyframes for animations, allowing for smooth transitions and animations without the need for JavaScript or Flash. This enhances user experience and engagement by providing visual feedback and interactive elements.

3. Custom Fonts and Typography

Use Case: Styling text with custom fonts and advanced typography to enhance the readability and aesthetic appeal of Web content.

Explanation: CSS3 allows for the use of custom fonts with the `@font-face` rule, enabling Web designers to move beyond the limited set of Web-safe fonts. This capability enhances the design and branding of Websites.

4. Box Model and Flexbox/Grid Layouts

Use Case: Creating complex, flexible layouts that are easier to manage and adapt to various screen sizes.

Explanation: CSS3 introduced Flexbox and Grid Layout modules, providing more efficient ways to design complex layouts. Flexbox is great for one-dimensional layouts, while CSS Grid excels in two-dimensional layouts. These tools offer greater control over alignment, distribution of space, and order of elements within a container.

5. Gradients, Shadows, and Rounded Corners

Use Case: Adding visual effects like gradients, shadows, and rounded corners to enhance the visual appeal of elements without using images.

Explanation: CSS3 simplifies the process of adding visual effects. Gradients (linear or radial), box and text shadows, and border-radius for rounded corners can be easily applied to elements. This reduces the need for additional image files, decreasing load times and simplifying maintenance.

6. Feature Detection and Progressive Enhancement

Use Case: Designing Web pages that progressively enhance according to the capabilities of the browser or device.

Explanation: With CSS3, developers can use feature detection techniques (like Modernizr) to identify if a browser supports certain CSS features. Based on this, they can provide fallback styles or enhancements, ensuring that the Web site is functional and aesthetically pleasing across different browsers.

7. Advanced Selectors and Pseudo-Classes
Use Case: Targeting specific elements in the HTML document more precisely for styling without changing the HTML structure.
Explanation: CSS3 introduces a range of advanced selectors and pseudo-classes (like nth-child, not, :hover, :focus). These allow for more specific and complex selections, enabling fine-grained control over the styling of elements based on their state or position in the document.

Conclusion
These use cases illustrate the versatility and power of CSS3 in Web design. By enabling responsive designs, interactive animations, advanced layouts, and more, CSS3 plays a pivotal role in creating modern, user-friendly, and visually appealing Web sites.

SECURITY ISSUES WITH CSS3

The following prompt was supplied to GPT-4 in order to describe potential security issues with CSS3:

Please provide a detailed description of potential security
issues involving CSS3.

ChatGPT:

CSS3 (Cascading Style Sheets Level 3) is primarily used
for styling Web pages and is not typically associated with
direct security vulnerabilities. However, in specific scenarios, particularly when CSS interacts with other Web technologies or user input, security considerations can arise.
Here's a detailed description of potential security issues
involving CSS3:

1. CSS Injection
  - **Issue:** Similar to Cross-Site Scripting (XSS), CSS Injection occurs when an attacker is able to insert malicious CSS into a Web page. This can happen if user input is improperly sanitized and used in inline styles or style sheets.
  - **Consequences:** While CSS cannot directly execute scripts, it can be used to alter the page's appearance in a way that can facilitate phishing attacks or hide malicious content.

2. Mixed Content Vulnerability
  - **Issue:** When a secure (HTTPS) Web page includes CSS files from insecure (HTTP) sources, it creates a mixed content vulnerability.

- **Consequences:** This can lead to man-in-the-middle attacks, where an attacker intercepts and alters the CSS being delivered, potentially changing the behavior or appearance of the Web site.

3. Third-Party CSS Libraries
- **Issue:** Using third-party CSS libraries or frameworks can introduce risks if the library is not well-maintained or is compromised.
- **Consequences**: An attacker could inject malicious code into the library, affecting all Web sites that use it.

4. Data URI Scheme in CSS
- **Issue:** The data URI scheme allows CSS to embed external resources as base64-encoded data directly within the stylesheet.
- **Consequences**: This can be exploited to include malicious content, such as phishing links or malware, within the encoded data.

5. CSS Selectors and Web Scraping
- **Issue:** CSS selectors can be used by Web scrapers to target and extract specific content from a Website.
- **Consequences:** While not a direct threat to the Web site, this can lead to data privacy issues or intellectual property theft.

6. Oversensitive CSS Queries
- **Issue:** CSS3 introduced features like attribute selectors that can be overly sensitive to changes in data attributes, potentially revealing sensitive information through style changes.
- **Consequences:** An attacker could use this to infer private data based on how the CSS renders different states.

7. Browser Fingerprinting
- **Issue:** Sophisticated CSS3 features can be used to aid in browser fingerprinting, where a user's browser and device information are collected to uniquely identify them.
- **Consequences:** This raises privacy concerns as it can be used for tracking users without their knowledge or consent.

8. Mitigation Strategies
- **Content Security Policy (CSP):** Implementing CSP can help mitigate the risk of CSS injection attacks by controlling the sources from which styles can be loaded.
- **Sanitizing User Input:** Any user input that might be included in CSS should be rigorously sanitized to prevent injection attacks.
- **Secure Resources:** Always use HTTPS for hosting and accessing CSS files and other resources.
- **Vet Third-Party Libraries:** Carefully assess and regularly update third-party CSS libraries to ensure they are secure and maintained.
- **Awareness of CSS Capabilities:** Understanding the full capabilities of CSS3, especially in terms of selectors and queries, can help in writing styles that don't inadvertently expose sensitive information.

Conclusion

While CSS3 is not inherently a high-risk technology in terms of security, certain aspects of its use and interaction with other Web technologies can pose security concerns. Awareness and proactive measures are key in mitigating these risks, ensuring that CSS contributes positively to both the functionality and security of Web applications.

TEXT WITH A CSS3 LINEAR GRADIENT

The following prompt was supplied to GPT-4 in order to generate an HTML Web page that contains CSS3:

Please generate an HTML Web page that contains a text string with linear gradient shading, along with an explanation of the code.

ChatGPT:

Creating an HTML Web page with a text string that has a linear gradient effect can be achieved using HTML and CSS. Below is an example of how this can be done, along with an explanation for each part of the code:

LISTING 5.2: gpt4_css3_text_linear_gradient.html

```
<!DOCTYPE html>
<html>
<head>
    <title>Gradient Text Example</title>
    <style>
        .gradient-text {
            font-size: 40px;
            font-weight: bold;
            background: linear-gradient(45deg, blue, red);
            -webkit-background-clip: text;
            color: transparent;
            background-clip: text;
        }
    </style>
</head>
<body>

    <div class="gradient-text">Gradient Text</div>

</body>
</html>
```

Explanation of the Code:

1. **<!DOCTYPE html>:** This line declares the document type and version of HTML (HTML5 in this case).
2. **<html>:** The root element of an HTML document.

3. **<head>**: Contains meta-information about the document.
   - **<title>**: Sets the title of the Web page, which appears in the browser's title bar or tab.
   - **<style>**: Contains CSS styles for the elements in the HTML document.
      o **.gradient-text**: This is a CSS class selector. The styles inside this block will apply to any HTML element with `class="gradient-text"`.
      o **font-size**: Sets the size of the font.
      o **font-weight**: Makes the text bold.
      o **background**: Applies a linear gradient to the background. The gradient is defined to start at a 45-degree angle, blending from blue to red.
      o **-webkit-background-clip**: This is a webkit-specific property that clips the background as per the text. It's necessary for the gradient effect on the text.
      o **color**: Set to transparent to allow the gradient background to show through the text.
      o **background-clip**: Clips the background to the foreground text. The `text` value makes the background only visible where the text is.
4. **<body>**: Contains the content of the HTML document.
      o **<div class="gradient-text">**: A `div` element with the class `gradient-text`. The text inside this `div` ("Gradient Text") will have the gradient effect applied to it based on the CSS styles defined above.

This code will display a Web page with the text "Gradient Text" shaded with a linear gradient that transitions from blue to red. This effect is primarily achieved through CSS, particularly the use of the `background-clip: text` and `linear-gradient` properties.

Now launch the Web page `gpt4_css3_text_linear_gradient.html` by navigating to the directory that contains this HTML Web page and then typing the following command:

```
open gpt4 css3 text linear gradient.html
```

After a few moments you will see the Web page in Figure 5.2 that displays a CSS3-based linear gradient text.

Gradient Text

FIGURE 5.2. A Web page with linear gradient text.

TEXT WITH A CSS3 RADIAL GRADIENT

The following prompt was supplied to GPT-4 in order to generate an HTML Web page that contains CSS3:

```
Please generate an HTML Web page that contains a text string
with linear gradient shading, along with an explanation of
the code.
```

ChatGPT:

Creating an HTML Web page with a text string that has a linear gradient effect can be achieved using HTML and CSS. Following is an example of how this can be done, along with an explanation for each part of the code.

LISTING 5.3: gpt4_css3_text_radial_gradient.html

```
<!DOCTYPE html>
<html>
<head>
    <title>Gradient Text Example</title>
    <style>
        .gradient-text {
            font-size: 40px;
            font-weight: bold;
            background: linear-gradient(45deg, blue, red);
            -webkit-background-clip: text;
            color: transparent;
            background-clip: text;
        }
    </style>
</head>
<body>

    <div class="gradient-text">Gradient Text</div>

</body>
</html>
```

Explanation of the Code:

1. **<!DOCTYPE html>:** This line declares the document type and version of HTML (HTML5 in this case).

2. **<html>:** The root element of an HTML document.

3. **<head>:** Contains meta-information about the document.

   • **<title>:** Sets the title of the Web page, which appears in the browser's title bar or tab.

   • **<style>:** Contains CSS styles for the elements in the HTML document.

     o **.gradient-text**: This is a CSS class selector. The styles inside this block will apply to any HTML element with class="gradient-text".

     o **font-size:** Sets the size of the font.

     o **font-weight:** Makes the text bold.

     o **background:** Applies a linear gradient to the background. The gradient is defined to start at a 45-degree angle, blending from blue to red.

     o **webkit-background-clip:** This is a webkit-specific property that clips the background as per the text. It's necessary for the gradient effect on the text.

     o **color:** Set to transparent to allow the gradient background to show through the text.

    o **background-clip:** Clips the background to the foreground text. The `text` value makes the background only visible where the text is.

4. **<body>:** Contains the content of the HTML document.

    • **<div class="gradient-text">:** A `div` element with the class `gradient-text`. The text inside this `div` ("Gradient Text") will have the gradient effect applied to it based on the CSS styles defined above.

This code will display a Web page with the text "Gradient Text" shaded with a linear gradient that transitions from blue to red. This effect is primarily achieved through CSS, particularly the use of the `background-clip: text` and `linear-gradient` properties.

Now launch the Web page `gpt4_css3_text_radial_gradient.html` by navigating to the directory that contains this HTML Web page and then typing the following command:

```
open gpt4_css3_text_radial_gradient.html
```

After a few moments you will see the Web page in Figure 5.3 that displays a CSS3-based radial gradient text.

Radial Gradient Text

FIGURE 5.3. A Web page with radial gradient text.

A ROUNDED RECTANGLE WITH A CSS3 RADIAL GRADIENT

The following prompt was supplied to GPT-4 in order to generate an HTML Web page that contains a rounded rectangle with a CSS3 radial gradient:

Please render a rounded rectangle of width 400 and height 200 that is rendered with a CSS3 radial gradient, and also an ellipse of comparable dimensions with a CSS3 radial gradient, as well as a box-shadow attribute with value inset 15px 12px 30px #000; and an explanation of the code.

ChatGPT:

To create a rounded rectangle and an ellipse each with a CSS3 radial gradient and an inset box-shadow, we'll use HTML and CSS. The rounded rectangle will be represented using a <div> element with border-radius styling for the rounded corners, while the ellipse will be created using another <div> with specific styling to give it an elliptical shape. Both shapes will have a radial gradient background and an inset box-shadow applied through CSS.

LISTING 5.4: css3_rounded_rect_radial_gradient2.html

```
<!DOCTYPE html>
<html lang="en">
```

```
<head>
    <meta charset="UTF-8">
    <title>CSS3 Radial Gradient and Box-Shadow on Shapes
        </title>
    <style>
        .rounded-rectangle {
            width: 400px;
            height: 200px;
            background: radial-gradient(circle, red,
                                       yellow);
            border-radius: 25px; /* Rounded corners */
            box-shadow: inset 15px 12px 30px #000;
                                    /* Inset shadow */
            margin-bottom: 20px;
        }

        .ellipse {
            width: 400px;
            height: 200px;
            background: radial-gradient(circle at center,
                                       blue, green);
            border-radius: 50%; /* Full ellipse */
            box-shadow: inset 15px 12px 30px #000;
                                    /* Inset shadow */
        }
    </style>
</head>
<body>

<div class="rounded-rectangle"></div>
<div class="ellipse"></div>

</body>
</html>
```

Explanation of the Code

HTML Structure:

Two <div> elements are created: one with the class rounded-rectangle and the other with the class ellipse.

CSS Styles:

.rounded-rectangle class: Styles a 400px by 200px rectangle with rounded corners (border-radius: 25px). The background property is set to a radial gradient that transitions from red at the center to yellow at the edges. The box-shadow property adds an inset shadow, creating an effect of depth inside the rectangle.

.ellipse class: Styles a 400px by 200px ellipse (border-radius: 50%). Its background has a radial gradient transitioning from blue at the center to green at the edges, and it also features the same inset box-shadow as the rectangle.

Radial Gradient and Box-Shadow Effect:

The background: radial-gradient (shape at position, color1, color2); property creates a smooth color transition in a circular pattern.

The box-shadow: inset 15px 12px 30px #000; property adds an inset shadow to the shape. The parameters 15px 12px 30px define the x-offset, y-offset, and blur radius of the shadow, respectively, and #000 sets the shadow color to black.

When this HTML and CSS code is rendered in a browser, it will display a rounded rectangle and an ellipse, each with a different radial gradient and a subtle inset box-shadow. This combination of radial gradients and shadow effects creates a visually compelling and three-dimensional appearance for the shapes.

Now launch the Web page css3_roundedrect_radial_gradient2. html by navigating to the directory that contains this HTML Web page and then typing the following command:

```
open css3_rounded_rect_radial_gradient2.html
```

After a few moments you will see the image in Figure 5.4 that displays a rounded rectangle as well as an ellipse with a CSS3 radial gradient.

FIGURE 5.4. A rounded rectangle and ellipse with CSS3 radial gradient.

DIAGONAL GRADIENTS AND MULTIGRADIENTS

The following prompt was supplied to GPT-4 in order to generate an HTML Web page that contains a diagonal gradient and a multigradient:

Please generate an HTML Web page with <div> elements that contains a <div> element with a diagonal gradient, and a <div> element with a gradient that contains at least 4 color stops, where all <div> elements are 250x250, along with an explanation of the code.

ChatGPT:

Certainly! Below is an HTML Web page that contains two <div> elements, each 250x250 pixels in size. One <div> will have a

diagonal gradient, and the other will have a gradient with
at least four color stops.

LISTING 5.5: gpt-4_css3_diagonal_multi_gradients.html

```html
<!DOCTYPE html>
<html>
<head>
    <style>
        .box {
            width: 250px;
            height: 250px;
            display: inline-block;
            margin: 10px;
        }


        /* Diagonal Gradient */
        .diagonal-gradient {
            background: linear-gradient(45deg, red, blue);
        }

        /* Gradient with Four Color Stops */
        .four-color-gradient {
            background: linear-gradient(to right, green,
                                yellow, orange, purple);
        }
    </style>
</head>
<body>

<div class="box diagonal-gradient"></div>
<div class="box four-color-gradient"></div>

</body>
</html>
```

Explanation:

- **Common Box Styling (box class)**: Both <div> elements share the box class. This class sets their width and height to 250px and displays them inline-block with some margin for spacing.
- **Diagonal Gradient (diagonal-gradient class)**: This <div> has a linear gradient background that goes diagonally. The gradient starts at 45 degrees, transitioning from red to blue. This creates a diagonal effect from the top left to the bottom right of the <div>.
- **Four-Color Gradient (four-color-gradient class)**: The second <div> features a linear gradient with four color stops. It transitions horizontally (from left to right) through green, yellow, orange, and purple.

When you open this HTML file in a browser, you'll see two squares with different gradient styles. Feel free to modify the colors or gradient directions as you like!

Now launch the Web page `gpt4_css3_diagonal_multi_gradients.html` by navigating to the directory that contains this HTML Web page and then typing the following command:

```
open gpt4_css3_diagonal_multi_gradients.html
```

After a few moments you will see a rectangle with a diagonal gradient and a second rectangle with a four-color gradient, as shown in Figure 5.5.

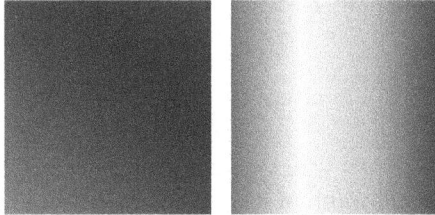

FIGURE 5.5. Rectangle with a diagonal gradient and multigradient.

MEDIA QUERIES

The following prompt was supplied to GPT-4 in order to generate an HTML Web page that contains a Media Query:

Please generate an HTML Web page that contains a media query in order to adjust styles based on screen size, along with an explanation of the code.

ChatGPT:

Sure! I'll create an HTML Web page that contains a media query to adjust styles based on the screen size. The media query will change the background color of a <div> element depending on whether the screen width is more or less than 600 pixels. This is a basic example to demonstrate how media queries can be used for responsive design.

LISTING 5.6: gpt4_css3_media_query.html

```
<!DOCTYPE html>
<html>
<head>
    <style>
        .responsive-div {
            width: 100%;
            height: 200px;
            background-color: lightblue; /* Default
                                     background color */
        }

        /* Media query for screens wider than 600 pixels */
        @media (min-width: 600px) {
```

```
            .responsive-div {
                background-color: lightgreen;
                    /* Background color for wider screens */
            }
        }
    </style>
</head>
<body>

<div class="responsive-div"></div>

</body>
</html>
```

Explanation:

Default Style: The <div> with class responsive-div is styled to have a width of 100% (taking the full width of its parent), a height of 200 pixels, and a light blue background color by default.

Media Query: The @media (min-width: 600px) rule applies to screens with a minimum width of 600 pixels. Inside this media query, the background color of elements with the responsive-div class changes to light green. This means that when the screen width is 600 pixels or wider, the <div> will have a light green background; otherwise, it will have a light blue background.

When you resize the browser window, you will see the background color of the <div> change based on the width of the window. This technique is widely used in responsive Web design to create layouts and styles that adapt to different screen sizes. You can expand upon this by adding more complex styles or more breakpoints to cater to different devices.

Now launch the Web page gpt4_css3_media_query.html by navigating to the directory that contains this HTML Web page and then typing the following command:

```
open gpt4_css3_media_query.html
```

After a few moments you will see a green <div> element whose width equals the width of your browser session. Now resize the size of your browser and watch how the <div> elements adjusts its width to match the width of the browser session.

KEYFRAME ANIMATION EFFECTS

The following prompt was supplied to GPT-4 in order to generate an HTML Web page that contains CSS3 animation:

```
Please generate an HTML Web page with a 300x300 <div> that
has keyframe animations, along with an explanation of the
code.
```

ChatGPT:

```
Certainly! Below is an HTML Web page that features a 300x300
<div> element with keyframe animations. This <div> will have
```

an animation that changes its background color and applies a rotation over a duration of 4 seconds. The animation will repeat infinitely.

LISTING 5.7: gpt4_css3_keyframe_animations1.html

```
<!DOCTYPE html>
<html>
<head>
    <style>
        @keyframes colorRotateAnimation {
            0% {
                background-color: red;
                transform: rotate(0deg);
            }
            25% {
                background-color: blue;
            }
            50% {
                background-color: green;
                transform: rotate(180deg);
            }
            75% {
                background-color: yellow;
            }
            100% {
                background-color: red;
                transform: rotate(360deg);
            }
        }

        .animated-box {
            width: 300px;
            height: 300px;
            margin: auto;
            animation: colorRotateAnimation 4s infinite;
        }
    </style>
</head>
<body>

<div class="animated-box"></div>

</body>
</html>
```

Explanation of the Code:
Keyframes (colorRotateAnimation): This is where the animation is defined. It's a set of keyframes that describe how properties of the <div> change over time.

At 0% (start), the background color is red, and it has no rotation.

At 25%, the background color changes to blue.

At 50%, the background color is green, and the <div> is rotated 180 degrees.

At 75%, the background color changes to yellow.

Finally, at 100% (end), it goes back to red with a full 360-degree rotation.

Animated Box (animated-box class): This class is applied to the <div> and sets its width and height to 300px. It also applies the animation using the animation property. The animation uses the colorRotateAnimation keyframes, lasts 4 seconds per cycle, and repeats infinitely.

When you open this HTML page in a web browser, you will see the 300x300 <div> changing its background color and rotating continuously. This is a simple demonstration of CSS keyframes and animations. You can adjust the keyframes to change the animation effects as desired.

Now launch the Web page `gpt4_css3_keyframe-animation1.html` by navigating to the directory that contains this HTML Web page and then typing the following command:

```
open gpt4_css3_keyframe_animation1.html
```

After a few moments you will see the Web page in Figure 5.6 that displays a snapshot of CSS3-based animation.

FIGURE 5.6. A rectangle with CSS3-based animation.

CSS3 ANIMATION EFFECTS

The following prompt was supplied to GPT-4 in order to generate an HTML Web page that contains CSS3 animation:

Please generate an HTML Web page that contains an animated text string with linear gradient shading, along with an explanation of the code.

ChatGPT:

Creating an HTML Web page with an animated text string that has linear gradient shading involves using HTML for the structure and CSS for the styling and animation. Following is an example with a brief explanation of each part of the code:

LISTING 5.8: gpt4_css3_animated.html

```
<!DOCTYPE html>
<html>
<head>
    <title>Animated Gradient Text</title>
    <style>
        @keyframes gradient-animation {
            0% { background-position: 0% 50%; }
            50% { background-position: 100% 50%; }
            100% { background-position: 0% 50%; }
        }

        .animated-gradient-text {
            font-size: 40px;
            font-weight: bold;
            background: linear-gradient(45deg, blue, red,
                                        green, yellow);
            background-size: 200% 200%;
            color: transparent;
            background-clip: text;
            -webkit-background-clip: text;
            -webkit-text-fill-color: transparent;
            animation: gradient-animation 5s ease infinite;
        }
    </style>
</head>
<body>

    <div class="animated-gradient-text">Animated Gradient
    Text</div>

</body>
</html>
```

Explanation of the Code:

1. **<!DOCTYPE html>:** Declares the document type and version (HTML5).
2. **<html>:** The root element of an HTML document.
3. **<head>:**
   - **<title>:** Sets the title of the Web page.
   - **<style>:** Contains the CSS styles.
     o **@keyframes gradient-animation:** Defines the animation keyframes for the gradient.
       ▪ The background position is animated over time to create a moving gradient effect.

o **.animated-gradient-text:** A class selector for applying styles to the specified HTML element.

- **font-size** and **font-weight:** Set the size and weight of the font.
- **background:** Applies a linear gradient. The gradient consists of multiple colors.
- **background-size:** Expands the size of the gradient background, important for the animation effect.
- **color:** Set to transparent to reveal the gradient background.
- **background-clip:** Clips the background to the foreground text.
- **-webkit-background-clip** and **-webkit-text-fill-color:** Webkit-specific properties for clipping the background and setting the text fill color.
- **animation:** Applies the defined animation to the text. It uses the gradient-animation defined above, lasts for 5 seconds, and iterates infinitely.

4. **<body>:**

- **<div class="animated-gradient-text">:** A div element with the animated-gradient-text class. The text inside this div ("Animated Gradient Text") will be displayed with the animated gradient effect.

This code creates a Web page showing the text "Animated Gradient Text" with a linear gradient that smoothly transitions between colors (blue, red, green, yellow). The gradient moves across the text, creating an eye-catching animation effect. The key aspects of this animation are defined within the @keyframes gradient-animation and applied to the text through the animation property in the CSS class .animated-gradient-text.

Launch the Web page gpt4_css3_animated.html by navigating to the directory that contains this HTML Web page and then typing the following command:

```
open gpt4_css3_animated.html
```

After a few moments you will see the image in Figure 5.7 that displays a snapshot of text that is rendered with CSS3-based animation.

Animated Gradient Text

FIGURE 5.7. Text with CSS3-based animation.

A CAROUSEL EFFECT WITH CSS3

The following prompt was supplied to GPT-4 to generate an HTML Web page that displays a carousel effect with PNG files:

```
Please generate an HTML Web page that contains a horizontal
carousel effect with multiple PNGs.
```

ChatGPT:

Sure, I'll create an HTML Web page that demonstrates CSS3-based 2D transform effects on three <div> elements. Each <div> will have a unique transformation: rotation, scaling, and skewing. This will help you understand how to apply and control these effects using CSS.

Listing 5.9 displays the contents of gpt4_css3_carousel.html that shows the code that GPT-4 generated in order to display a carousel effect with multiple PNGs.

LISTING 5.9: gpt4_css3_carousel1.html

```
<!DOCTYPE html>
<html lang="en">
<head>
    <meta charset="UTF-8">
    <title>Image Carousel</title>
    <style>
        .carousel-container {
            width: 100%;
            white-space: nowrap; /* Keep images in a line
*/
        }

        .carousel-container img {
            width: 20%; /* Adjust based on the number of
                        images and container size */
            height: auto;
        }
    </style>
</head>
<body>

<!-- NB: the sample images were added manually -->

<div class="carousel-container" id="carousel">
    <img src="Clown1.png" alt="Image 1">
    <img src="Avocadoes1.png" alt="Image 2">
    <img src="sample3.png" alt="Image 3">
    <img src="Clown1.png" alt="Image 4">
    <img src="Avocadoes1.png" alt="Image 5">
    <img src="sample3.png" alt="Image 6">
    <img src="Clown1.png" alt="Image 7">
    <img src="Avocadoes1.png" alt="Image 8">
    <img src="sample3.png" alt="Image 9">
    <!-- Add more images here -->
</div>

<script>
    const carousel = document.getElementById('carousel');

    // NB: the scrollBy() functions were manually reversed
    window.addEventListener('keydown', function(event) {
        console.log("pressed key:",event.key)
```

```
        if (event.key === 'ArrowRight') {
            carousel.scrollBy(-100, 0); // Scroll right
            //console.log("scroll right")
        } else if (event.key === 'ArrowLeft') {
            carousel.scrollBy(100, 0); // Scroll left
            //console.log("scroll left")
        }
    });
</script>

</body>
</html>
```

Explanation of the Code

HTML Structure:

A <div> with the class carousel-container acts as the container for the carousel. It contains <img> tags for each image in the carousel.

CSS Styles:

.carousel-container: Sets the width to 100% of the viewport and hides any overflow along the x-axis. It also ensures that the images are displayed in a horizontal line.

.carousel-container img: Styles the images to have a consistent width and automatic height to maintain aspect ratio.

JavaScript for Carousel Control:

We add an event listener for keydown events to the window object. When an arrow key is pressed, the scrollBy method is called on the carousel container.

If the right arrow key (ArrowRight) is pressed, the carousel scrolls horizontally to the right by 100 pixels. If the left arrow key (ArrowLeft) is pressed, it scrolls left by 100 pixels.

When you view this HTML page in a browser and press the arrow keys, the carousel will scroll horizontally to reveal more images. You can adjust the scroll amount and image sizes as needed for your specific layout and design needs.

Keep in mind that the following overflow attribute was manually removed from .carousel-container:

```
overflow-x: auto; /* Hide horizontal overflow */
```

Now launch the Web page gpt4_css3_carousel1.html by navigating to the directory that contains this HTML Web page and then typing the following command:

```
open gpt4_css3_carousel1.html
```

After a few moments you will see a set of PNG files displayed horizontally in a Web page. Now hover over any image and press the left arrow key or the right arrow key and you will see the row of images shift to the left or to the right, respectively, as shown in Figure 5.8.

FIGURE 5.8. A web page with a carousel effect.

CSS3 AND 2D TRANSFORMS

The following prompt was supplied to GPT-4 to generate an HTML Web page that contains CSS3-based 2D transforms on HTML <div> elements:

Please generate an HTML Web page that contains CSS3-based 2D transform effects on three HTML <div> elements, along with an explanation of the code.

ChatGPT:

Sure, I'll create an HTML Web page that demonstrates CSS3-based 2D transform effects on three <div> elements. Each <div> will have a unique transformation: rotation, scaling, and skewing. This will help you understand how to apply and control these effects using CSS.

Listing 5.10 displays the contents of gpt4_css3_2d_transforms.html that shows the code that GPT-4 generated in order to display a Web page that contains an SVG rectangle with linear gradient shading, an SVG polygon with radial gradient shading, and an SVG circle with radial gradient shading.

LISTING 5.10: gpt4_css3_2d_transforms.html

```
<!DOCTYPE html>
<html lang="en">
<head>
    <meta charset="UTF-8">
    <title>CSS3 2D Transformations</title>
    <style>
        .box {
            width: 100px;
            height: 100px;
            margin: 20px;
            display: inline-block;
            background-color: #4CAF50;
            color: white;
            text-align: center;
```

```
            line-height: 100px;
            transition: transform 0.5s ease;
        }
        .rotate:hover {
            transform: rotate(45deg);
        }
        .scale:hover {
            transform: scale(1.5);
        }
        .skew:hover {
            transform: skewX(20deg);
        }
    </style>
</head>
<body>

    <div class="box rotate">Rotate</div>
    <div class="box scale">Scale</div>
    <div class="box skew">Skew</div>

</body>
</html>
```

Explanation of the Code
    HTML Structure:
        Three <div> elements are created, each with
the class box and an additional class specific to the
transformation it will undergo (rotate, scale, skew).

    CSS:
        The .box class sets common styles for all divs,
like size, background color, text alignment, and transition
effect for smooth transformation.

        The .rotate, .scale, and .skew classes are targeted
by the :hover pseudo-class, which means the transformation
occurs when the mouse hovers over the div.

        The transform property is used with different values
for each class:
        rotate(45deg) rotates the element 45 degrees
        clockwise.
        scale(1.5) increases the size of the element by 50%.
        skewX(20deg) skews the element along the X-axis by
        20 degrees.

    Interactivity:
        The transition property in .box class ensures the
transformation occurs smoothly over 0.5 seconds.
        When you hover over each box, it will perform the
specified transformation.
This simple example demonstrates how to use CSS3 2D
transforms to create interactive and visually appealing
effects on Web elements. The :hover pseudo-class adds an
interactive aspect, allowing users to see the effects in
action with a simple mouse-over.

Now launch the Web page `gpt4_css3_2d_transforms.html` by navigating to the directory that contains this HTML Web page and then typing the following command:

```
open gpt4_css3_2d_transforms.html
```

After a few moments you will see a Web page that displays three green HTML <div> elements that contain the text Rotate, Scale, and Skew, respectively. Now hover over each of these <div> elements and you will see a corresponding 2D transform effect that is shown in Figure 5.9, Figure 5.10, and Figure 5.11, respectively.

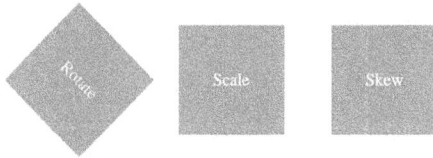

FIGURE 5.9. A Web page with a CSS3-based rotation effect.

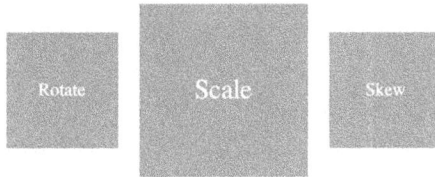

FIGURE 5.10. A Web page with a CSS3-based scaling effect.

FIGURE 5.11. A Web page with a CSS3-based skew effect.

CSS3 QUADRATIC BEZIER CURVES

The following prompt was supplied to GPT-4 to generate an HTML Web page that contains cubic Bezier curves with random radial gradients:

Please generate CSS3 code to display twenty quadratic Bezier curves that are rendered with a random CSS3 radial gradient, along with an explanation of the code.

GPT-4:

Creating twenty quadratic Bezier curves, each rendered with a random CSS3 radial gradient and an inset box-shadow, can be achieved using HTML and CSS. For simplicity and randomness, we'll use JavaScript to generate random colors for the gradients. Each curve will be represented by a <div> element styled to approximate a quadratic Bezier curve using CSS transformations.

Listing 5.11 displays the contents of gpt4_css3_quadratic_bezier. html that shows the code that GPT-4 generated in order to display a Web page that contains an artistic pattern of quadratic Bezier curves with random radial gradients.

LISTING 5.11: gpt4_css3_quadratic_bezier.html

```
<!DOCTYPE html>
<html lang="en">
<head>
    <meta charset="UTF-8">
    <title>CSS3 Quadratic Bezier Curves</title>
    <style>
      .bezier-curve svg {
        box-shadow: inset 15px 12px 30px #000;
      }
    </style>
</head>

<body>
 <div class="bezier-curve">
  <svg width="200" height="200" xmlns="http://www.
w3.org/2000/svg">
    <path d="M10 80 Q 95 10 180 80"
stroke="url(#gradient1)" stroke-width="2" fill="none"/>
    <defs>
      <radialGradient id="gradient1">
        <stop offset="0%" stop-color="#ff0000"/>
        <stop offset="100%" stop-color="#ffff00"/>
      </radialGradient>
    </defs>
  </svg>
 </div>
</body>
</html>
```

Explanation:

- **SVG Path for Quadratic Bezier Curve**: The path element's d attribute defines the curve. M moves the pen to the start point, Q defines a quadratic Bezier curve with a control point and an end point. The coordinates after M and Q set these points.
- **Radial Gradient**: Defined within the defs element, it specifies the gradient colors. The id attribute links the gradient to the stroke of the path. stop-color defines the colors at various points in the gradient.
- **CSS Box Shadow:** Applied to the SVG element, creating a shadow effect that appears to inset the curve into the page. The values define the shadow's offsets, blur radius, and color.
- **To create twenty curves with random gradients:** You would replicate the SVG structure within different div elements, each with its own

gradient definitions in the `defs` section. The CSS for the box shadow can remain the same, or you can customize it for each curve.

```
This example provides a base. For truly random gradients and
multiple curves, you'd programmatically generate the SVG
paths and gradient colors, possibly through a server-side
script or JavaScript, to inject varying colors and curve co-
ordinates into the HTML structure.
```

Launch the Web page `gpt4_css3_quadratic_bezier.html` by navigating to the directory that contains this HTML Web page and then typing the following command:

```
open gpt4_css3_quadratic_bezier.html
```

After a few moments you will see the image displayed in Figure 5.12.

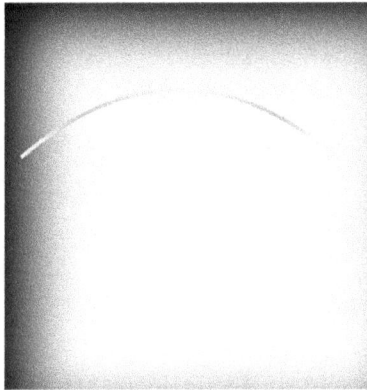

FIGURE 5.12. Quadratic Bezier Curves CSS3-based rotation effect.

CSS3 CUBIC BEZIER CURVES

The following prompt was supplied to GPT-4 to generate an HTML Web page that contains cubic Bezier curves with random radial gradients:

```
Please generate CSS3 code to display 20 cubic Bezier curves
that are rendered with a random CSS3 radial gradient, along
with an explanation of the code.
```

```
GPT-4:
```

```
Creating an artistic design with 20 cubic Bezier curves, each
rendered with a random CSS3 radial gradient and an inset box-
shadow, can be achieved using HTML and CSS. For simplicity
and randomness, we'll use JavaScript to generate random
colors for the gradients. Each curve will be represented by
a <div> element styled to approximate a cubic Bezier curve
using CSS transformations.
```

Listing 5.12 displays the contents of gpt4_css3_cubic_bezier.html that shows the code that GPT-4 generated in order to display a Web page that contains an artistic pattern of cubic Bezier curves with random radial gradients.

LISTING 5.12: gpt4_css3_cubic_bezier.html

```html
<!DOCTYPE html>
<html lang="en">
<head>
    <meta charset="UTF-8">
    <title>CSS3 2D Transformations</title>
    <style>
        .box {
            width: 100px;
            height: 100px;
            margin: 20px;
            display: inline-block;
            background-color: #4CAF50;
            color: white;
            text-align: center;
            line-height: 100px;
            transition: transform 0.5s ease;
        }
        .rotate:hover {
            transform: rotate(45deg);
        }
        .scale:hover {
            transform: scale(1.5);
        }
        .skew:hover {
            transform: skewX(20deg);
        }
    </style>
</head>
<body>

    <div class="box rotate">Rotate</div>
    <div class="box scale">Scale</div>
    <div class="box skew">Skew</div>

</body>
</html>
```

Launch the Web page gpt4_css3_cubic_bezier.html by navigating to the directory that contains this HTML Web page and then typing the following command:

```
open gpt4_css3_cubic_bezier.html
```

After a few moments you will see the image displayed in Figure 5.13.

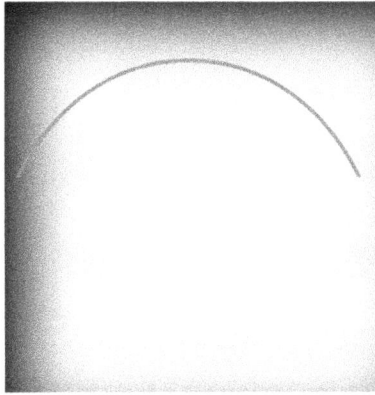

FIGURE 5.13. Cubic Bezier curves with a CSS3-based rotation effect.

ARTISTIC CSS3 CUBIC BEZIER CURVES

The following prompt was supplied to GPT-4 to generate an HTML Web page that contains cubic Bezier curves with random radial gradients:

Please generate at least 20 cubic Bezier curves that are rendered with a random CSS3 radial gradient, as well as a box-shadow attribute with value inset 15px 12px 30px #000; to create an artistic design.

GPT-4:

Creating an artistic design with 20 cubic Bezier curves, each rendered with a random CSS3 radial gradient and an inset box-shadow, can be achieved using HTML and CSS. For simplicity and randomness, we'll use JavaScript to generate random colors for the gradients. Each curve will be represented by a <div> element styled to approximate a cubic Bezier curve using CSS transformations.

Listing 5.13 displays the contents of gpt4_css3_artistic_bezier.html that shows the code that GPT-4 generated in order to display a Web page that contains an artistic pattern of cubic Bezier curves with random radial gradients.

LISTING 5.13: gpt4_css3_artistic_bezier.html

```
<!DOCTYPE html>
<html lang="en">
<head>
    <meta charset="UTF-8">
    <title>Artistic Cubic Bezier Curves</title>
    <style>
        .bezier-curve-container {
            position: relative;
            width: 100vw;
```

```
                height: 100vh;
                overflow: hidden;
            }

        .bezier-curve {
                position: absolute;
                width: 200px;
                height: 200px;
                border-radius: 50%;
                box-shadow: inset 15px 12px 30px #000;
                transform: rotate(-45deg) skewX(-30deg);
                transform-origin: bottom left;
            }
    </style>
</head>
<body>

<div class="bezier-curve-container" id="container"></div>

<script>
    function getRandomColor() {
        var letters = '0123456789ABCDEF';
        var color = '#';
        for (var i = 0; i < 6; i++) {
            color += letters[Math.floor(Math.random() * 16)];
        }
        return color;
    }

    function createBezierCurve() {
        var curve = document.createElement('div');
        curve.className = 'bezier-curve';
        curve.style.background = 'radial-gradient(circle,
                ${getRandomColor()}, ${getRandomColor()})';
        curve.style.top = '${Math.random() * 100}%';
        curve.style.left = '${Math.random() * 100}%';
        return curve;
    }

    const container = document.getElementById('container');
    for (let i = 0; i < 20; i++) {
        container.appendChild(createBezierCurve());
    }
</script>
</body>
</html>
```

Explanation of the Code

HTML Structure:
A single container <div> with the ID container is used to hold all the Bezier curve elements.

CSS Styles:
.bezier-curve-container: Sets up a full viewport container to hold the curves.

.bezier-curve: Styles each curve. The dimensions, border-radius, box-shadow, and transformation are set to create the approximate Bezier curve shape.

JavaScript for Randomization:
getRandomColor(): A function to generate random hex color codes.
createBezierCurve(): Creates a new div element styled as a Bezier curve with a random radial gradient background. It also randomly positions each curve within the container.
A loop creates 20 Bezier curves by calling createBezierCurve() and appending each to the container.

When rendered in a browser, this code will display 20 randomly colored and positioned cubic Bezier curves with inset box-shadows, creating a dynamic and artistic design. Each curve's appearance and position are randomized for variety.

Launch the Web page gpt4_css3_cubic_bezier.html by navigating to the directory that contains this HTML Web page and then typing the following command:

open gpt4_css3_artistic_bezier.html

After a few moments you will see the image in Figure 5.14 that displays the rendered cubic Bezier curves.

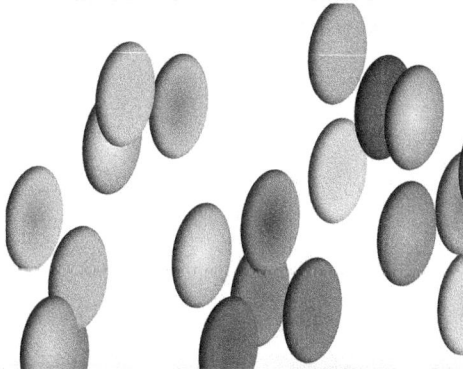

FIGURE 5.14. Multiple cubic Bezier curves.

CSS3 FILTERS

Filter effects in HTML Web pages can greatly enhance the visual experience. CSS3 supports the following filter types:

- blur
- drop-shadow
- brightness

- contrast
- grayscale
- hue-rotate
- invert
- opacity
- saturate
- sepia
- url

Note that SVG supports a larger set of filter effects, some of which you will see in the next chapter. Now let's take a look at some examples of CSS3 filter effects as shown in the following subsections.

CSS3 BLUR FILTER

The following prompt was supplied to GPT-4 to generate an HTML Web page that contains an HTML <div> element that is rendered with a CSS3 blur filter:

```
Please generate an HTML Web page that contains a <div> ele-
ment of width 400 and height 200, with a box-shadow attribute
with value inset 15px 12px 30px #000;
```

Listing 5.14 displays the contents of gpt4_css3_blur_filter.html that shows the code that GPT-4 generated in order to display a Web page that contains an artistic pattern of cubic Bezier curves with random radial gradients.

LISTING 5.14: gpt4_css3_blur_filter.html

```
<!DOCTYPE html>
<html lang="en">
<head>
    <meta charset="UTF-8">
    <title>Div with Box-Shadow and Blur Filter</title>
    <style>
        .shadow-blur-box {
            width: 400px;
            height: 200px;
            background-color: lightblue; /* Example
                                    background color */
            box-shadow: inset 15px 12px 30px #000;
            filter: blur(5px);
            margin: 20px;
        }
    </style>
</head>
<body>

<div class="shadow-blur-box"></div>

</body>
</html>
```

Explanation of the Code

HTML Structure:
A single <div> element with the class shadow-blur-box is used to create the box.

CSS Styles:

.shadow-blur-box: This class styles the <div> to have a width of 400px and a height of 200px.

background-color: lightblue; sets a light blue background color for the box. You can change this to any color of your choice.

box-shadow: inset 15px 12px 30px #000; adds an inset box-shadow to the element. The shadow is 15px to the right, 12px down, with a blur radius of 30px, and in black color (#000).

filter: blur(5px); applies a blur filter to the box, giving it a blurred appearance with a radius of 5px.

margin: 20px; adds some space around the box for better visibility.

When this HTML and CSS code is rendered in a browser, it displays a box with a specified width and height, an inset shadow, and a blur effect, creating a unique visual style. The blur filter adds a soft, unfocused effect to the box, while the inset shadow gives it a sense of depth.

Launch the Web page gpt4_css3_blur_filter.html by navigating to the directory that contains this HTML Web page and then typing the following command:

open gpt4_css3_blur_filter.html

After a few moments you will see the image in Figure 5.15 that displays a CSS3 blur filter effect.

FIGURE 5.15. CSS3 blur filter effect.

CSS3 DROP SHADOW

The following prompt was supplied to GPT-4 to generate an HTML Web page that contains an HTML <div> element that is rendered with a CSS3 drop shadow effect:

Please generate an HTML Web page that contains a <div> element of width 400 and height 200, with a a box-shadow attribute with value inset 15px 12px 30px #000; that is displayed with a CSS3 blur filter.

GPT-4:To create a rectangle and an ellipse each with a CSS3 drop shadow filter, we will use HTML and CSS. The rectangle will be made using a <div> element, while the ellipse will be created using another <div> with specific styling to make it elliptical. Both will have a drop shadow effect applied through CSS.

Listing 5.14 displays the contents of gpt4_css3_drop_shadow.html that shows the code that GPT-4 generated in order to display a Web page that contains an artistic pattern of cubic Bezier curves with random radial gradients.

LISTING 5.14: gpt4_css3_drop_shadow.html

```
<!DOCTYPE html>
<html lang="en">
<head>
    <meta charset="UTF-8">
    <title>CSS3 Drop Shadow on Shapes</title>
    <style>
        .rectangle {
            width: 400px;
            height: 200px;
            background-color: blue;
            box-shadow: 10px 10px 5px grey;
            margin-bottom: 20px;
        }

        .ellipse {
            width: 400px;
            height: 200px;
            background-color: red;
            border-radius: 50%;
            box-shadow: 10px 10px 5px grey;
        }
    </style>
</head>
<body>

<div class="rectangle"></div>
<div class="ellipse"></div>

</body>
</html>
```

Explanation of the Code

HTML Structure:
Two <div> elements are created: one with the class rectangle and the other with the class ellipse.

CSS Styles:
.rectangle class: This styles a 400px by 200px rectangle with a blue background. The box-shadow property applies a drop shadow effect. The shadow is offset by 10px horizontally and 10px vertically, has a blur radius of 5px, and is colored grey.
.ellipse class: This class also styles a shape of 400px by 200px, but the border-radius: 50%; makes it elliptical. It has a red background and the same drop shadow effect as the rectangle.

Drop Shadow Effect:
The box-shadow property in both classes creates a drop shadow for the shapes. The syntax box-shadow: horizontal-offset ver-tical-offset blur-radius color; defines the appearance and position of the shadow.

When this HTML and CSS code is rendered in a browser, it will display a blue rectangle and a red ellipse, each with a grey drop shadow, demonstrating a simple yet effective way to add depth and dimension to HTML elements using CSS3.

Launch the Web page gpt4_css3_drop_shadow.html by navigating to the directory that contains this HTML Web page and then typing the following command:

```
open gpt4_css3_drop_shadow.html
```

After a few moments you will see the image in Figure 5.16 that displays a CSS3 drop shadow effect:

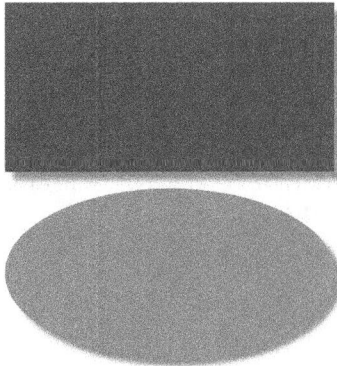

FIGURE 5.16. CSS3 drop shadow effect.

DALLE-3 AND GPT-4

The following prompt was supplied to GPT-4 in order to describe its support for DALLE-3:

```
Please describe the features of DALLE-3 that you support.
```

ChatGPT:

As of my last update in April 2023, here are the key features of DALLE-3 that I support:

1. **Image Generation from Descriptive Text:** I can create images based on detailed text descriptions. These descriptions can include a variety of elements like objects, scenes, styles, emotions, actions, and more. The more detailed the description, the more accurately the generated image will likely match your request.

2. **Adjustment to Image Descriptions:** I can modify image prompts based on your feedback to refine the output. If the first image doesn't quite match what you're looking for, you can provide more details or specify adjustments, and I can generate a new image based on that refined description.

3. **Policy Compliance:** My image generation follows specific guidelines. For instance, I don't create images of copyrighted characters, specific private individuals unless described, or content that violates OpenAI's use-case policy.

4. **Image Sizes:** I can generate images in three different sizes: 1024×1024 (square), 1792×1024 (wide), and 1024×1792 (full-body portraits).

5. **Single Image Generation:** I generate one image per request. This helps in focusing on creating a single, well-defined image based on your description.

```
Please note that while DALLE-3 is powerful, it might not
always perfectly interpret or visualize very complex or ab-
stract concepts. It's also important to provide a detailed
description for the best results.
```

DALLE-3 SAMPLE IMAGES

The following prompt was supplied to GPT-4 in order to generate an image of a pirate steering a cigar boat:

```
Please generate a pirate steering a cigar boat engulfed in
swirling ocean waters.
```

After a short delay you will see the image in Figure 5.17 that displays the

FIGURE 5.17. A pirate steering a cigar boat.

The following prompt was supplied to GPT-4 in order to generate an image of a movie star steering a cigar boat.

```
Please generate a movie star steering a cigar boat engulfed
in swirling ocean waters.
```

After a short delay you will see the image in Figure 5.18 that displays a movie star steering a cigar boat.

FIGURE 5.18. A movie star steering a cigar boat.

As can see from the two markedly different preceding images, the text in a prompt can significantly affect the type of image that GPT-4 will generate for you.

SUMMARY

This chapter started with a brief description of the strengths and weaknesses of HTML, as well as popular use cases for HTML. Then you saw a GPT-4-generated HTML Web page that contains a drop-down list with the days of the week.

Next, you learned about the strengths and weaknesses of CSS3, as well as use cases and potential security issues with CSS3. In addition, you saw code samples of CSS3 linear gradients, CSS3 radial gradients, rounded rectangles, diagonal gradients, and multigradients.

In addition, you learned how to create CSS3 animation effects, keyframe animation effects, and a carousel with CSS3. Furthermore, you learned how to use CSS3 2D transforms, quadratic Bezier curves, and cubic Bezier curves.

There were examples of CSS3 filters, such as blur filters and drop shadow filter effects. Finally, you saw examples of images that were generated using DALLE-3, which is accessible from GPT-4 (currently only for paid monthly subscriptions).

CHAPTER 6

SCALABLE VECTOR GRAPHICS (SVG)

This chapter gives you an overview of scalable vector graphics (SVG), along with examples of how to reference SVG documents in CSS3 selectors. Keep in mind that the CSS3 examples in this book are for WebKit-based browsers, but you can insert the code for other browsers by using browser-specific prefixes, which were discussed briefly in Chapter 3.

OVERVIEW OF SVG

This section contains various examples that illustrate some of the 2D shapes and effects that you can create with SVG. This section gives you a compressed overview, and if you want to learn more about SVG, you can perform an Internet search for details about books and many online tutorials.

SVG is an XML-based technology for rendering 2D shapes. SVG supports linear gradients, radial gradients, filter effects, transforms (translate, scale, skew, and rotate), and animation effects using an XML-based syntax. Although SVG does not support 3D effects, SVG provides functionality that is unavailable in CSS3, such as support for arbitrary polygons and more advanced filters beyond CSS3 filters.

Fortunately, you can reference SVG documents in CSS selectors via the CSS url() function, and the third part of this chapter contains examples of combining CSS3 and SVG in an HTML page. Moreover, the combination of CSS3 and SVG gives you a powerful mechanism for leveraging the functionality of SVG in CSS3 selectors. After reading this chapter you can learn more about SVG by performing an Internet search and then choosing from the many online tutorials that provide many SVG code samples.

Basic 2D Shapes in SVG

SVG supports a `<line>` element for rendering line segments, and its syntax looks like this:

```
<line x1="20" y1="20" x2="100" y2="150".../>
```

SVG `<line>` elements render line segments that connect the two points `(x1,y1)` and `(x2,y2)`.

SVG also supports a `<rect>` element for rendering rectangles, and its syntax looks like this:

```
<rect width="200" height="50" x="20" y="50".../>
```

The SVG `<rect>` element renders a rectangle whose width and height are specified in the width and height attributes. The upper-left vertex of the rectangle is specified by the point with coordinates (x,y). Listing 6.1 displays the contents of `BasicShapes1.svg` that illustrates how to render line segments and rectangles.

LISTING 6.1: BasicShapes1.svg

```
<?xml version="1.0" encoding="iso-8859-1"?>
<!DOCTYPE svg PUBLIC "-//W3C//DTD SVG 20001102//EN"
"http://www.w3.org/TR/2000/CR-SVG-20001102/DTD
                                /svg-20001102.dtd">

<svg xmlns="http://www.w3.org/2000/svg"
     xmlns:xlink="http://www.w3.org/1999/xlink"
     width="100%" height="100%">
<g>
<!-- left-side figures -->
<line x1="20" y1="20" x2="220" y2="20"
        stroke="blue" stroke-width="4"/>

<line x1="20" y1="40" x2="220" y2="40"
        stroke="red" stroke-width="10"/>

<rect width="200" height="50" x="20" y="70"
        fill="red" stroke="black" stroke-width="4"/>

<path d="M20,150 1200,0 10,50 1-200,0 z"
        fill="blue" stroke="red" stroke-width="4"/>

<!-- right-side figures -->

<path d="M250,20 1200,0 1-100,50 z"
        fill="blue" stroke="red" stroke-width="4"/>

<path d="M300,100 1100,0 150,50 1-50,50 1-100,0 1-50,-50 z"
        fill="yellow" stroke="red" stroke-width="4"/>
</g>
</svg>
```

The first SVG <line> element in Listing 6.1 specifies the color blue and a stroke-width (i.e., line width) of 4, whereas the second SVG <line> element specifies the color red and a stroke-width of 10.

Notice that the first SVG <rect> element renders a rectangle that looks the same (except for the color) as the second SVG <line> element and shows you that you can use more than one SVG element to render a rectangle (or a line segment).

The SVG <path> element is probably the most flexible and powerful element, because you can create arbitrarily complex shapes, based on a concatenation of other SVG elements. Later in this chapter you will see an example of how to render multiple Bezier curves in an SVG <path> element.

An SVG <path> element contains a d attribute that specifies the points in the desired path. For example, the first SVG <path> element in Listing 6.1 contains the following d attribute:

```
d="M20,150 l200,0 10,50 l-200,0 z"
```

This is how to interpret the contents of the d attribute:

- move to the absolute point (20,150)
- draw a horizontal line segment 200 pixels to the right
- draw a line segment 10 pixels to the right and 50 pixels down
- draw a horizontal line segment 200 pixels toward the left
- draw a line segment to the initial point (z)

Similar comments apply to the other two <path> elements in Listing 6.1. One thing to keep in mind is that uppercase letters (C, L, M, and Q) refer to absolute positions, whereas lowercase letters (c, l, m, and q) refer to relative positions with respect to the element that is to the immediate left. Experiment with the code in Listing 6.1 by using combinations of lowercase and uppercase letters to gain a better understanding of how to create different visual effects. Figure 6.1 displays the result of rendering the SVG document BasicShapes1.svg.

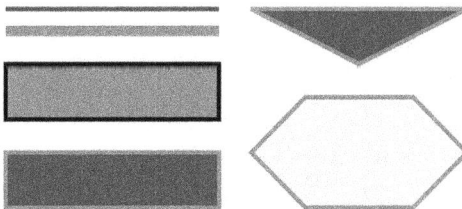

FIGURE 6.1. SVG line segments and rectangles.

SVG Gradients

As you have probably surmised, SVG supports linear gradients as well as radial gradients that you can apply to 2D shapes. For example, you can use the SVG <path> element to define elliptic arcs (using the d attribute) and then specify gradient effects. Note that SVG supports the stroke-dasharray attribute and the <polygon> element, neither of which is available in HTML5 Canvas.

Listing 6.2 displays the contents of `BasicShapesLRG1.svg` that illustrates how to render 2D shapes with linear gradients and with radial gradients.

LISTING 6.2: BasicShapesLRG1.svg

```
<?xml version="1.0" encoding="iso-8859-1"?>
<!DOCTYPE svg PUBLIC "-//W3C//DTD SVG 20001102//EN"
 "http://www.w3.org/TR/2000/CR-SVG-20001102/DTD
                                    /svg-20001102.dtd">

<svg xmlns="http://www.w3.org/2000/svg"
     xmlns:xlink="http://www.w3.org/1999/xlink"
     width="100%" height="100%">
<defs>
<linearGradient id="pattern1"
                   x1="0%" y1="100%" x2="100%" y2="0%">
<stop offset="0%"   stop-color="yellow"/>
<stop offset="40%"  stop-color="red"/>
<stop offset="80%"  stop-color="blue"/>
</linearGradient>

<radialGradient id="pattern2">
<stop offset="0%"   stop-color="yellow"/>
<stop offset="40%"  stop-color="red"/>
<stop offset="80%"  stop-color="blue"/>
</radialGradient>
</defs>

<g>
<ellipse cx="120" cy="80" rx="100" ry="50"
            fill="url(#pattern1)"/>

<ellipse cx="120" cy="200" rx="100" ry="50"
            fill="url(#pattern2)"/>

<ellipse cx="320" cy="80" rx="50" ry="50"
            fill="url(#pattern2)"/>

<path d="M 505,145 v -100 a 250,100 0 0,1 -200,100"
         fill="black"/>

<path d="M 500,140 v -100 a 250,100 0 0,1 -200,100"
         fill="url(#pattern1)"
         stroke="black" stroke-thickness="8"/>

<path d="M 305,165 v  100 a 250,100 0 0,1  200,-100"
         fill="black"/>

<path d="M 300,160 v  100 a 250,100 0 0,1  200,-100"
         fill="url(#pattern1)"
         stroke="black" stroke-thickness="8"/>

<ellipse cx="450" cy="240" rx="50" ry="50"
            fill="url(#pattern1)"/>
</g>
</svg>
```

Listing 6.2 contains an SVG <defs> element that specifies a <linearGradient> element (whose id attribute has value pattern1) with three stop values using an XML-based syntax, followed by a <radialGradient> element with three <stop> elements and an id attribute whose value is pattern2.

The SVG <g> element contains four <ellipse> elements, the first of which specifies the point (120,80) as its center (cx,cy), with a major radius of 100, a minor radius of 50, filled with the linear gradient pattern1, as shown here:

```
<ellipse cx="120" cy="80" rx="100" ry="50"
         fill="url(#pattern1)"/>
```

Similar comments apply to the other three SVG <ellipse> elements.

The SVG <g> element also contains four <path> elements that render elliptic arcs. The first <path> element specifies a black background for the elliptic arc defined with the following d attribute:

```
 d="M 505,145 v -100 a 250,100 0 0,1 -200,100"
```

Unfortunately, the SVG syntax for elliptic arcs is nonintuitive, and it's based on the notion of major arcs and minor arcs that connect two points on an ellipse. This example is only for illustrative purposes, so we won't delve into a detailed explanation of elliptic arcs work in SVG. If you need to learn the details, you can perform an Internet search and read the information found at the various links (be prepared to spend some time experimenting with how to generate various types of elliptic arcs).

The second SVG <path> element renders the same elliptic arc with a slight offset, using the linear gradient pattern1, which creates a shadow effect. Similar comments apply to the other pair of SVG <path> elements that render an elliptic arc with the radial gradient pattern2 (also with a shadow effect). Figure 6.2 displays the result of rendering BasicShapesLRG1.svg.

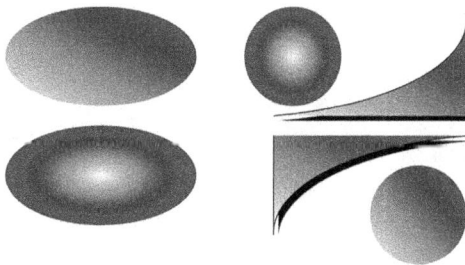

FIGURE 6.2. SVG elliptic arcs with linear and radial gradients.

SVG <polygon> Element

The SVG <polygon> element contains a polygon attribute in which you can specify points that represent the vertices of a polygon. The SVG <polygon> element is most useful when you want to create polygons with an arbitrary number of sides, but you can also use this element to render line segments and rectangles. Listing 6.3 displays the contents of SvgCube1.svg that illustrates how to render a cube in SVG.

LISTING 6.3: SvgCube1.svg

```
<?xml version="1.0" encoding="iso-8859-1"?>
<!DOCTYPE svg PUBLIC "-//W3C//DTD SVG 20001102//EN"
  "http://www.w3.org/TR/2000/CR-SVG-20001102/DTD/svg-
                                            20001102.dtd">

<svg xmlns="http://www.w3.org/2000/svg"
     xmlns:xlink="http://www.w3.org/1999/xlink"
     width="100%" height="100%">
<defs>
<linearGradient id="pattern1">
<stop offset="0%"   stop-color="yellow"/>
<stop offset="40%"  stop-color="red"/>
<stop offset="80%"  stop-color="blue"/>
</linearGradient>

<radialGradient id="pattern2">
<stop offset="0%"   stop-color="yellow"/>
<stop offset="40%"  stop-color="red"/>
<stop offset="80%"  stop-color="blue"/>

</radialGradient>
<radialGradient id="pattern3">
<stop offset="0%"   stop-color="red"/>
<stop offset="30%"  stop-color="yellow"/>
<stop offset="60%"  stop-color="white"/>
<stop offset="90%"  stop-color="blue"/>
</radialGradient>
</defs>

<!-- top face (counter clockwise) -->
<polygon fill="url(#pattern1)"
            points="50,50 200,50 240,30 90,30"/>

<!-- front face -->
<rect width="150" height="150" x="50" y="50"
         fill="url(#pattern2)"/>

<!-- right face (counter clockwise) -->
<polygon fill="url(#pattern3)"
            points="200,50 200,200 240,180 240,30"/>
</svg>
```

Listing 6.3 contains an SVG <defs> element that defines a linear gradient and two radial gradients. Next, the SVG <g> element contains the three faces of a cube: an SVG <polygon> element renders the top face (a parallelogram), an SVG <rect> element renders the front face, and another SVG <polygon> element renders the right face (which is also a parallelogram). The three faces of the cube are rendered with the linear gradient and the two radial gradients defined in the SVG <defs> element at the beginning of Listing 6.3. Figure 6.3 displays the result of rendering the SVG document SvgCube1.svg.

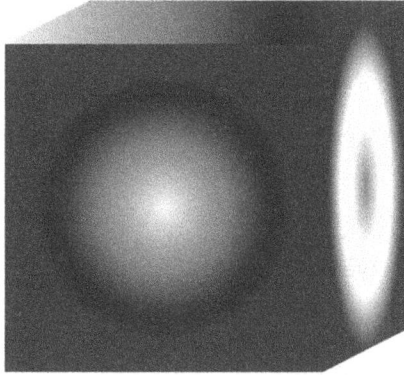

FIGURE 6.3. An SVG cube with gradient shading.

Bezier Curves

SVG supports quadratic and cubic Bezier curves that you can render with linear gradients or radial gradients. You can also concatenate multiple Bezier curves using an SVG <path> element. Listing 6.4 displays the contents of BezierCurves1.svg that illustrates how to render various Bezier curves.

LISTING 6.4: BezierCurves1.svg

```
<?xml version="1.0" encoding="iso-8859-1"?>
<!DOCTYPE svg PUBLIC "-//W3C//DTD SVG 20001102//EN"
  "http://www.w3.org/TR/2000/CR-SVG-20001102/DTD/svg-
                                        20001102.dtd">

<svg xmlns="http://www.w3.org/2000/svg"
     xmlns:xlink="http://www.w3.org/1999/xlink"
     width="100%" height="100%">
<defs>
<linearGradient id="pattern1"
                x1="0%" y1="100%" x2="100%" y2="0%">
<stop offset="0%"    stop-color="yellow"/>
<stop offset="40%"   stop-color="red"/>
<stop offset="80%"   stop-color="blue"/>
</linearGradient>

<linearGradient id="pattern2"
                gradientTransform="rotate(90)">
<stop offset="0%"    stop-color="#C0C040"/>
<stop offset="30%"   stop-color="#303000"/>
<stop offset="60%"   stop-color="#FF0F0F"/>
<stop offset="90%"   stop-color="#101000"/>
</linearGradient>
</defs>

<g transform="scale(1.5,0.5)">
```

```
<path d="m 0,50 C 400,200 200,-150 100,350"
        stroke="black" stroke-width="4"
        fill="url(#pattern1)"/>
</g>

<g transform="translate(50,50)">
<g transform="scale(0.5,1)">
<path d="m 50,50 C 400,100 200,200 100,20"
        fill="red" stroke="black" stroke-width="4"/>
</g>

<g transform="scale(1,1)">
<path d="m 50,50 C 400,100 200,200 100,20"
        fill="yellow" stroke="black" stroke-width="4"/>
</g>
</g>

<g transform="translate(-50,50)">
<g transform="scale(1,2)">
<path d="M 50,50 C 400,100 200,200 100,20"
        fill="blue" stroke="black" stroke-width="4"/>
</g>
</g>

<g transform="translate(-50,50)">
<g transform="scale(0.5, 0.5) translate(195,345)">
<path d="m20,20 C20,50 20,450 300,200 s-150,-250 200,100"
        fill="blue" style="stroke:#880088;
                                        stroke-width:4;"/>
</g>

<g transform="scale(0.5, 0.5) translate(185,335)">
<path d="m20,20 C20,50 20,450 300,200 s-150,-250 200,100"
        fill="url(#pattern2)"
style="stroke:#880088;stroke-width:4;"/>
</g>

<g transform="scale(0.5, 0.5) translate(180,330)">
<path d="m20,20 C20,50 20,450 300,200 s-150,-250 200,100"
    fill="blue" style="stroke:#880088;stroke-width:4;"/>
</g>

<g transform="scale(0.5, 0.5) translate(170,320)">
<path d="m20,20 C20,50 20,450 300,200 s-150,-250 200,100"
        fill="url(#pattern2)" style="stroke:black;
                                        stroke-width:4;"/>
</g>
</g>

<g transform="scale(0.8,1) translate(380,120)">
<path d="M0,0 C200,150 400,300 20,250"
        fill="url(#pattern2)" style="stroke:blue;
                                        stroke-width:4;"/>
</g>

<g transform="scale(2.0,2.5) translate(150,-80)">
```

```
<path d="M200,150 C0,0 400,300 20,250"
        fill="url(#pattern2)" style="stroke:blue;stroke-
                                        width:4;"/>
</g>
</svg>
```

Listing 6.4 contains an SVG <defs> element that defines two linear gradients, followed by 10 SVG <path> elements, each of which renders a cubic Bezier curve. The SVG <path> elements are enclosed in SVG <g> elements whose transform attributes contain the SVG scale() function or the SVG translate() functions (or both).

The first SVG <g> element invokes the SVG scale() function to scale the cubic Bezier curve that is specified in an SVG<path> element, as shown here:

```
<g transform="scale(1.5,0.5)">
<path d="m 0,50 C 400,200 200,-150 100,350"
        stroke="black" stroke-width="4"
        fill="url(#pattern1)"/>
</g>
```

The cubic Bezier curve has an initial point (0,50), with control points (400,200) and (200,-150), followed by the second control point (100,350). The Bezier curve is black, with a width of 4, and its fill color is defined in the <linearGradient> element (whose id attribute is pattern1) that is contained in the SVG <defs> element. The remaining SVG <path> elements are similar to the first SVG <path> element, so they will not be described. Figure 6.4 displays the result of rendering the Bezier curves that are defined in the SVG document BezierCurves1.svg.

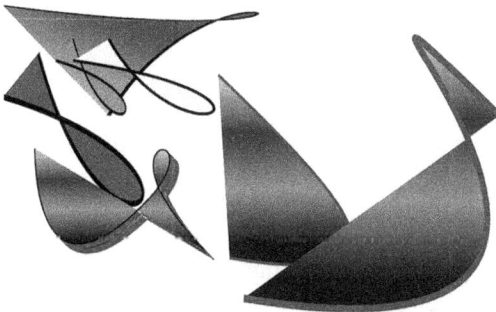

FIGURE 6.4. SVG Bezier curves.

SVG FILTERS, SHADOW EFFECTS, AND TEXT PATHS

You can create filter effects that you can apply to 2D shapes and also to text strings; this section contains three SVG-based examples of creating such effects. Listing 6.5, Listing 6.6, and Listing 6.7 display the contents of the SVG documents BlurFilterText1.svg, ShadowFilterText1.svg, and TextOnQBezierPath1.svg, respectively.

LISTING 6.5: BlurFilterText1.svg

```
<?xml version="1.0" encoding="iso-8859-1"?>
<!DOCTYPE svg PUBLIC "-//W3C//DTD SVG 20001102//EN"
 "http://www.w3.org/TR/2000/CR-SVG-20001102/DTD/svg-
                                            20001102.dtd">

<svg xmlns="http://www.w3.org/2000/svg"
     xmlns:xlink="http://www.w3.org/1999/xlink"
     width="100%" height="100%">
<defs>
<filter
     id="blurFilter1"
     filterUnits="objectBoundingBox"
     x="0" y="0"
     width="100%" height="100%">
<feGaussianBlur stdDeviation="4"/>
</filter>
</defs>

<g transform="translate(50,100)">
<text id="normalText" x="0" y="0"
      fill="red" stroke="black" stroke-width="4"
      font-size="72">
    Normal Text
</text>

<text id="horizontalText" x="0" y="100"
      filter="url(#blurFilter1)"
      fill="red" stroke="black" stroke-width="4"
      font-size="72">
    Blurred Text
</text>
</g>
</svg>
```

The SVG <defs> element in Listing 6.5 contains an SVG <filter> element that specifies a Gaussian blur with the following line:

```
<feGaussianBlur stdDeviation="4"/>
```

You can specify larger values for the stdDeviation attribute if you want to create more diffuse filter effects.

The first SVG <text> element that is contained in the SVG <g> element renders a normal text string, whereas the second SVG <text> element contains a filter attribute that references the filter (defined in the SVG <defs> element) in order to render the same text string, as shown here:

```
filter="url(#blurFilter1)"
```

Figure 6.5 displays the result of rendering `BlurFilterText1.svg` that creates a filter effect.

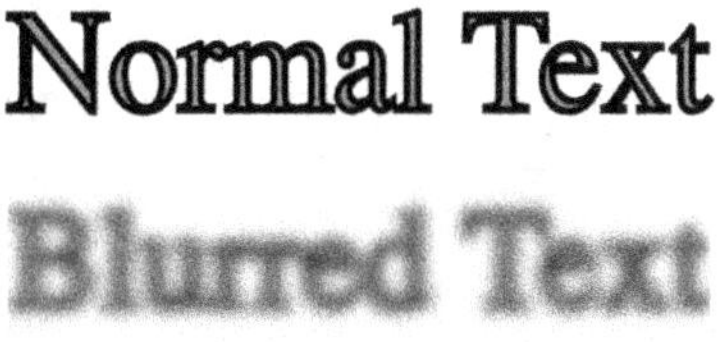

Normal Text

Blurred Text

FIGURE 6.5. SVG filter effect.

LISTING 6.6 : *ShadowFilterText1.svg*

```
<?xml version="1.0" encoding="iso-8859-1"?>
<!DOCTYPE svg PUBLIC "-//W3C//DTD SVG 20001102//EN"
 "http://www.w3.org/TR/2000/CR-SVG-20001102/DTD/svg-
                                        20001102.dtd">

<svg xmlns="http://www.w3.org/2000/svg"
     xmlns:xlink="http://www.w3.org/1999/xlink"
     width="100%" height="100%">
<defs>
<filter
     id="blurFilter1"
     filterUnits="objectBoundingBox"
     x="0" y="0"
     width="100%" height="100%">
<feGaussianBlur stdDeviation="4"/>
</filter>
</defs>

<g transform="translate(50,150)">
<text id="horizontalText" x="15" y="15"
      filter="url(#blurFilter1)"
      fill="red" stroke="black" stroke-width="2"
      font-size="72">
    Shadow Text
</text>

<text id="horizontalText" x="0" y="0"
      fill="red" stroke="black" stroke-width="4"
      font-size="72">
    Shadow Text
</text>
</g>
</svg>
```

Listing 3.5 is very similar to the code in Listing 6.10, except that the relative offset for the second SVG `<text>` element is slightly different, thereby creating a shadow effect.

Figure 6.6 displays the result of rendering `ShadowFilterText1.svg` that creates a shadow effect.

Shadow Text

FIGURE 6.6 SVG text with a shadow effect.

LISTING 6.7: *TextOnQBezierPath1.svg*

```
<?xml version="1.0" encoding="iso-8859-1"?>
<!DOCTYPE svg PUBLIC "-//W3C//DTD SVG 20001102//EN"
 "http://www.w3.org/TR/2000/CR-SVG-20001102/DTD/svg-
                                          20001102.dtd">

<svg xmlns="http://www.w3.org/2000/svg"
     xmlns:xlink="http://www.w3.org/1999/xlink"
     width="100%" height="100%">
<defs>
<path id="pathDefinition"
        d="m0,0 Q100,0 200,200 T300,200 z"/>
</defs>

<g transform="translate(100,100)">
<text id="textStyle" fill="red"
        stroke="blue" stroke-width="2"
        font-size="24">

<textPath xlink:href="#pathDefinition">
        Sample Text that follows a path specified by a
                                Quadratic Bezier curve
</textPath>
</text>
</g>
</svg>
```

The SVG `<defs>` element in Listing 6.7 contains an SVG `<path>` element that defines a quadratic Bezier curve (note the `Q` in the `d` attribute). This SVG `<path>` element has an `id` attribute whose value is `pathDefinition`, which is referenced later in this code sample.

The SVG `<g>` element contains an SVG`<text>` element that specifies a text string to render, as well as an SVG `<textPath>` element that specifies the path along which the text is rendered, as shown here:

```
<textPath xlink:href="#pathDefinition">
        Sample Text that follows a path specified by a
                                Quadratic Bezier curve
</textPath>
```

Notice that the SVG `<textPath>` element contains the attribute `xlink:href` whose value is `pathDefinition`, which is also the `id` of the SVG`<path>` element that is defined in the SVG `<defs>` element. As a result, the text string is rendered along the path of a quadratic Bezier curve instead of rendering the text string horizontally (which is the default behavior). Figure 6.7 displays the result of rendering `TextOnQBezierPath1.svg` that renders a text string along the path of a quadratic Bezier curve.

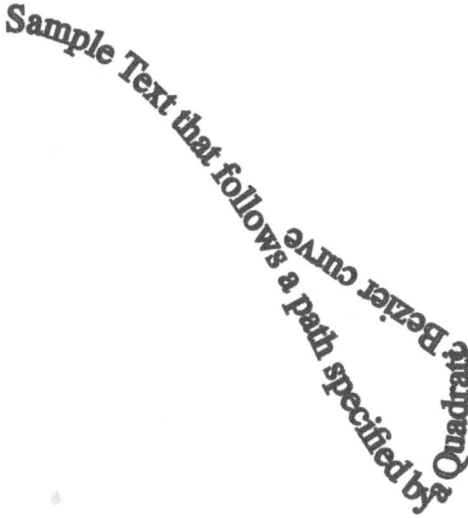

FIGURE 6.7. SVG text on a quadratic Bezier curve.

SVG TRANSFORMS

Earlier in this chapter you saw some examples of SVG transform effects. In addition to the SVG functions `scale()`, `translate()`, and `rotate()`, SVG provides the `skew()` function to create skew effects. Listing 6.8 displays the contents of `TransformEffects1.svg` that illustrates how to apply transforms to rectangles and circles in SVG.

LISTING 6.8: *TransformEffects1.svg*

```
<?xml version="1.0" encoding="iso-8859-1"?>
<!DOCTYPE svg PUBLIC "-//W3C//DTD SVG 20001102//EN"
 "http://www.w3.org/TR/2000/CR-SVG-20001102/DTD/svg-
                                         20001102.dtd">

<svg xmlns="http://www.w3.org/2000/svg"
     xmlns:xlink="http://www.w3.org/1999/xlink"
     width="100%" height="100%">
<defs>
<linearGradient id="gradientDefinition1"
     x1="0" y1="0" x2="200" y2="0"
     gradientUnits="userSpaceOnUse">
<stop offset="0%"   style="stop-color:#FF0000"/>
<stop offset="100%" style="stop-color:#440000"/>
</linearGradient>
```

```
<pattern id="dotPattern" width="8" height="8"
         patternUnits="userSpaceOnUse">
<circle id="circle1" cx="2" cy="2" r="2"
        style="fill:red;"/>
</pattern>
</defs>

<!-- full cylinder -->
<g id="largeCylinder" transform="translate(100,20)">
<ellipse cx="0"  cy="50" rx="20" ry="50"
         stroke="blue" stroke-width="4"
         style="fill:url(#gradientDefinition1)"/>

<rect x="0" y="0" width="300" height="100"
      style="fill:url(#gradientDefinition1)"/>

<rect x="0" y="0" width="300" height="100"
      style="fill:url(#dotPattern)"/>

<ellipse cx="300" cy="50" rx="20"  ry="50"
         stroke="blue" stroke-width="4"
         style="fill:yellow;"/>
</g>

<!-- half-sized cylinder -->
<g transform="translate(100,100) scale(.5)">
<use xlink:href="#largeCylinder" x="0" y="0"/>
</g>

<!-- skewed cylinder -->
<g transform="translate(100,100) skewX(40) skewY(20)">
<use xlink:href="#largeCylinder" x="0" y="0"/>
</g>

<!-- rotated cylinder -->
<g transform="translate(100,100) rotate(40)">
<use xlink:href="#largeCylinder" x="0" y="0"/>
</g>
</svg>
```

The SVG <defs> element in Listing 6.8 contains a <linearGradient> element that defines a linear gradient, followed by an SVG <pattern> element that defines a custom pattern as shown here:

```
<pattern id="dotPattern" width="8" height="8"
         patternUnits="userSpaceOnUse">
<circle id="circle1" cx="2" cy="2" r="2"
        style="fill:red;"/>
</pattern>
```

As you can see, the SVG <pattern> element contains an SVG <circle> element that is repeated in a grid-like fashion inside an 8x8 rectangle (note the values of the width attribute and the height attribute). The SVG <pattern> element has an id attribute whose value is dotPattern because, as you will see, this element creates a "dotted" effect.

Listing 6.8 contains four SVG <g> elements, each of which renders a cylinder that references the SVG <pattern> element that is defined in the SVG <defs> element. The first SVG <g> element in Listing 6.8 contains two <ellipse> elements and two SVG <rect> elements. The first <ellipse> element renders the left-side "cover" of the cylinder with the linear gradient that is defined in the SVG<defs> element. The first <rect> element renders the "body" of the cylinder with a linear gradient, and the second <rect> element renders the "dot pattern" on the body of the cylinder. Finally, the second <ellipse> element renders the right-side "cover" of the ellipse.

The other three cylinders are easy to create: they simply reference the first cylinder and apply a transformation to change the size, shape, and orientation. Specifically, these three cylinders reference the first cylinder with the following code:

```
<use xlink:href="#largeCylinder" x="0" y="0"/>
```

and then they apply scale, skew, and rotate functions in order to render scaled, skewed, and rotated cylinders. Figure 6.8 displays the result of rendering TransformEffects1.svg.

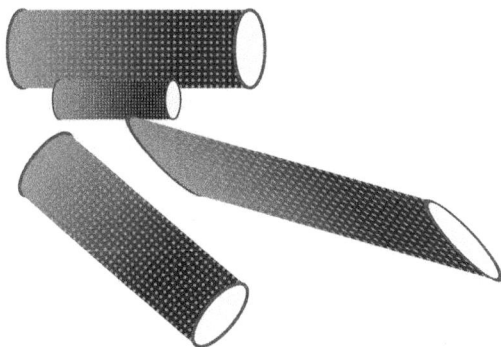

FIGURE 6.8. SVG transform effects.

SVG ANIMATION

SVG supports animation effects that you can specify as part of the declaration of SVG elements. Listing 6.9 displays the contents of the SVG document AnimateMultiRect1.svg that illustrates how to create an animation effect with four rectangles.

LISTING 6.9: AnimateMultiRect1.svg

```
<?xml version="1.0" encoding="iso-8859-1"?>
<!DOCTYPE svg PUBLIC "-//W3C//DTD SVG 20010904//EN"
   "http://www.w3.org/TR/2001/REC-SVG-20010904/DTD/svg10.dtd">

<svg xmlns="http://www.w3.org/2000/svg"
     xmlns:xlink="http://www.w3.org/1999/xlink"
     width="100%" height="100%">
```

```
<defs>
<rect id="rect1" width="100" height="100"
        stroke-width="1" stroke="blue"/>
</defs>

<g transform="translate(10,10)">
<rect width="500" height="400"
        fill="none" stroke-width="4" stroke="black"/>
</g>

<g transform="translate(10,10)">
<use xlink:href="#rect1" x="0" y="0" fill="red">
<animate attributeName="x" attributeType="XML"
                begin="0s" dur="4s"
                fill="freeze" from="0" to="400"/>
</use>

<use xlink:href="#rect1" x="400" y="0" fill="green">
<animate attributeName="y" attributeType="XML"
                begin="0s" dur="4s"
                fill="freeze" from="0" to="300"/>
</use>

<use xlink:href="#rect1" x="400" y="300" fill="blue">
<animate attributeName="x" attributeType="XML"
                begin="0s" dur="4s"
                fill="freeze" from="400" to="0"/>
</use>

<use xlink:href="#rect1" x="0" y="300" fill="yellow">
<animate attributeName="y" attributeType="XML"
                begin="0s" dur="4s"
                fill="freeze" from="300" to="0"/>
</use>
</g>
</svg>
```

The SVG <defs> element in Listing 6.9 contains an SVG <rect> element that defines a blue rectangle, followed by an SVG <g> element that renders the border of a large rectangle that "contains" the animation effect that involves the movement of four rectangles in a clockwise fashion along the perimeter of an outer rectangle.

The second SVG <g> element contains four <use> elements that perform a parallel animation effect on four rectangles. The first <use> element references the rectangle defined in the SVG <defs> element and then animates the x attribute during a four-second interval as shown here:

```
<use xlink:href="#rect1" x="0" y="0" fill="red">
<animate attributeName="x" attributeType="XML"
                begin="0s" dur="4s"
                fill="freeze" from="0" to="400"/>
</use>
```

Notice that the x attribute varies from 0 to 400, which moves the rectangle horizontally from left to right. The second SVG <use> element also references the rectangle defined in the SVG <defs> element, except that the animation involves changing the y attribute from 0 to 300 in order to move the rectangle downward, as shown here:

```
<use xlink:href="#rect1" x="400" y="0" fill="green">
<animate attributeName="y" attributeType="XML"
                begin="0s" dur="4s"
                fill="freeze" from="0" to="300"/>
</use>
```

In a similar fashion, the third SVG <use> element moves the referenced rectangle horizontally from right to left, and the fourth SVG <use> element moves the referenced rectangle vertically and upward.

If you want to create a sequential animation effect (or a combination of sequential and parallel), then you need to modify the values of the begin attribute (and possibly the dur attribute) in order to achieve your desired animation effect. Figure 6.9 displays the result of rendering AnimateMultiRect1.svg.

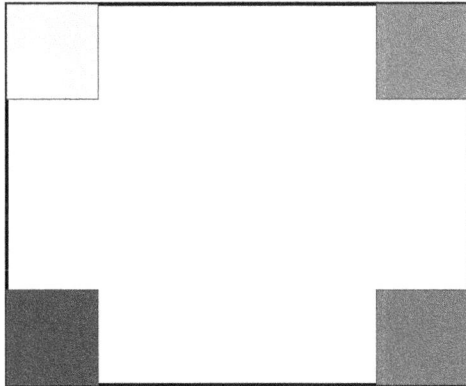

FIGURE 6.9. SVG animation effect with four rectangles.

Listing 6.10 displays the contents of the SVG documentAnimateText1.svg that illustrates how to animate a text string.

LISTING 6.10: AnimateText1.svg

```
<?xml version="1.0" encoding="iso-8859-1"?>
<!DOCTYPE svg PUBLIC "-//W3C//DTD SVG 20010904//EN"
  "http://www.w3.org/TR/2001/REC-SVG-20010904/DTD/svg10.dtd">

<svg xmlns="http://www.w3.org/2000/svg"
     xmlns:xlink="http://www.w3.org/1999/xlink"
     width="100%" height="100%">
```

```
<g transform="translate(100,100)">
<text x="0" y="0" font-size="48" visibility="hidden"
        stroke="black" stroke-width="2">
    Animating Text in SVG
<set attributeName="visibility"
            attributeType="CSS" to="visible"
            begin="2s" dur="5s" fill="freeze"/>

<animateMotion path="M0,0 L50,150"
            begin="2s" dur="5s" fill="freeze"/>

<animateColor attributeName="fill"
            attributeType="CSS"
            from="yellow" to="red"
            begin="2s" dur="8s" fill="freeze"/>

<animateTransform attributeName="transform"
            attributeType="XML"
            type="rotate" from="-90" to="0"
            begin="2s" dur="5s" fill="freeze"/>

<animateTransform attributeName="transform"
            attributeType="XML"
            type="scale" from=".5" to="1.5" additive="sum"
            begin="2s" dur="5s" fill="freeze"/>
</text>
</g>
</svg>
```

Listing 6.10 contains an SVG <text> element that specifies four different effects. The <set> element specifies the visibility of the text string for a five-second interval with an initial offset of two seconds.

The SVG <animateMotion> element shifts the upper-left corner of the text string from the point (0,0) to the point (50,150) in a linear fashion. This effect is combined with two other motion effects: rotation and scaling.

The SVG <animateColor> element changes the text color from yellow to red, and because the dur attribute has value 8s, this effect lasts three seconds longer than the other animation effects, whose dur attributes have values 5s. Note that all the animation effects start at the same time.

The first SVG <animateTransform> element performs a clockwise rotation of 90 degrees from vertical to horizontal. The second SVG <animate-Transform> element performs a scaling effect that occurs in parallel with the first SVG <animateTransform> element because they have the same values for the begin attribute and the dur attribute. Figure 6.10 displays the result of rendering AnimateText1.svg.

Animating Text in SVG

FIGURE 6.10. SVG text animation effect.

SVG AND JAVASCRIPT

SVG allows you to embed JavaScript in a CDATA section, which means that you can programmatically create SVG elements. Listing 6.11 displays the contents of the SVG document `ArchEllipses1.svg` that illustrates how to render a set of ellipses that follow the path of an Archimedean spiral.

LISTING 6.11: `ArchEllipses1.svg`

```
<?xml version="1.0" standalone="no"?>
<!DOCTYPE svg PUBLIC "-//W3C//DTD SVG 20010904//EN"
  "http://www.w3.org/TR/2001/REC-SVG-20010904/DTD/svg10.dtd">

<svg xmlns="http://www.w3.org/2000/svg"
     xmlns:xlink="http://www.w3.org/1999/xlink"
     onload="init(evt)"
     width="100%" height="100%">

<script type="text/ecmascript">
<![CDATA[
    var basePointX    = 250;
    var basePointY    = 200;
    var currentX      = 0;
    var currentY      = 0;
    var offsetX       = 0;
    var offsetY       = 0;
    var radius        = 0;
    var minorAxis     = 60;
    var majorAxis     = 30;
    var spiralCount   = 4;
    var Constant      = 0.25;
    var angle         = 0;
    var maxAngle      = 720;
    var angleDelta    = 2;
    var strokeWidth   = 1;
    var redColor      = "rgb(255,0,0)";

    var ellipseNode   = null;
    var svgDocument   = null;
    var target        = null;
    var gcNode        = null;

    var svgNS         = "http://www.w3.org/2000/svg";

    function init(event)
    {
        svgDocument = event.target.ownerDocument;
        gcNode = svgDocument.getElementById("gc");

        drawSpiral(event);
    }
```

```
    function drawSpiral(event)
    {
        for(angle=0; angle<maxAngle; angle+=angleDelta)
        {
            radius   = Constant*angle;
            offsetX  = radius*Math.cos(angle*Math.PI/180);
            offsetY  = radius*Math.sin(angle*Math.PI/180);
            currentX = basePointX+offsetX;
            currentY = basePointY-offsetY;

            ellipseNode = svgDocument.createElementNS
                                    (svgNS, "ellipse");

            ellipseNode.setAttribute("fill", redColor);
            ellipseNode.setAttribute("stroke-width",
                                            strokeWidth);

            if( angle % 3 == 0 ) {
               ellipseNode.setAttribute("stroke", "yellow");
            } else {
               ellipseNode.setAttribute("stroke", "green");
            }

            ellipseNode.setAttribute("cx", currentX);
            ellipseNode.setAttribute("cy", currentY);
            ellipseNode.setAttribute("rx", majorAxis);
            ellipseNode.setAttribute("ry", minorAxis);

            gcNode.appendChild(ellipseNode);
        }
    } // drawSpiral
  ]]></script>
<!-- ============================= -->
<g id="gc" transform="translate(10,10)">
<rect x="0" y="0"
         width="800" height="500"
         fill="none" stroke="none"/>
</g>
</svg>
```

Notice that the SVG <svg> element in Listing 6.11 contains an onload attribute that references the JavaScript function init(), and as you can surmise, the init() function is executed when you launch this SVG document in a browser. In this example, the purpose of the init() function is to reference the graphics context that is defined in the SVG <g> element at the bottom of Listing 6.11, and then to invoke the drawSpiral() function.

Whenever you want to include JavaScript in an SVG document, place the JavaScript code inside a CDATA section that is embedded in a <script> element. The CDATA section in Listing 6.11 initializes some variables, along with the definition of the init() function and the drawSpiral() function.

The code in the drawSpiral() function consists of a loop that renders a set of dynamically created SVG <ellipse> elements. Each SVG <ellipse> element is created in the SVG namespace that is specified in the variable svgNS, after which values are assigned to the required attributes of an ellipse, as shown here:

```
ellipseNode = svgDocument.createElementNS(svgNS, "ellipse");
ellipseNode.setAttribute("fill", redColor);
ellipseNode.setAttribute("stroke-width", strokeWidth);

// conditional logic omitted
ellipseNode.setAttribute("cx", currentX);
ellipseNode.setAttribute("cy", currentY);
ellipseNode.setAttribute("rx", majorAxis);
ellipseNode.setAttribute("ry", minorAxis);
```

After each SVG <ellipse> element is dynamically created, the element is appended to the DOM with one line of code, as shown here:

```
gcNode.appendChild(ellipseNode);
```

Finally, the SVG <g> element at the bottom of Listing 6.11 acts as a canvas on which the dynamically generated ellipses are rendered. Figure 6.11 displays the result of rendering ArchEllipses1.svg.

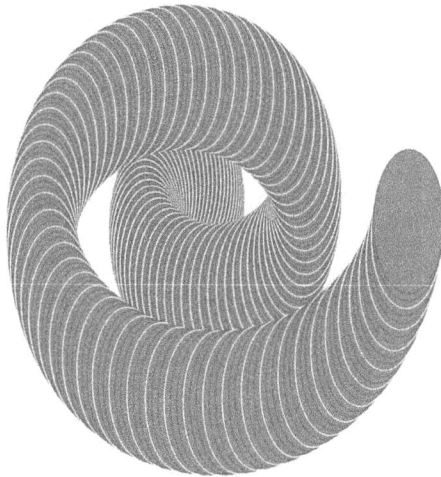

FIGURE 6.11. Dynamically generated SVG <ellipse> elements.

CSS3 AND SVG BAR CHARTS

Now that you know how to reference SVG documents in CSS3 selectors, let's look at an example of referencing an SVG-based bar chart in a CSS3 selector. Listing 6.12 displays the contents of the HTML5 page CSS3SVGBarChart1. html, Listing 6.13 displays the contents of the CSS3 stylesheet CSS3SVGBarChart1.css (whose selectors are applied to the contents of Listing 6.13), and Listing 6.14 displays the contents of the SVG document CSS3SVGBarChart1. svg (referenced in a selector in Listing 6.13) that contains the SVG code for rendering a bar chart.

LISTING 6.12: CSS3SVGBarChart1.html

```
<!doctype html>
<html en>
<head>
<title>CSS Multi Column Text and SVG Bar Chart</title>
<meta charset="utf-8" />
<link href="CSS3SVGBarChart1.css" rel="stylesheet"
type="text/css">
</head>

<body>
<div id="outer">
<article>
<p id="line1">.</p>
<div id="columns">
<p>
CSS enables you to define so-called "selectors" that specify
the style or the manner in which you want to render
elements in an HTML page.  CSS helps you modularize your
HTML content and since you can place your CSS definitions in
a separate file, you can also re-use the same CSS definitions
in multiple HTML files.</p>
<p>
Moreover, CSS also enables you to simplify the updates that
you need to make to elements in HTML pages.  For example,
suppose that multiple HTML table elements use a CSS rule
that specifies the color red.  If you later need to change
the color to blue, you can effect such a change simply by
making one change (i.e., changing red to blue) in one CSS
rule.</p>
<p>
Without a CSS rule, you would be forced to manually update
the color attribute in every HTML table element that
is affected, which is error-prone, time-consuming, and
extremely inefficient.</p>
<p>
 As you can see, it's very easy to reference an SVG
document in CSS selectors, and in this example, an SVG-
based bar chart is rendered on the left-side of the
screen.</p>
</div>

<p id="line1">.</p>
</article>
</div>
<div id="chart1">
</div>
</body>
</html>
```

In Chapter 4, you saw an example of rendering multicolumn text, and the contents of Listing 6.12 are essentially the same as the contents of that example. There is an additional HTML <div> element (whose id attribute has value chart1), however, that is used for rendering an SVG bar chart via a CSS selector in Listing 6.13.

LISTING 6.13: *CSS3SVGBarChart1.css*

```
#columns {
-webkit-column-count : 4;
-webkit-column-gap : 40px;
-webkit-column-rule : 1px solid rgb(255,255,255);
column-count : 3;
column-gap : 40px;
column-rule : 1px solid rgb(255,255,255);
}

#line1 {
color: red;
font-size: 24px;
background-image: -webkit-gradient(linear, 0% 0%, 0% 100%,
from(#fff), to(#f00));
background-image: -gradient(linear, 0% 0%, 0% 100%,
from(#fff), to(#f00));
-webkit-border-radius: 4px;
border-radius: 4px;
}

#chart1 {
opacity: 0.5;
color: red;
width: 800px;
height: 50%;
position: absolute; top: 20px; left: 20px;
font-size: 24px;
-webkit-border-radius: 4px;
-moz-border-radius: 4px;
border-radius: 4px;
border-radius: 4px;
-webkit-background: url(CSS3SVGBarChart1.svg) top right;
-moz-background: url(CSS3SVGBarChart1.svg) top right;
background: url(CSS3SVGBarChart1.svg) top right;
}
```

The #chart selector contains various attributes, along with a reference to an SVG document that renders an actual bar chart, as shown here:

```
-webkit-background: url(CSS3SVGBarChart1.svg) top right;
-moz-background: url(CSS3SVGBarChart1.svg) top right;
background: url(CSS3SVGBarChart1.svg) top right;
```

Now that you've see the contents of the HTML5 page and the selectors in the CSS stylesheet, let's take a look at the SVG document that renders the bar chart.

LISTING 6.14: CSS3SVGBarChart1.svg

```
<?xml version="1.0" encoding="iso-8859-1"?>
<!DOCTYPE svg PUBLIC "-//W3C//DTD SVG 20001102//EN"
 "http://www.w3.org/TR/2000/CR-SVG-20001102/DTD/svg-
                                      20001102.dtd">

<svg xmlns="http://www.w3.org/2000/svg"
     xmlns:xlink="http://www.w3.org/1999/xlink"
     width="100%" height="100%">
<defs>
<linearGradient id="pattern1">
<stop offset="0%"   stop-color="yellow"/>
<stop offset="40%"  stop-color="red"/>
<stop offset="80%"  stop-color="blue"/>
</linearGradient>

<radialGradient id="pattern2">
<stop offset="0%"   stop-color="yellow"/>
<stop offset="40%"  stop-color="red"/>
<stop offset="80%"  stop-color="blue"/>
</radialGradient>

<radialGradient id="pattern3">
<stop offset="0%"   stop-color="red"/>
<stop offset="30%"  stop-color="yellow"/>
<stop offset="60%"  stop-color="white"/>
<stop offset="90%"  stop-color="blue"/>
</radialGradient>
</defs>

<g id="chart1" transform="translate(0,0) scale(1,1)">
<rect width="30" height="235" x="15"  y="15"  fill="black"/>
<rect width="30" height="240" x="10"  y="10"
 fill="url(#pattern1)"/>

<rect width="30" height="145" x="45"  y="105" fill="black"/>
<rect width="30" height="150" x="40"  y="100"
fill="url(#pattern2)"/>

<rect width="30" height="195" x="75"  y="55"  fill="black"/>
<rect width="30" height="200" x="70"  y="50"
fill="url(#pattern1)"/>

<rect width="30" height="185" x="105" y="65"  fill="black"/>
<rect width="30" height="190" x="100" y="60"
fill="url(#pattern3)"/>

<rect width="30" height="145" x="135" y="105" fill="black"/>
<rect width="30" height="150" x="130" y="100"
 fill="url(#pattern1)"/>

<rect width="30" height="225" x="165" y="25"  fill="black"/>
<rect width="30" height="230" x="160" y="20"
fill="url(#pattern2)"/>
```

```
<rect width="30" height="145" x="195" y="105" fill="black"/>
<rect width="30" height="150" x="190" y="100"
fill="url(#pattern1)"/>

<rect width="30" height="175" x="225" y="75"  fill="black"/>
<rect width="30" height="180" x="220" y="70"
 fill="url(#pattern3)"/>
</g>

<g id="chart2" transform="translate(250,125) scale(1,0.5)"
             width="100%" height="100%">
<use xlink:href="#chart1"/>
</g>
</svg>
```

Listing 6.14 contains an SVG `<defs>` element in which three gradients are defined (one linear gradient and two radial gradients), whose `id` attribute has values `pattern1`, `pattern2`, and `pattern3`, respectively. These gradients are referenced by their `id` in the SVG `<g>` element that renders a set of rectangular bars for a bar chart. The second SVG `<g>` element (whose `id` attribute has value `chart2`) performs a transform involving the SVG `translate()` and `scale()` functions, and then renders the actual bar chart, as shown in this code:

```
<g id="chart2" transform="translate(250,125) scale(1,0.5)"
             width="100%" height="100%">
<use xlink:href="#chart1"/>
</g>
```

Figure 6.12 displays the result of applying `CSS3SVGBarChart1.css` to the elements in the HTML page `CSS3SVGBarChart1.html`.

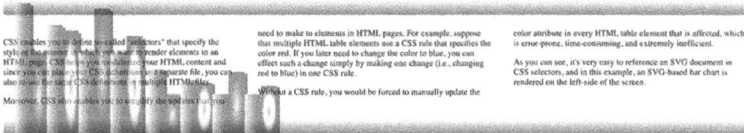

FIGURE 6.12. CSS3 with SVG applied to an HTML page.

SUMMARY

This chapter gave you an introduction to SVG, and you saw several code samples that illustrated the graphics capabilities of SVG. You also learned how to render 2D shapes and how to combine the functionality of SVG with CSS3. In particular, you learned how to do the following:

- create SVG linear gradients and radial gradients
- apply SVG gradients to ellipses and elliptic arcs
- render quadratic Bezier curves and cubic Bezier curves in SVG
- reference SVG documents in CSS3 selectors

CSS3 and SVG support additional features for creating sophisticated effects, and you can perform an Internet search to find links that discuss those features.

CHAPTER 7

SVG AND *GPT-4*

This chapter provides an assortment of SVG-based code samples that are generated by GPT-4, based on prompts that are supplied to GPT-4. Some of the code samples will be familiar: the difference is that almost all the code samples in this chapter are all generated by GPT-4.

The first portion of this chapter describes the strengths and weaknesses of SVG, followed by SVG use cases, SVG accessibility, and potential security issues with SVG.

The second portion of this chapter contains examples of GPT-4 generating linear gradients, radial gradients, and various SVG 2D shapes and gradients. You will also see how to render a bar chart in SVG.

The third section shows you how to render quadratic Bezier curves and cubic Bezier curves, as well as how to add animation effects for Bezier curves. In addition, you will learn how to create hover effects.

The fourth section compares SVG with CSS3 and also compares SVG with PNGs. Then you will learn how to work with SVG filters, such as blur filters and turbulence filters.

The fifth section contains code samples that combine SVG and CSS3 in an HTML Web page, as well we combine SVG and JavaScript in an HTML Web page. You will learn how to create other effects that involve JavaScript and SVG, such as rendering elliptic arts, checkerboard patterns, and finally a master detail HTML Web page that involves SVG.

One more detail to keep in mind: the SVG code samples involving Bezier curves (toward the end of the chapter) are created by Python code that is generated by GPT-4. Many laptops have Python already installed, and if need be, you can search online with the keywords "install Python Windows" to find links where you can download Python onto your laptop (and also replace "Windows" with your operating system).

WORKING WITH SVG

The following prompt was supplied to GPT-4 to describe SVG and its various features.

```
Please provide a description of the features of SVG, along
with its strengths and weaknesses.
```

Scalable vector graphics (SVG) is a versatile image format used on the Web and in various applications. Here is a description of its features, along with its strengths and weaknesses:

Features of SVG

1. **Vector-Based:** Unlike raster images like JPEGs or PNGs, SVGs are composed of vectors, which are mathematical descriptions of the image's shapes and paths. This allows them to scale infinitely without losing quality.

2. **XML-Based:** SVG images are written in XML (extensible markup language), making them easily readable and modifiable by both humans and machines.

3. **Interactive and Dynamic:** SVGs can be manipulated using CSS and JavaScript, allowing for interactivity, animation, and dynamic changes.

4. **DOM Integration:** SVG elements are part of the Document Object Model (DOM), meaning they can be interacted with just like HTML elements, offering a wide range of manipulation possibilities.

5. **Styling and Animation:** SVG supports styling with CSS and can be animated using CSS animations or SMIL (Synchronized Multimedia Integration Language).

6. **Accessibility:** Texts in SVG images are selectable and searchable, improving accessibility and SEO.

7. **Compact File Size:** Generally, SVG files are smaller in size compared to high-quality raster images, especially for graphics like logos, icons, and geometric shapes.

8. **Print Quality:** SVGs are resolution-independent, so they can be printed with high quality at any size.

Strengths

1. **Scalability:** Perfect for responsive Web design; images look sharp at any size or resolution.

2. **Editable:** Easily edited with text editors or vector graphic software.

3. **Performance:** Can reduce load times due to smaller file sizes compared to high-resolution raster images.

4. **Interactivity and Animation:** Offers dynamic and interactive capabilities, enhancing user experience.

5. **Accessibility and SEO Benefits:** Texts in SVGs are readable by screen readers and search engines.

Weaknesses

1. **Complexity for Detailed Images:** Not ideal for complex images like photographs; can become complex and large in file size.
2. **Browser Compatibility:** Some older browsers or specific features might have compatibility issues, although this is becoming less of a problem.
3. **Learning Curve:** Requires knowledge of XML and possibly CSS/JavaScript for advanced features.
4. **Security Concerns:** Being XML-based, SVG files can potentially contain harmful JavaScript, so they require careful handling and sanitization.
5. **Limited Editing Software:** While widely supported, not all graphic editing software are equally proficient at handling SVGs.

In summary, SVG is a powerful format for Web and graphic design, especially suited for logos, icons, and other designs that require scalability and interactivity. Its weaknesses are more apparent in handling complex images and require a bit of technical knowledge to fully utilize its capabilities.

USE CASES FOR SVG

The following prompt was supplied to GPT-4 in order to describe use cases for SVG in HTML Web pages:

```
Please describe significant use cases that involve SVG in HTML
Web pages, along with an explanation of the use cases.

ChatGPT:

Scalable vector graphics (SVG) is a powerful tool in modern
Web development, offering precision, scalability, and flex-
ibility for graphical elements. Here are some significant use
cases of SVG in HTML Web pages, along with explanations for
each:
```

1. High-Quality Scalable Icons and Logos
Use Case: Using SVG for icons, logos, and other vector graphics that need to retain high quality at any scale.
Explanation: Unlike raster images (like PNG or JPEG), SVGs are resolution-independent and remain crisp and clear at any size. This makes them ideal for logos and icons, especially in responsive designs where the image size adjusts to different screen resolutions.

2. Interactive and Animated Graphics
Use Case: Creating interactive diagrams, charts, and animations that respond to user actions.

Explanation: SVG can be manipulated with CSS and JavaScript, allowing for interactive and dynamic graphics. For instance, an SVG-based chart can be animated or updated in response to user inputs or data changes. This interactivity enhances user engagement and experience.

3. Complex Illustrations

Use Case: Embedding detailed illustrations and artwork that are zoomable without loss of quality.

Explanation: SVG is perfect for complex illustrations like technical diagrams, architectural plans, or detailed artwork. These graphics can be zoomed in on or scaled down while maintaining their quality, which is essential for conveying detailed information.

4. Data Visualization

Use Case: Creating dynamic data visualizations like graphs, pie charts, and maps.

Explanation: SVG's ability to scale and its support for interactivity make it suitable for data visualization. It can be used to create dynamic, data-driven charts and graphs that are both informative and visually appealing.

5. UI Elements and Controls

Use Case: Designing custom user interface elements like buttons, sliders, and progress bars.

Explanation: SVG provides more flexibility than traditional CSS in designing complex UI elements. With SVG, you can create detailed, scalable, and interactive UI components that enhance the user interface.

6. Text Manipulation and Accessibility

Use Case: Incorporating text within graphics that remains selectable and accessible.

Explanation: Texts in SVG are selectable and can be read by screen readers, unlike texts in raster images. This is particularly useful for accessibility and for scenarios where text and graphics need to work together, in infographics, for example.

7. Clipping and Masking Effects

Use Case: Applying complex clipping and masking effects to elements.

Explanation: SVG supports advanced clipping and masking capabilities, allowing for creative visual effects where parts of images or elements are hidden or revealed in specific shapes.

8. Web Typography and Decorative Text

Use Case: Creating artistic and decorative text effects.

Explanation: SVG offers extensive capabilities for stylizing and animating text, going beyond what CSS can achieve. This is useful for decorative purposes, such as fancy headings or stylized text in logos.

Conclusion

SVG's integration into HTML Web pages opens up a world of possibilities for high-quality graphics, interactive elements, and dynamic visualizations. Its strengths in scalability, interactivity, and precision make it an invaluable tool for creating engaging and effective Web content.

ACCESSIBILITY AND SVG

The following prompt was supplied to GPT-4 in order to describe the level of support for accessibility in SVG:

Please provide a detailed description of the level of support for accessibility in SVG.

ChatGPT:

Scalable vector graphics (SVG) offer a significant degree of support for accessibility, which is crucial for ensuring that Web content is available to all users, including those with disabilities. Here's a detailed description of the level of support for accessibility in SsVG:

Semantic Structure
- **Descriptive Tags:** SVG allows the use of descriptive tags like `<title>` and `<desc>`, which can provide context or descriptions for screen readers. This is similar to providing `alt` text in HTML `<img>` elements.
- **Use of Text:** Unlike text in raster images, text in SVG is selectable and searchable, which is beneficial for screen readers and SEO.

ARIA (Accessible Rich Internet Applications) Integration
- **ARIA Roles and Properties:** SVG integrates well with ARIA roles and properties. ARIA attributes can be used within SVG to enhance the accessibility of SVG elements, particularly for dynamic or complex graphics.
- **Hidden Attribute:** The `aria-hidden` attribute can be used to hide decorative SVG elements from screen readers, focusing on the more content-relevant parts.

Keyboard Navigation
- **Focusable Elements:** SVG elements can be made focusable and navigable using keyboard navigation, which is essential for users who cannot use a mouse. The `tabindex` attribute can be used to include or exclude elements from the tab order.

Zoom and Scalability
- **Scalable Graphics:** One of the inherent advantages of SVG is its scalability. Users with visual impairments can zoom in without loss of quality, which is not possible with raster images.

Color and Contrast

- **Customization:** SVGs can be styled and manipulated with CSS. This means that colors and contrasts can be dynamically adjusted to meet various accessibility standards or user preferences.

Dynamic Updates

- **JavaScript Interaction:** SVGs can be dynamically updated with JavaScript, which means they can be made to reflect changes in real time. This is particularly useful for users relying on assistive technology to access up-to-date information.

Text Alternatives

- **Complex Images:** For complex SVG images like charts or graphs, providing a text alternative is crucial. This can be done using HTML elements alongside the SVG or within the SVG using tags like <desc>.

Assistive Technology Support

- **Compatibility:** Modern screen readers and assistive technologies generally support SVG. However, the level of support can vary, and keeping SVGs simple and well-structured improves accessibility.

Challenges and Considerations

- **Complexity:** Complex SVGs (like detailed graphs) can be challenging to make fully accessible. In such cases, providing textual descriptions or alternative content is important.
- **Browser and Assistive Technology Variability:** Different browsers and assistive technologies may interpret SVG accessibility features differently, so testing across various platforms is important.

Conclusion

SVG provides various features that support accessibility, making it a viable option for creating accessible Web graphics. Proper use of semantic elements, ARIA roles, and text alternatives, along with careful design considerations, can enhance the accessibility of SVG content. As with any Web technology, the key to effective accessibility in SVGs lies in thoughtful implementation and thorough testing across different devices and assistive technologies.

SECURITY ISSUES WITH SVG

The following prompt was supplied to GPT-4 in order to describe potential security issues with SVG:

Please provide a detailed description of potential security issues involving SVG.

ChatGPT:

Scalable vector graphics (SVG) is a powerful XML-based markup language for describing two-dimensional vector graphics. SVG is widely used on the Web due to its scalability and flexibility, but like many Web technologies, it comes with its own set of security considerations. Here's a detailed description of potential security issues involving SVG:

1. Cross-Site Scripting (XSS) Attacks
- **Issue:** SVG files can contain JavaScript, which can be executed in the user's browser. If an SVG file is not properly sanitized and is allowed to include malicious scripts, it can lead to XSS attacks when the SVG is embedded in a Web page.
- **Consequences:** This can allow attackers to steal cookies, session tokens, or even take over a user's session.

2. Malicious Payloads
- **Issue:** SVG files can contain various types of potentially harmful content, including JavaScript, CSS, and even embedded raster images. This versatility makes it possible for SVG files to carry malicious payloads.
- **Consequences:** If the SVG file is not properly validated and sanitized, it can be used to deliver various types of exploits.

3. Phishing and Social Engineering
- **Issue:** SVGs can be crafted to look like legitimate interactive elements or familiar brands, tricking users into clicking on them or providing sensitive information.
- **Consequences:** This can lead to phishing attacks where users are misled into giving away personal data or credentials.

4. Resource Consumption
- **Issue:** SVGs can be designed to be computationally intensive to render, either intentionally or by accident.
- **Consequences:** Loading complex SVGs can lead to significant performance hits on a user's device, potentially causing Denial of Service (DoS) like conditions.

5. External Resource References
Issue: SVGs can reference external resources, which can be used maliciously.

Consequences: This can lead to information leakage (through referrer headers), or the loading of malicious resources if the external resource is controlled by an attacker.

6. Privacy Leaks
- **Issue:** SVGs can contain scripting or external resource references that send user data to remote servers without the user's knowledge.
- **Consequences:** This can be a privacy concern, as it can be used to track users or collect sensitive information.

Mitigation Strategies

- **Content Sanitization:** Any SVG content uploaded by users should be properly sanitized to remove potentially malicious scripts or payloads. This is especially important for Web applications that allow user-uploaded content.
- **CSP (Content Security Policy):** Implementing a robust CSP can help prevent the execution of unauthorized scripts within SVGs.
- **Limiting SVG Features:** Restricting features like scripting, external resource loading, and embedding within SVGs can reduce the attack surface.
- **User Awareness and Education:** Educating users about the risks associated with unknown SVG files and encouraging caution can be an effective line of defense.

Conclusion

SVG, while being a versatile and powerful technology for Web graphics, brings its own set of security challenges. Awareness of these issues and implementing proper security measures and best practices are key to mitigating the risks associated with using SVG in Web applications.

SVG LINEAR GRADIENTS

The following prompt was supplied to GPT-4 in order to generate an HTML Web page that contains an SVG rectangle with a linear gradient:

```
Please generate an SVG rectangle of width 500 and height 300
that is rendered with an SVG linear gradient, along with an
explanation of the code.
```

ChatGPT:

```
To create an SVG rectangle of width 500 and height 300 ren-
dered with a linear gradient, you can use SVG's <rect> ele-
ment for the rectangle and define a linear gradient for its
fill. Here's an example of how to achieve this:
```

Listing 7.1 displays the contents of gpt4_svg_linear_gradient.html that shows the code that GPT-4 generated in order to display a Web page that contains an SVG rectangle with linear gradient shading, an SVG polygon with radial gradient shading, and an SVG circle with radial gradient shading.

LISTING 7.1: gpt4_svg_linear_gradient.html

```
<!DOCTYPE html>
<html lang="en">
<head>
    <meta charset="UTF-8">
    <title>SVG Rectangle with Linear Gradient</title>
</head>
```

```
<body>

<svg width="500" height="300" xmlns="http://www.
w3.org/2000/svg">
    <!-- Define a linear gradient -->
    <defs>
        <linearGradient id="gradient">
            <stop offset="0%" stop-color="lightblue" />
            <stop offset="100%" stop-color="blue" />
        </linearGradient>
    </defs>

    <!-- Draw a rectangle with the linear gradient fill -->
    <rect width="500" height="300" fill="url(#gradient)" />
</svg>

</body>
</html>
```

Explanation of the Code

1. SVG Container:
  - An <svg> element sets up an SVG container with a specified width of 500 and a height of 300 to hold the rectangle.

2. Linear Gradient Definition:
  - Inside the <defs> element, a <linearGradient> with the ID gradient is defined. This gradient is used for the fill of the rectangle.
  - The gradient includes two <stop> elements, defining the color transition. The gradient transitions from light blue at the start (0% offset) to blue at the end (100% offset).

3. Rectangle with Linear Gradient Fill:
  - The <rect> element draws the rectangle. It is given a width of 500 and a height of 300.
  - The fill attribute applies the defined linear gradient to the rectangle using the url(#gradient) reference.

When rendered in a browser, this HTML will display a rectangle with a linear gradient fill, showcasing how SVG and its gradient capabilities can be used to create visually appealing graphics with smooth color transitions.

Launch the Web page gpt4_svg_rect_poly.html by navigating to the directory that contains this HTML Web page and then typing the following command:

```
open gpt4_svg_linear_gradient.html
```

After a few moments you will see the Web page in Figure 7.1 that displays a snapshot of SVG-based graphics.

FIGURE 7.1. A Web page with SVG-based graphics.

SVG RADIAL GRADIENTS

The following prompt was supplied to GPT-4 in order to generate an HTML Web page that contains an SVG rectangle with a radial gradient:

Please generate an SVG rectangle of width 500 and height 300 that is rendered with an SVG radial gradient, along with an explanation of the code.

ChatGPT:

To create an SVG rectangle of width 500 and height 300 rendered with a radial gradient, you can use SVG's <rect> element for the rectangle and define a linear gradient for its fill. Here's an example of how to achieve this:

Listing 7.2 displays the contents of gpt4_svg_radial_gradient.html that shows the code that GPT-4 generated in order to display a Web page that contains an SVG rectangle with radial gradient shading.

LISTING 7.2: gpt4_svg_radial_gradient.html

```
<!DOCTYPE html>
<html lang="en">
<head>
    <meta charset="UTF-8">
    <title>SVG Rectangle with Radial Gradient</title>
</head>
<body>

<svg width="500" height="300" xmlns="http://www.
w3.org/2000/svg">
    <!-- Define a radial gradient -->
    <defs>
        <radialGradient id="gradient">
            <stop offset="0%" stop-color="lightblue" />
            <stop offset="100%" stop-color="blue" />
        </radialGradient>
    </defs>

    <!-- Draw a rectangle with the radial gradient fill -->
```

```
    <rect width="500" height="300" fill="url(#gradient)" />
</svg>
</body>
</html>
```

Explanation of the Code

1. SVG Container:
- An `<svg>` element creates a container for the rectangle, specifying its width as 500 and height as 300.

2. Radial Gradient Definition:
- Inside the `<defs>` element, a `<radialGradient>` with the ID `gradient` is defined. This gradient is used to fill the rectangle.
- The gradient includes two `<stop>` elements, each specifying a color at a particular offset. It transitions from light blue at the center (0% offset) to blue at the edges (100% offset).

3. Rectangle with Radial Gradient Fill:
- The `<rect>` element draws the rectangle with the specified width and height.
- The `fill` attribute applies the radial gradient to the rectangle. The gradient reference `url(#gradient)` is used to link the rectangle to the defined gradient.

When rendered in a browser, this HTML will display a rectangle with a radial gradient fill, demonstrating how SVG can be utilized to create visually appealing graphics with smooth color transitions that radiate from the center.

Launch the Web page `gpt4_svg_radial_gradient.html` by navigating to the directory that contains this HTML Web page and then typing the following command:

```
open gpt4_svg_radial_gradient.html
```

After a few moments you will see the Web page in Figure 7.2 that displays a rectangle rendered with a radial gradient.

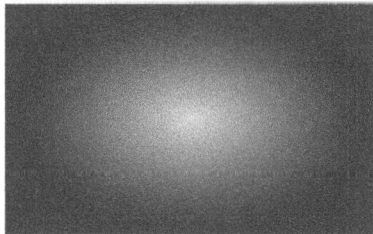

FIGURE 7.2. A rectangle with a radial gradient.

A TRIANGLE WITH A RADIAL GRADIENT

The following prompt was supplied to GPT-4 in order to generate SVG code for a triangle that is rendered with a radial gradient in an HTML Web page:

Please generate a triangle with width 200 and height 400 that is rendered with a radial gradient and a drop shadow, along with an explanation of the code.

ChatGPT:

To create an SVG triangle with a width of 200 and a height of 400, rendered with a radial gradient and a drop shadow, you can use SVG's <polygon> element for the triangle, define a radial gradient for the fill, and apply a drop shadow using SVG's filter functionality. Here's an example of how this can be done:

LISTING 7.3: triangleRG1.html

```
<!DOCTYPE html>
<html lang="en">
<head>
    <meta charset="UTF-8">
    <title>SVG Triangle with Radial Gradient and Drop
                                            Shadow</title>
</head>
<body>

<svg width="300" height="450" xmlns="http://www.
w3.org/2000/svg">
    <!-- Define radial gradient -->
    <defs>
        <radialGradient id="gradient">
            <stop offset="0%" stop-color="lightblue" />
            <stop offset="100%" stop-color="blue" />
        </radialGradient>

        <!-- Define drop shadow filter -->
        <filter id="dropshadow" x="-20%" y="-20%"
                                 width="140%" height="140%">
            <feGaussianBlur in="SourceAlpha"
                                            stdDeviation="3" />
            <feOffset dx="5" dy="5" />
            <feMerge>
                <feMergeNode />
                <feMergeNode in="SourceGraphic" />
            </feMerge>
        </filter>
    </defs>

    <!-- Draw a triangle with gradient fill and drop
                                            shadow -->
    <polygon points="50,50 250,50 150,450"
fill="url(#gradient)" filter="url(#dropshadow)" />
</svg>

</body>
</html>
```

Explanation of the Code

SVG Container:
The <svg> element sets up an SVG container with a width of
300 and a height of 450, which is large enough to encompass
the triangle and its drop shadow.

Radial Gradient Definition:
      Inside the <defs> element, a <radialGradient> with
the ID gradient is defined. It includes two <stop> elements
to define the color transition of the gradient, going from
light blue at the center to blue at the edges.

Drop Shadow Filter:
A <filter> element with the ID dropshadow is also defined in
the <defs> element. It uses <feGaussianBlur> for blurring,
<feOffset> for offsetting the shadow, and <feMerge> to
combine the effects with the original graphic.

Triangle with Gradient Fill and Drop Shadow:
The <polygon> element is used to draw the triangle. The
points attribute defines the vertices of the triangle,
calculated to create a triangle with the desired width and
height.
  The fill attribute applies the radial gradient to the
triangle.
  The filter attribute applies the drop shadow effect.

When rendered in a browser, this HTML will display a
triangle with a radial gradient fill and a drop shadow,
showcasing how SVG can create complex shapes with visually
appealing effects. The size of the SVG container and the
coordinates of the triangle's points are adjusted to
accommodate the desired dimensions and shadow effect.

Launch the Web page triangleRG1.html by navigating to the directory that
contains this HTML Web page and then typing the following command:

open triangleRG1.html

After a few moments you will see the Web page in Figure 7.3 that displays a
triangle with a radial gradient.

FIGURE 7.3. An SVG triangle with a radial gradient.

SVG 2D SHAPES AND GRADIENTS

The following prompt was supplied to GPT-4 in order to generate an HTML Web page that contains several SVG-based elements:

Please generate an HTML Web page that contains an SVG triangle, SVG circle, SVG ellipse, and an 8-sided SVG polygon that are rendered with either a linear gradient or a radial gradient, along with an explanation of the code.

GPT-4:

Certainly! I'll create an HTML Web page featuring SVG elements—a triangle, a circle, an ellipse, and an 8-sided polygon—each filled with either a linear or a radial gradient. SVG gradients allow for smooth color transitions within SVG shapes.

Listing 7.4 displays the contents of gpt4_svg_2d_shapes.html that shows the code that GPT-4 generated in order to display a Web page that contains an SVG rectangle with linear gradient shading, an SVG polygon with radial gradient shading, and an SVG circle with radial gradient shading.

LISTING 7.4: gpt4_svg_2d_shapes.html

```
<!DOCTYPE html>
<html lang="en">
<head>
    <meta charset="UTF-8">
    <title>SVG Shapes with Gradients</title>
</head>
<body>

    <svg width="300" height="300">
        <!-- Linear Gradient Definition -->
        <defs>
            <linearGradient id="linear-gradient" x1="0%"
                            y1="0%" x2="100%" y2="100%">
                <stop offset="0%" style="stop-
                    color:rgb(255,255,0); stop-opacity:1" />
                <stop offset="100%" style="stop-
                    color:rgb(255,0,0); stop-opacity:1" />
            </linearGradient>
        </defs>

        <!-- SVG Triangle -->
        <polygon points="50,5 100,95 0,95"
                            fill="url(#linear-gradient)" />
    </svg>

    <svg width="300" height="300">
        <!-- Radial Gradient Definition -->
```

```
    <defs>
        <radialGradient id="radial-gradient" cx="50%"
                    cy="50%" r="50%" fx="50%" fy="50%">
            <stop offset="0%" style="stop-
                color:rgb(0,255,0); stop-opacity:1" />
            <stop offset="100%" style="stop-
                color:rgb(0,0,255); stop-opacity:1" />
        </radialGradient>
    </defs>

    <!-- SVG Circle -->
    <circle cx="150" cy="150" r="100" fill="url(#radial-
                                    gradient)" />
</svg>
<svg width="300" height="300">
    <!-- SVG Ellipse with the same Radial Gradient -->
    <ellipse cx="150" cy="150" rx="80" ry="50"
                        fill="url(#radial-gradient)" />
</svg>

<svg width="300" height="300">
    <!-- SVG 8-sided Polygon with the same Linear
                                    Gradient -->
    <polygon points="150,10 190,60 240,70 190,120
      150,170 110,120 60,70 110,60" fill="url(#linear-
                                    gradient)" />
</svg>

</body>
</html>
```

Explanation of the Code

1. SVG Triangle with Linear Gradient:
- The `<polygon>` element creates a triangle using the `points` attribute.
- A linear gradient is defined within `<defs>` with the ID `linear-gradi-ent`. This gradient transitions from yellow to red.
- The `fill` attribute of the triangle references this gradient.

2. SVG Circle with Radial Gradient:
- The `<circle>` element creates a circle.
- A radial gradient is defined with the ID `radial-gradient`. This gradient transitions from green at the center to blue at the edges.
- The circle's `fill` attribute uses this radial gradient.

3. SVG Ellipse with Radial Gradient:
- The `<ellipse>` element creates an ellipse.
- The same radial gradient used for the circle is applied to the ellipse.

4. SVG 8-sided Polygon with Linear Gradient:
- The `<polygon>` element is used again to create an 8-sided polygon.
- The points for the polygon are defined to create an octagonal shape.
- The same linear gradient used for the triangle is applied to the polygon.

This example demonstrates the versatility of SVG for creating various shapes and the use of gradients to enhance their appearance with smooth color transitions. The `defs` element is used to define reusable gradients, which can then be applied to multiple SVG shapes.

Launch the Web page `gpt4_svg_2d_shapes.html` in Listing 7.4 by navigating to the directory that contains this HTML Web page and then typing the following command:

```
open gpt4_svg_2d_shapes.html
```

After a few moments you will see the contents of Figure 7.4 that displays a triangle, circle, ellipse, and polygon with gradient shading.

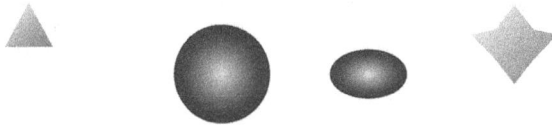

FIGURE 7.4 SVG-based 2D shapes.

A BAR CHART IN SVG

Before you read this section, keep in mind that the GPT-4-generated code in Listing 7.5 that is is shown below is incorrect, whereas Listing 7.6 contains a manually modified of Listing 7.5 that does display an SVG-based bar chart.

The following prompt was supplied to GPT-4 in order to generate SVG code for a bar chart in an HTML Web page:

Please generate synthetic data in order to render an SVG bar chart in an HTML Web page, along with an explanation of the code.

ChatGPT:

The generated synthetic data for the SVG bar chart is as follows:

- Category A: 18
- Category B: 13
- Category C: 98
- Category D: 11
- Category E: 55

Create an SVG bar chart in an HTML page using this data. Listing 7.5 contains the SVG and HTML code.

LISTING 7.5: gpt4_svg_barchart.html

```
<!DOCTYPE html>
<html>
```

```
<head>
    <title>SVG Bar Chart</title>
</head>
<body>
  <svg width="500" height="300">
    <!-- Bars for the chart -->
    <rect x="10" y="10" width="20" height="${18 * 2}"
                                style="fill:blue;" />
    <rect x="60" y="10" width="20" height="${13 * 2}"
                                style="fill:green;" />
    <rect x="110" y="10" width="20" height="${98 * 2}"
                                style="fill:red;" />
    <rect x="160" y="10" width="20" height="${11 * 2}"
                                style="fill:orange;" />
    <rect x="210" y="10" width="20" height="${55 * 2}"
                                style="fill:purple;" />

    <!-- Labels for the chart -->
    <text x="10" y="280" font-family="Verdana" font-
                                size="15">A</text>
    <text x="60" y="280" font-family="Verdana" font-
                                size="15">B</text>
    <text x="110" y="280" font-family="Verdana" font-
                                size="15">C</text>
    <text x="160" y="280" font-family="Verdana" font-
                                size="15">D</text>
    <text x="210" y="280" font-family="Verdana" font-
                                size="15">E</text>
  </svg>
</body>
</html>
```

Explanation of the Code:

1. **SVG Container:** The `<svg>` element with a specified width and height acts as a container for the bar chart.
2. **Bars:** Each `<rect>` element represents a bar in the chart.
   - x and y attributes set the position of the bar.
   - `width` attribute is set to a fixed value (20) for all bars.
   - `height` is dynamically set based on the data value (multiplied by 2 for better visibility).
   - `style` attribute assigns a color to each bar.
3. **Labels:** The `<text>` elements are used to label each category (A, B, C, D, E) under the bars.
   - x and y attributes position the text labels.
   - `font-family` and `font-size` attributes style the text.

This SVG bar chart represents the synthetic data visually, with different colors for each category and scaled heights corresponding to the data values. The multiplication factor (2) for height is chosen arbitrarily to make the bars visibly distinct. You can adjust it as needed for your display requirements.

As noted in the beginning this section, the code in Listing 7.5 is incorrect, so let's ask GPT-4 to fix the code.

The code that you generated is incorrect. Please generate a corrected version of this code.

Listing 7.6 displayed a modified version of Listing 7.5 that correctly displays an SVG-based bar chart.

LISTING 7.6: *gpt4_svg_barchart2.html*

```
<!DOCTYPE html>
<html>
<head>
  <title>SVG Bar Chart</title>
</head>
<body>
  <svg width="500" height="300">
    <!-- Bars for the chart -->
    <rect x="10"  y="65" width="20" height="135"
                                     style="fill:blue;" />
    <rect x="60"  y="75" width="20" height="125"
                                     style="fill:green;" />
    <rect x="110" y="10" width="20" height="190"
                                     style="fill:red;" />
    <rect x="160" y="80" width="20" height="120"
                                     style="fill:orange;"/>
    <rect x="210" y="45" width="20" height="155"
                                     style="fill:purple;"/>

    <!-- Labels for the chart -->
    <text x="10"  y="220" font-family="Verdana" font-
                                     size="15">A</text>
    <text x="60"  y="220" font-family="Verdana" font-
                                     size="15">B</text>
    <text x="110" y="220" font-family="Verdana" font-
                                     size="15">C</text>
    <text x="160" y="220" font-family="Verdana" font-
                                     size="15">D</text>
    <text x="210" y="220" font-family="Verdana" font-
                                     size="15">E</text>
  </svg>
</body>
</html>
```

Now launch the Web page gpt4_svg_barchart2.html by navigating to the directory that contains this HTML Web page and then typing the following command:

```
open gpt4_svg_barchart2.html
```

After a few moments you will see the image displayed in Figure 7.5 that shows an SVG-based bar chart.

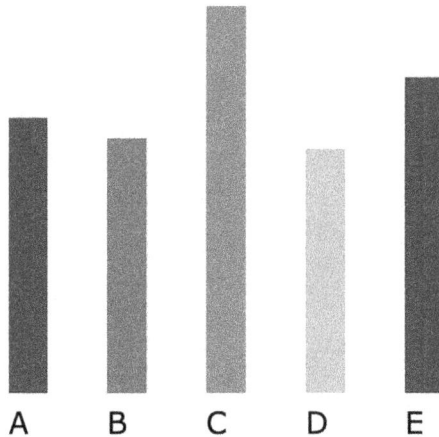

FIGURE 7.5 An SVG-based bar chart.

SVG QUADRATIC BEZIER CURVES

The following prompt was supplied to GPT-4 in order to create an HTML Web page that contains fifty random SVG quadratic Bezier curves:

Please generate a set of fifty random SVG quadratic Bezier curves with a fill pattern alternating between two different radial gradients, with a maximum width of 600 and a maximum height of 400, along with an explanation of the code.

GPT-4: I have created an SVG file containing fifty random quadratic Bezier curves, adhering to your specifications. The maximum dimensions are 600x400. Here's a breakdown of the code:

1. **SVG Drawing Initialization:** A new SVG drawing is created with the specified size (600x400) using `svgwrite.Drawing`.
2. **Radial Gradients Definition:** Two different radial gradients are defined. The first gradient transitions from red to yellow, and the second from blue to green. These gradients are added to the SVG's definitions section for reuse.
3. **Random Quadratic Bezier Curve Generation:** The `generate_random_quadratic_bezier_curve` function creates a single quadratic Bezier curve. It randomly chooses the start and end points, along with a control point, all within the SVG's dimensions. The stroke color is randomly selected, and the stroke width is set to 2.
4. **Adding Curves With Alternating Fill Patterns:** The script adds fifty Bezier curves to the SVG. Each curve's fill pattern alternates between the two defined radial gradients.
5. **Saving the SVG:** The SVG is saved to a file.

Listing 7.7 displays the contents of the Python file `gpt4_svg_random_quad-ratic_bezier_curves.py` that generates an SVG document that contains randomly generated quadratic Bezier curves.

LISTING 7.7: gpt4_svg_random_quadratic_bezier_curves.py

```python
import random
import svgwrite

def generate_random_quadratic_bezier_curve(dwg, width,
height):
    # Starting point
    start = (random.randint(0, width), random.randint(0,
                                                height))

    # Control point
    control = (random.randint(0, width), random.randint(0,
                                                height))

    # Ending point
    end = (random.randint(0, width), random.randint(0,
                                                height))

    # Create a quadratic bezier curve
    path = dwg.path(d='M {} {} Q {} {}, {} {}'.
                            format(*start, *control, *end),
                        fill='none', stroke=svgwrite.rgb(random.
                        randint(0, 255), random.randint(0, 255),
                    random.randint(0, 255), '%'), stroke_width=2)
    return path

def create_svg_with_quadratic_bezier_curves(file_name,
                            num_curves, width, height):
    dwg = svgwrite.Drawing(file_name, size=(width, height))

    # Define two different radial gradients
    gradient1 = dwg.defs.add(dwg.radialGradient())
    gradient1.add_stop_color(0, 'red')
    gradient1.add_stop_color(1, 'yellow')

    gradient2 = dwg.defs.add(dwg.radialGradient())
    gradient2.add_stop_color(0, 'blue')
    gradient2.add_stop_color(1, 'green')

    # Add curves with alternating fill patterns
    for i in range(num_curves):
        curve = generate_random_quadratic_bezier_curve(dwg,
                                        width, height)
        if i % 2 == 0:
            curve.fill(gradient1.get_paint_server())
        else:
            curve.fill(gradient2.get_paint_server())
        dwg.add(curve)

    dwg.save()
```

```
# Create an SVG file with random quadratic Bezier curves
file_name_quadratic = "random_quadratic_bezier_curves.svg"
create_svg_with_quadratic_bezier_curves(file_name_quadratic,
50, 600, 400)
```

Launch the Python file from the command line as follows:

```
python gpt4_svg_random_quadratic_bezier_curves.py
```

After a few moments you will see the image (or something similar) that is displayed in Figure 7.6.

FIGURE 7.6 SVG-based quadratic Bezier curves.

SVG CUBIC BEZIER CURVES

The following prompt was supplied to GPT-4 in order to create an HTML Web page that contains fifty random SVG cubic Bezier curves:

Please generate a set of fifty random SVG cubic Bezier curves with a fill pattern alternating between two different radial gradients, with a maximum width of 600 and a maximum height of 400, along with an explanation of the code.

GPT-4: I have generated an SVG file containing fifty random cubic Bezier curves with the specifications you provided. The maximum dimensions of the SVG are 600x400. Here's an explanation of the code:

1. **SVG Drawing Initialization:** We use `svgwrite.Drawing` to create a new SVG drawing with the specified dimensions (600x400).

2. **Radial Gradients Definition:** Two radial gradients are defined. The first gradient transitions from red to yellow, and the second from blue to green. These gradients are added to the SVG's definition section, allowing them to be reused.

3. **Random Bezier Curve Generation:** The `generate_random_bezier_curve` function creates a single cubic Bezier curve. It randomly selects start and end points, as well as two control points, all within the

SVG's dimensions. The stroke color of the curve is also randomly chosen, and the stroke width is set to 2.

4. **Adding Curves with Alternating Fill Patterns:** The script iteratively adds fifty Bezier curves to the SVG. For each curve, it alternates the fill pattern between the two defined radial gradients.

5. **Saving the SVG:** Finally, the SVG is saved to a file.

Listing 7.8 displays the contents of `gpt4_svg_cubic_bezier_curves.py` (a Python file) that generates an SVG document that contains randomly generated cubic Bezier curves.

LISTING 7.8: *gpt4_svg_random_cubic_bezier_curves.py*

```python
import random
import svgwrite

def generate_random_bezier_curve(dwg, width, height):
    # Starting point
    start = (random.randint(0, width), random.randint
                                              (0, height))

    # Control points
    control1 = (random.randint(0, width), random.randint
                                              (0, height))
    control2 = (random.randint(0, width), random.randint
                                              (0, height))

    # Ending point
    end = (random.randint(0, width), random.randint
                                              (0, height))

    # Create a cubic bezier curve
    path = dwg.path(d='M {} {} C {} {}, {} {}, {} {}'.
                format(*start, *control1, *control2, *end),
                    fill='none', stroke=svgwrite.rgb(random.
                    randint(0, 255), random.randint(0, 255),
                            random.randint(0, 255), '%'),
                    stroke_width=2)
    return path

def create_svg_with_bezier_curves(file_name, num_curves,
                                          width, height):
    dwg = svgwrite.Drawing(file_name, size=(width, height))

    # Define two different radial gradients
    gradient1 = dwg.defs.add(dwg.radialGradient())
    gradient1.add_stop_color(0, 'red')
    gradient1.add_stop_color(1, 'yellow')

    gradient2 = dwg.defs.add(dwg.radialGradient())
    gradient2.add_stop_color(0, 'blue')
    gradient2.add_stop_color(1, 'green')
```

```
    # Add curves with alternating fill patterns
    for i in range(num_curves):
        curve = generate_random_bezier_curve(dwg, width,
                                                      height)
        if i % 2 == 0:
            curve.fill(gradient1.get_paint_server())
        else:
            curve.fill(gradient2.get_paint_server())
        dwg.add(curve)

    dwg.save()

# Create an SVG file with random bezier curves
file_name = "random_cubic_bezier_curves.svg"
create_svg_with_bezier_curves(file_name, 50, 600, 400)
```

Launch the Python file in Listing 7.8 from the command line as follows:

```
python gpt4_svg_random_cubic_bezier_curves.py
```

After a few moments you will see the image (or something similar) that is displayed in Figure 7.7.

FIGURE 7.7. SVG-based cubic Bezier curves.

SVG AND 2D TRANSFORMS

The following prompt was supplied to GPT-4 in order to generate SVG-based 2D transformation effects:

Please generate an HTML Web page that contains an SVG-based rectangle with animated rotation, an SVG triangle with an animated skew effect, an SVG polygon with animated scaling effect, and an SVG-based ellipse with an animated rotation and also an animated scaling effect, along with an explanation of the SVG code.

ChatGPT:

Certainly! I'll provide you with an HTML Web page that includes several SVG elements with different animations. SVG

(Scalable vector graphics) is a great way to include high-quality, scalable graphics in Web pages. We'll use SVG for creating shapes and CSS animations to animate them.

Here's a breakdown of the components:
    SVG Rectangle with Animated Rotation
    SVG Triangle with Animated Skew Effect
    SVG Polygon with Animated Scaling Effect
    SVG Ellipse with Animated Rotation and Scaling Effect

Listing 7.9 displays the contents of gpt4_svg_2d_transforms.html that contains GPT-4-generated SVG code that performs 2D transform-based animation effects on four 2D shapes.

LISTING 7.9: gpt4_svg_2d_transforms.html

```
<!DOCTYPE html>
<html lang="en">
<head>
    <meta charset="UTF-8">
    <title>SVG Animations</title>
    <style>
        svg {
            width: 100px;
            height: 100px;
            margin: 20px;
            display: inline-block;
        }
        .rotate {
            animation: rotate 4s linear infinite;
        }
        .skew {
            animation: skew 3s linear infinite;
        }
        .scale {
            animation: scale 5s linear infinite;
        }
        .rotate-scale {
            animation: rotateScale 6s linear infinite;
        }
        @keyframes rotate {
            from { transform: rotate(0deg); }
            to { transform: rotate(360deg); }
        }

        @keyframes skew {
            0%, 100% { transform: skewX(0deg); }
            50% { transform: skewX(20deg); }
        }

        @keyframes scale {
            0%, 100% { transform: scale(1); }
            50% { transform: scale(1.5); }
        }
```

```
        @keyframes rotateScale {
            0% { transform: rotate(0deg) scale(1); }
            50% { transform: rotate(180deg) scale(1.5); }
            100% { transform: rotate(360deg) scale(1); }
        }
    </style>
</head>
<body>

    <svg viewBox="0 0 100 100">
        <rect x="10" y="10" width="80" height="80"
                            fill="red" class="rotate" />
    </svg>
    <svg viewBox="0 0 100 100">
        <polygon points="50,15 100,85 0,85" fill="green"
                                        class="skew" />
    </svg>

    <svg viewBox="0 0 100 100">
        <polygon points="50,5 90,95 10,95" fill="blue"
                                        class="scale" />
    </svg>

    <svg viewBox="0 0 100 100">
        <ellipse cx="50" cy="50" rx="40" ry="30"
                        fill="purple" class="rotate-scale" />
    </svg>

</body>
</html>
```

Explanation of the SVG Code

SVG Rectangle with Animated Rotation:
```
        <rect x="10" y="10" width="80" height="80"
            fill="red" class="rotate" /> creates a
                                    red rectangle.
```

The class rotate applies a continuous rotation animation.
    SVG Triangle with Animated Skew Effect:
```
        <polygon points="50,15 100,85 0,85" fill="green"
            class="skew" /> creates a green triangle.
```

The class skew applies an animation that skews the triangle
back and forth.
    SVG Polygon with Animated Scaling Effect:
```
        <polygon points="50,5 90,95 10,95" fill="blue"
            class="scale" /> creates a blue polygon.
```

The class scale applies a scaling animation, making the
polygon grow and shrink.
    SVG Ellipse with Animated Rotation and Scaling Effect:
```
        <ellipse cx="50" cy="50" rx="40" ry="30"
            fill="purple" class="rotate-scale" /> creates a
            purple ellipse.
```

The class rotate-scale applies both rotation and scaling
animations simultaneously.

The viewBox attribute in each SVG element defines the coordinate system and the area of the scene. The CSS @keyframes are used to define the steps of each animation, specifying the starting and ending points, and any intermediate steps.

This Web page will display four SVG shapes with different animated effects, showing the versatility of SVG and CSS animations for Web graphics.

Now launch the Web page `gpt4_svg_2d_transforms.html` by navigating to the directory that contains Listing 7.9 and then typing the following command:

```
open gpt4_svg_2d_transforms.html
```

After a few moments you will see the Web page in Figure 7.8 that displays a snapshot of SVG-based animation of various polygonal shapes.

FIGURE 7.8. SVG-based animation with polygonal shapes.

ANIMATED SVG CUBIC BEZIER CURVES

The following prompt was supplied to GPT-4 in order to generate animated cubic Bezier curves:

Please generate an HTML Web page that contains fifty random cubic SVG-based Bezier curves with random radial gradients.

ChatGPT:

I have created an SVG file with an animation effect involving fifty random cubic Bezier curves. Each curve alternates between two different radial gradients as a fill pattern. The maximum dimensions of the SVG are 600x400, and the animation duration for each curve is set to 5 seconds. Here's an explanation of the code:

1. **SVG Drawing Initialization:** A new SVG drawing is created with the specified dimensions (600x400) using `svgwrite.Drawing`.

2. **Radial Gradients Definition:** Two different radial gradients are defined. The first gradient transitions from red to yellow, and the second from blue to green. These gradients are stored in the SVG's definitions section.

3. **Bezier Curve Generation and Animation:** The script creates fifty cubic Bezier curves with random start, end, and control points. Each curve is given a stroke color and width. The fill pattern of each curve alternates between the two defined gradients.

4. **Animation Addition:** An opacity animation is added to each curve using `animate.Animate`. This animation makes each curve fade in and out over a duration of 5 seconds. The `repeatCount` is set to "indefinite," causing the animation to loop continuously.

5. **Saving the SVG:** The SVG file is saved with the animations.

You can download and view the animated SVG file here: animated Bezier curves SVG. When you open the file in a Web browser, you will see the animation effect of the Bezier curves fading in and out.

Listing 7.10 displays the contents of `gpt4_svg_animated_cubic_bezier_curves.py` (a Python file) that generates an SVG document that contains randomly generated quadratic Bezier curves.

LISTING 7.10: gpt4_svg_animated_cubic_bezier_curves.py

```
import svgwrite
from svgwrite import animate

def create_svg_with_animated_bezier_curves(file_name, num_
            curves, width, height, animation_duration):
    dwg = svgwrite.Drawing(file_name, size=(width, height))

    # Define two different radial gradients
    gradient1 = dwg.defs.add(dwg.radialGradient())
    gradient1.add_stop_color(0, 'red')
    gradient1.add_stop_color(1, 'yellow')

    gradient2 = dwg.defs.add(dwg.radialGradient())
    gradient2.add_stop_color(0, 'blue')
    gradient2.add_stop_color(1, 'green')

    for i in range(num_curves):
        # Randomly generate the points for a cubic bezier
                                                    curve
        start = (random.randint(0, width),
                            random.randint(0, height))
        control1 - (random.randint(0, width),
                            random.randint(0, height))
        control2 = (random.randint(0, width),
                            random.randint(0, height))
        end = (random.randint(0, width),
                            random.randint(0, height))

        # Create the path for the bezier curve
        path = dwg.path(d='M {} {} C {} {}, {} {}, {} {}'.
                format(*start, *control1, *control2, *end),
                            fill='none', stroke=svgwrite.
            rgb(random.randint(0, 255), random.randint(0, 255),
                            random.randint(0, 255), '%'),
                            stroke_width=2)

        # Alternate fill pattern with gradients
        if i % 2 == 0:
```

```
        path.fill(gradient1.get_paint_server())
    else:
        path.fill(gradient2.get_paint_server())

    # Add an animation effect to each path
    animation = animate.Animate(attributeName=
'opacity', begin='0s', dur=str(animation_duration)+'s',
              values='0;1;0', repeatCount='indefinite')
    path.add(animation)
    dwg.add(path)

dwg.save()
```

Create an SVG file with animated bezier curves

```
animated_file_name = "animated_cubic_bezier_curves.svg"
create_svg_with_animated_bezier_curves(animated_file_name,
50, 600, 400, 5) # 5 seconds animation duration
```

Launch the Python file in Listing 7.10 from the command line as follows:

```
python gpt4_svg_animated_cubic_bezier_curves.py
```

After a few moments you will see the image (or something similar) that is displayed in Figure 7.9.

FIGURE 7.9. Animation with cubic Bezier curves.

HOVER EFFECTS

The following prompt was supplied to GPT-4 in order to generate an HTML Web page that contains SVG and a hover animation effect:

```
Please generate an HTML Web page with a 300x300 SVG rectangle
that has a rotating animation effect on a hover event.
```

```
GPT-4:
```

```
To create an HTML Web page with a 300x300 SVG rectangle that
has a rotating animation effect when you hover over it, you'll
need to use HTML for the basic structure, SVG for the rec-
tangle, and CSS for the hover effect and animation. Here's an
example of how to do this:
```

HTML: Provides the structure and includes the SVG element.
 SVG: A rectangle element (<rect>) is defined within the SVG.
 CSS: Applies a rotating animation to the rectangle on hover.

LISTING 7.11: gpt4_svg_hover.html

```
<!DOCTYPE html>
<html>
<head>
    <style>
        /* Initial fill color */
        rect {
            fill: blue;
        }

        /* Fill color on hover */
        rect:hover {
            fill: red;
        }
    </style>
</head>
<body>

<svg width="300" height="300">
    <rect width="300" height="300"/>
</svg>

</body>
</html>
```

Now launch the Web page `gpt4_svg_hover.html` by navigating to the directory that contains this HTML Web page and then typing the following command:

```
open gpt4_svg_hover.html
```

After a few moments you will see the image in Figure 7.10 that displays a snapshot of a SVG-based hover effect.

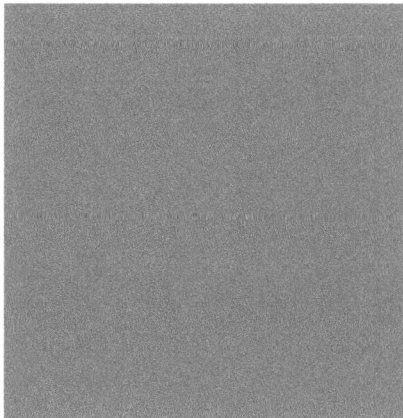

FIGURE 7.10. SVG-based hover effect.

HOVER ANIMATION EFFECTS

The following prompt was supplied to GPT-4 in order to generate an HTML
Web page that contains SVG and a hover animation effect:

Please generate an HTML Web page with a 300x300 SVG rectangle
that has a rotating animation effect on a hover event.

GPT-4:

To create an HTML Web page with a 300x300 SVG rectangle that
has a rotating animation effect when you hover over it, you'll
need to use HTML for the basic structure, SVG for the rectangle, and CSS for the hover effect and animation. Here's an
example of how to do this:

HTML: Provides the structure and includes the SVG element.
  SVG: A rectangle element (<rect>) is defined within the SVG.
  CSS: Applies a rotating animation to the rectangle on hover.

LISTING 7.12: gpt4_svg_hover_rotate.html

```
<!DOCTYPE html>
<html>
<head>
    <style>
        svg {
            display: block;
            margin: auto;
            background-color: lightgrey;
            border: 1px solid black;
        }

        rect {
            fill: blue;
            transition: transform 0.5s ease;
        }

        svg:hover rect {
            transform: rotate(180deg);
            transform-origin: center;
        }
    </style>
</head>
<body>

<svg width="300" height="300" viewBox="0 0 300 300">
    <rect x="50" y="50" width="200" height="200"/>
</svg>

</body>
</html>
```

Launch the Web page `gpt4_svg_hover_rotate.html` by navigating to the directory that contains this HTML Web page and then typing the following command:

```
open gpt4_svg_hover_rotate.html
```

After a few moments you will see the Web page in Figure 7.11 that displays a snapshot of SVG-based hover animation.

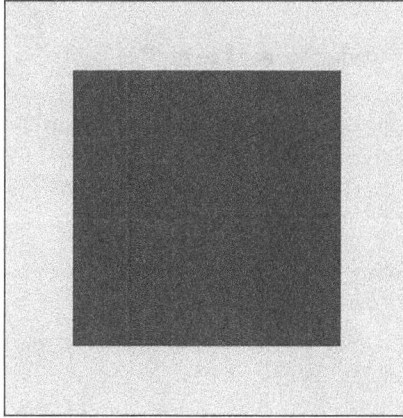

FIGURE 7.11. A Web page with SVG-based hover animation.

SVG VERSUS CSS3: A COMPARISON

The following prompt was supplied to GPT-4 in order to describe scenarios where it's better to use SVG instead of CSS3, as well as scenarios where it's better to use CSS3 instead of SVG:

```
Please provide a detailed comparison of SVG and CSS3, along
with scenarios where it's better to use SVG instead of CSS3,
and scenarios where it's better to use CSS3 instead of SVG.
```

```
ChatGPT:
    Scalable vector graphics (SVG) and Cascading Style Sheets
Level 3 (CSS3) are both essential tools in modern Web design,
but they serve different purposes and have unique charac-
teristics. Understanding their differences can guide you in
choosing the right tool for specific scenarios.
```

SVG (Scalable Vector Graphics)

Nature and Use:
- SVG is an XML-based image format used to define vector-based graphics for the Web.
- It allows for the creation of complex graphics including paths, shapes, text, and embedded raster graphics.

Key Features:
- **Scalability:** SVG images can be scaled to any size without loss of quality, making them ideal for responsive design.
- **Manipulation:** SVG elements can be manipulated via CSS and JavaScript.
- **Interactivity:** Supports user interactions and animations.
- **Accessibility:** Texts within SVGs are selectable and searchable, beneficial for accessibility and SEO.

CSS3 (Cascading Style Sheets Level 3)
Nature and Use:
- CSS3 is a style sheet language used for describing the presentation of a document written in a markup language like HTML.
- It's primarily used for styling and laying out Web pages.

Key Features:

Advanced Styling: Includes advanced properties for text effects, box models, animations, transitions, and transforms.

Responsiveness: CSS3 has features like media queries for responsive Web design.

Browser Compatibility: Widely supported across modern Web browsers.

Scenarios for Using SVG over CSS3

1. **Complex Shapes and Icons:** SVG is more suited for detailed and complex shapes like logos and icons that need to scale without losing quality.
2. **Graphs and Charts:** For interactive and dynamic charts where scalability and precise rendering are crucial.
3. **Illustrations and Artwork:** Detailed illustrations and artistic elements are best created with SVG.
4. **Interactive Graphics:** SVG's ability to integrate with JavaScript makes it ideal for graphics requiring interactivity.
5. **Text Inside Images:** If you need selectable and searchable text within your images.

Scenarios for Using CSS3 over SVG

1. **Styling Web Content:** CSS3 is the standard for styling and laying out Web pages, including typography, color schemes, and spacing.
2. **Simple Animations and Transitions:** For basic animations like hover effects, transitions, and transformations on HTML elements.
3. **Responsive Layouts:** CSS3's media queries are essential for creating responsive designs that adjust to different screen sizes.
4. **Performance:** For basic shapes and effects, CSS3 can be less resource intensive than SVG.

5. **Browser Rendering:** While SVG is widely supported, some complex SVG graphics can have compatibility issues in older browsers, whereas CSS3 properties often have fallback options.

Conclusion
- **Use SVG** when dealing with complex, scalable vector graphics, interactive elements, and when image quality is a priority.
- **Use CSS3** for styling, simple animations, responsive layout design, and when working with standard Web content.

By understanding the strengths and limitations of both SVG and CSS3, you can make more informed decisions about which tool to use for specific design requirements.

SVG VERSUS PNG: A COMPARISON

The following prompt was supplied to GPT-4 in order to describe scenarios where it's better to use SVG instead of PNG, as well as scenarios where it's better to use PNG instead of SVG:

```
Please provide a detailed comparison of SVG and PNG, along
with scenarios where it's better to use SVG instead of PNG,
and scenarios where it's better to use PNG instead of SVG.
```

ChatGPT:

```
SVG (scalable vector graphics) and PNG (Portable Network
Graphics) are both popular image formats used on the Web,
each with its own strengths and ideal use cases. Here's a
detailed comparison of the two, along with scenarios where
one might be preferred over the other.
```

SVG (Scalable Vector Graphics)
- **Nature:** SVG is a vector image format. It uses mathematical equations to define the graphics, such as shapes, lines, and colors.
- **File Size:** SVG files are often smaller, especially for simpler designs. Their size doesn't increase with the complexity of the image.
- **Scalability:** Being vector-based, SVG images can be scaled to any size without loss of quality.
- **Manipulation:** SVG can be manipulated and animated using CSS and JavaScript.
- **Interactivity:** SVG supports interactivity and dynamic updates, making it suitable for interactive Web applications.
- **Accessibility:** Text in SVG images is selectable and searchable, which is better for accessibility and SEO.
- **Browser Rendering:** SVGs are rendered by the browser, making them resolution-independent and always crisp.

PNG (Portable Network Graphics)

- **Nature:** PNG is a raster (or bitmap) image format. It represents images in a grid of pixels.
- **File Size:** File size increases with the resolution and color depth. PNGs can be larger for high-resolution images.
- **Scalability:** Scaling up can lead to loss of quality (pixelation), while scaling down is generally fine.
- **Manipulation:** Cannot be easily manipulated or animated like SVG. Requires image editing software for any changes.
- **Interactivity:** PNGs do not support interactivity or dynamic changes.
- **Transparency:** Supports transparency, which is useful for overlays, logos, and Web graphics.
- **Image Quality:** Excellent for complex images like photographs due to its support for high color depths and lossless compression.

When to Use SVG

1. **Logos and Icons:** For scalable graphics that need to stay sharp at any size.
2. **Graphs and Charts:** For interactive and dynamic data visualizations.
3. **Responsive Web Design:** In designs that need to adapt to various screen sizes.
4. **Simple Animations:** For graphics that require basic animations or transitions.
5. **Web Applications:** Where interactivity and dynamic updates to the graphic elements are necessary.

When to Use PNG

1. **Photographs:** For complex images with subtle color variations, like photos.
2. **Images with Transparency:** For graphics that require a transparent background.
3. **Detailed Imagery:** When image details must remain exact at a specific resolution.
4. **Print Materials:** For high-quality print documents where image clarity is crucial and resizing is not required.
5. **Compatibility:** When absolute compatibility with older systems or browsers is necessary.

Conclusion

- **Use SVG** for graphics that need scalability, interactivity, and are generally simpler in color composition (like logos, icons, charts).
- **Use PNG** for static images where color depth and detail are important, like photographs, or when transparency is required.

Both formats have their place in Web design and development, and the choice often depends on the specific needs of the project regarding scalability, image complexity, and interactivity.

SVG FILTERS

As you know from the previous Chapter 3, filter effects can significantly enhance the visual experience of the contents of an HTML Web page. In Chapter 3, you learned about learned about CSS3 filters, and in this chapter, you will learn about SVG Filters, as shown in the following list:

- `<feBlend>` - filter for combining images
- `<feColorMatrix>` - filter for color transforms
- `<feComponentTransfer>`
- `<feComposite>`
- `<feConvolveMatrix>`
- `<feDiffuseLighting>`
- `<feDisplacementMap>`
- `<feFlood>`
- `<feGaussianBlur>`
- `<feTurbulence>`

The following subsections contain examples of some of the filters in the preceding bullet list of filters.

SVG BLUR FILTER

The following prompt was supplied to GPT-4 in order to generate an HTML Web page with an SVG blur filter:

Please generate an HTML Web page that contains a rectangle that is rendered with an SVG blur filter, along with an explanation of the code.

ChatGPT:

Creating an SVG rectangle with a blur filter involves defining the rectangle using SVG's `<rect>` element and applying a blur effect with SVG's filter functionality. Here's an example of how to do this:

Listing 7.13 displays the contents of gpt4_svg_blur_filter.html that contains GPT-4-generated SVG rectangle with a blur filter effect.

LISTING 7.13: gpt4_svg_blur1.html

```
<!DOCTYPE html>
<html lang="en">
<head>
    <meta charset="UTF-8">
```

```
        <title>SVG Rectangle with Blur Filter</title>
</head>
<body>

<svg width="500" height="300"
                        xmlns="http://www.w3.org/2000/svg">
    <!-- Define a blur filter -->
    <defs>
        <filter id="blurFilter" x="0" y="0">
            <feGaussianBlur in="SourceGraphic"
                                stdDeviation="5" />
        </filter>
    </defs>

    <!-- Draw a rectangle with the blur filter applied -->
    <rect x="50" y="50" width="400" height="200"
                fill="green" filter="url(#blurFilter)"/>

</svg>
</body>
</html>
```

Explanation of the Code

```
SVG Container:
The <svg> element creates an SVG container with a width of
500 and a height of 300. These dimensions ensure there's
enough space around the rectangle to display the blur
effect.

Blur Filter Definition:
Inside the <defs> element, a <filter> is defined with the ID
blurFilter.
The <feGaussianBlur> element is used to create the blur
effect. The stdDeviation attribute controls the amount of
blur. Here, stdDeviation="5" provides a moderate blur
effect.

SVG Rectangle:
The <rect> element draws a rectangle. It is positioned at
(50, 50) and has a width of 400 and a height of 200.
The fill attribute sets the rectangle's color to green.
The filter attribute applies the blur filter to the rectangle
by referencing the blurFilter ID.
```

When this SVG is rendered, it displays a green rectangle with a blur effect applied, demonstrating how SVG filters can be used to create interesting visual effects.

Now launch the Web page gpt4_svg_blur1.html by navigating to the directory that contains this HTML Web page and then typing the following command:

```
open gpt4_svg_blur1.html
```

After a few moments you will see an SVG rectangle rendered with an SVG blur filter.

FIGURE 7.12. An SVG rectangle with a blur filter.

SVG TURBULENCE FILTER

The following prompt was supplied to GPT-4 in order to generate an HTML Web page with an SVG turbulence filter.

Please generate an HTML Web page that contains a rectangle that is rendered with an SVG turbulence filter, along with an explanation of the code.

ChatGPT:

Creating an SVG rectangle with an SVG turbulence filter involves defining the rectangle using SVG's <rect> element and applying a blur effect with SVG's filter functionality. Here's an example of how to do this:

Listing 7.14 displays the contents of gpt4_svg_turbulence1.html that contains GPT-4-generated SVG rectangle with a blur filter effect.

LISTING 7.14: gpt4_svg_turbulence1.html

```
<!DOCTYPE html>
<html lang="en">
<head>
    <meta charset="UTF-8">
    <title>SVG Rectangle with Turbulence Filter</title>
</head>
<body>

<svg width="500" height="300" xmlns="http://www.w3.org/2000/svg">

    <!-- Define a turbulence filter -->
    <defs>
        <filter id="turbulenceFilter" x="0" y="0">
            <feTurbulence type="turbulence"
            baseFrequency="0.05" numOctaves="2" result="turb"/>
            <feDisplacementMap in="SourceGraphic"
                                in2="turb" scale="20" />
```

```
        </filter>
    </defs>

    <!-- Draw a rectangle with the turbulence filter applied -->
    <rect x="50" y="50" width="400" height="200" fill="green"
                            filter="url(#turbulenceFilter)"/>

</svg>
</body>
</html>
```

Explanation of the Code

SVG Container:
The <svg> element creates an SVG container with a width of
500 and a height of 300. These dimensions ensure there's
enough space around the rectangle to display the blur
effect.

Blur Filter Definition:
Inside the <defs> element, a <filter> is defined with the ID
blurFilter.
The <feGaussianBlur> element is used to create the blur
effect. The stdDeviation attribute controls the amount of
blur. Here, stdDeviation="5" provides a moderate blur
effect.

SVG Rectangle:
The <rect> element draws a rectangle. It is positioned at
(50, 50) and has a width of 400 and a height of 200.
The fill attribute sets the rectangle's color to green.
The filter attribute applies the blur filter to the rectangle
by referencing the blurFilter ID.

When this SVG is rendered, it displays a green rectangle with a turbulence effect applied, demonstrating how SVG filters can be used to create interesting visual effects.

Now launch the Web page `gpt4_svg_css3.html` by navigating to the directory that contains this HTML Web page and then typing the following command:

```
open gpt4_svg_turbulence1.html
```

After a few moments you will see an SVG rectangle rendered with an SVG turbulence filter as shown in Figure 7.13.

FIGURE 7.13. An SVG rectangle with a turbulence filter.

SVG AND CSS3 IN HTML WEB PAGES

The following prompt was supplied to GPT-4 in order to generate an HTML Web page with SVG-based 2D shapes and CSS3 effects:

Please generate an HTML Web page that contains SVG-based 2D shapes and CSS3 effects, along with an explanation of the code.

ChatGPT:

Sure, I'll create an HTML Web page that includes SVG-based 2D shapes enhanced with CSS3 effects. We'll use a combination of SVG for the shapes and CSS for the effects, such as color changes on hover.

Here's a simple example that includes a few SVG shapes: a circle, a rectangle, and a polygon (triangle), each with a different CSS3 effect applied.

Listing 7.15 displays the contents of `gpt4_svg_css3.html` that contains GPT-4-generated SVG code with CSS3 effects.

LISTING 7.15: *gpt4_svg_css3.html*

```html
<!DOCTYPE html>
<html lang="en">
<head>
    <meta charset="UTF-8">
    <title>SVG Shapes with CSS3 Effects</title>
    <style>
        svg {
            width: 100px;
            height: 100px;
            margin: 20px;
        }

        .shape {
            transition: all 0.3s ease;
        }

        .circle:hover {
            fill: blue;
        }

        .rectangle:hover {
            stroke: red;
            stroke-width: 4;
        }

        .polygon:hover {
            fill-opacity: 0.5;
        }
    </style>
</head>
<body>
```

```
<svg viewBox="0 0 100 100">
    <circle cx="50" cy="50" r="40" fill="green"
                            class="shape circle"/>
</svg>

<svg viewBox="0 0 100 100">
    <rect x="10" y="10" width="80" height="80"
            fill="yellow" stroke="black" stroke-width="2"
                            class="shape rectangle"/>
</svg>

<svg viewBox="0 0 100 100">
    <polygon points="50,15 100,85 0,85" fill="red"
                            class="shape polygon"/>
</svg>

</body>
</html>
```

Explanation of the Code

SVG Shapes:
A <circle> element creates a circle, positioned at (50,50) with a radius of 40.

A <rect> element creates a rectangle, positioned at (10,10) with a width and height of 80.

A <polygon> element creates a triangle using points to define its vertices.

CSS3 Effects:
The .shape class applies a common transition effect to all shapes, making any changes smooth and gradual.

The :hover pseudo-class is used to change properties of each shape when the mouse hovers over them:

The .circle:hover changes the fill color of the circle to blue.

The .rectangle:hover changes the stroke color to red and increases the stroke width of the rectangle.

The .polygon:hover changes the fill opacity of the polygon, making it semitransparent.

Interactivity and Aesthetics:
The transition property in .shape ensures that the hover effects occur smoothly.

The viewBox attribute in each SVG element defines the coordinate system and the drawable area, ensuring that the shapes are properly scaled and positioned.

This Web page will display SVG shapes that react to user interactions, demonstrating how SVG and CSS3 can be combined to create interactive and visually appealing Web graphics.

Now launch the Web page `gpt4_svg_css3.html` by navigating to the directory that contains this HTML Web page and then typing the following command:

```
open gpt4_svg_css3.html
```

After a few moments you will see an SVG green circle, an SVG yellow square, and an SVG red triangle.

FIGURE 7.14. Three SVG shapes.

Hover over each of these three shapes and you will see the green circle turn blue; the border of the yellow rectangle changes from blue to red; and the red triangle becomes partially transparent.

SVG AND JAVASCRIPT IN HTML WEB PAGES

There are several ways to render SVG in an HTML Web page, as listed in the following bullet list:

- "Pure" SVG code
- SVG and CSS3 code
- SVG and JavaScript code

You have already seen examples of the first two techniques, and the remaining code samples in this chapter show you how to use the third technique. Specifically, you will see examples of combining SVG and JavaScript to perform the following tasks:

- Render a set of SVC elliptic arcs with a radial gradient.
- Render an SVG checkerboard pattern.
- Render an SVG checkerboard pattern with an SVG filter.
- Render a master/detail HTML Web page.
- Render quadratic Bezier curves.
- Render cubic Bezier curves.

Recall that you have already seen SVG Filters in a previous section in this chapter.

ELLIPTIC ARCS WITH A RADIAL GRADIENT

The following prompt was supplied to GPT-4 in order to generate SVG code for elliptic arcs that are rendered with a radial gradient in an HTML Web page:

Please generate a random set of fifty elliptic arcs in a screen of width 600 and height 400 where each elliptic arc has a fill pattern of a radial gradient and a drop shadow, along with an explanation of the code.

Creating fifty random elliptic arcs in an SVG screen with a width of 600 and a height of 400, where each arc has a fill pattern of a radial gradient and a drop shadow, involves using JavaScript to dynamically generate these arcs within an SVG container. Each arc will be an SVG <path> element with random attributes, and we'll apply radial gradients and drop shadows to them.

LISTING 7.16: *gpt4_svg_elliptic_arcs.html*

```
<!DOCTYPE html>
<html lang="en">
<head>
    <meta charset="UTF-8">
    <title>Random Elliptic Arcs with Gradients and
                                    Shadows</title>
</head>
<body>

<svg width="600" height="400"
                    xmlns="http://www.w3.org/2000/svg">
    <!-- Define radial gradient -->
    <defs>
        <radialGradient id="gradient">
            <stop offset="0%" stop-color="lightblue" />
            <stop offset="100%" stop-color="blue" />
        </radialGradient>

        <!-- Define drop shadow filter -->
        <filter id="dropshadow" x="-20%" y="-20%"
                            width="140%" height="140%">
            <feGaussianBlur in="SourceAlpha"
stdDeviation="3" />
            <feOffset dx="5" dy="5" />
            <feMerge>
                <feMergeNode />
                <feMergeNode in="SourceGraphic" />
            </feMerge>
        </filter>
    </defs>

    <!-- JavaScript to generate elliptic arcs -->
    <script>
        const svgNS = "http://www.w3.org/2000/svg";
        const svg = document.querySelector('svg');
```

```
        function randomArc() {
            const rx = Math.random() * 100 + 20;
                        // Radius x between 20 and 120
            const ry = Math.random() * 100 + 20;
                        // Radius y between 20 and 120
            const xAxisRotation = Math.random() * 360;
                    // Rotation between 0 and 360 degrees
            const largeArcFlag = Math.round(Math.random());
                    // 0 or 1
            const sweepFlag = Math.round(Math.random());
                    // 0 or 1
            const x = Math.random()* (600 - 2 * rx) + rx;
                    // Position x
            const y = Math.random()* (400 - 2 * ry) + ry;
                    // Position y

            const d = 'M ${x - rx},${y} A ${rx},${ry}
          ${xAxisRotation} ${largeArcFlag} ${sweepFlag}
                                    ${x + rx},${y}';
            return d;
        }

        for (let i = 0; i < 50; i++) {
            let path = document.createElementNS(svgNS,
                                            'path');
            path.setAttribute('d', randomArc());
            path.setAttribute('fill', 'url(#gradient)');
            path.setAttribute('filter', 'url(#dropshadow)');
            svg.appendChild(path);
        }
    </script>
</svg>
</body>
</html>
```

Explanation of the Code
SVG Container:
The <svg> element sets up a container for the arcs, with a width of 600 and a height of 400.

Radial Gradient and Drop Shadow Definitions:
A <radialGradient> and a <filter> for the drop shadow are defined within the <defs> element. The gradient transitions from light blue to blue, and the filter applies a Gaussian blur and offset to create a shadow effect.

JavaScript for Arc Generation:
The <script> tag contains JavaScript to dynamically generate elliptic arcs.
The randomArc function creates a random SVG path command for an elliptic arc.
A loop runs fifty times, creating fifty <path> elements with random attributes.

The setAttribute method sets the path data (d), applies the radial gradient fill, and adds the drop shadow filter.

Dynamic Arc Creation:
Each iteration of the loop creates a unique elliptic arc with randomized attributes for size, position, and arc flags.
The arcs are filled with the radial gradient and have drop shadows.

When this HTML is rendered in a browser, it displays fifty unique elliptic arcs with varying sizes and positions, each filled with a radial gradient and having a drop shadow. This creates a colorful and dynamic arrangement of shapes across the SVG canvas.

Launch the Web page gpt4_svg_elliptic_arcs.html by navigating to the directory that contains this HTML Web page and then typing the following command:

```
open gpt4_svg_elliptic_arcs.html
```

After a few moments you will see the image in Figure 7.15 that displays a set of elliptic arcs.

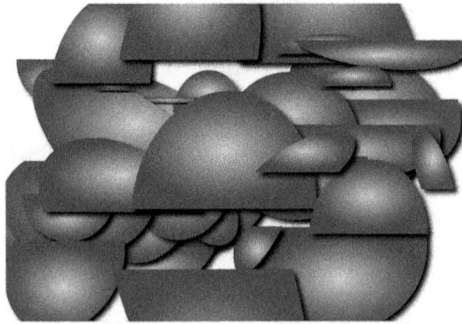

FIGURE 7.15. SVG elliptic arcs.

AN SVG CHECKERBOARD PATTERN

The following prompt was supplied to GPT-4 in order to generate SVG-based 2D transformation effects:

Please generate an HTML Web page that contains an 8x8 checkerboard pattern of red and yellow rectangles whose width is 60 and whose height is 60 that are rendered with an SVG drop shadow, along with an explanation of the code.

ChatGPT:

To create an 8x8 checkerboard pattern using SVG with red and yellow rectangles, each having a width and height of 60 units and rendered with a drop shadow, you can use the following HTML and SVG code. This code will create a checkerboard by alternating the colors of the rectangles in an 8x8 grid and applying an SVG drop shadow to each rectangle.

Listing 7.17 displays the contents of gpt4_svg_checkerboard1.html that contains GPT-4-generated SVG code that performs 2D transform-based animation effects on four 2D shapes.

LISTING 7.17: gpt4_svg_checkerboard1.html

```
<!DOCTYPE html>
<html lang="en">
<head>
    <meta charset="UTF-8">
    <title>SVG Checkerboard</title>
</head>
<body>

<svg width="480" height="480"
                    xmlns="http://www.w3.org/2000/svg">
    <!-- Define a drop shadow filter -->
    <defs>
        <filter id="dropShadow" x="-20%" y="-20%"
                            width="140%" height="140%">
            <feGaussianBlur in="SourceAlpha"
                                    stdDeviation="3" />
            <feOffset dx="2" dy="2" />
            <feMerge>
                <feMergeNode />
                <feMergeNode in="SourceGraphic" />
            </feMerge>
        </filter>
    </defs>

    <!-- Create checkerboard pattern -->
    <g filter="url(#dropShadow)">
        <!-- Loop to create rectangles -->
        <!-- JavaScript to generate SVG elements is a
                    placeholder for actual SVG elements -->
        <script>
            const svgNS = "http://www.w3.org/2000/svg";
            let checkerboard = document.querySelector
                                            ('svg g');

            for (let i = 0; i < 8; i++) {
                for (let j = 0; j < 8; j++) {
                    let rect = document.
                            createElementNS(svgNS, 'rect');
                    rect.setAttribute('x', i * 60);
                    rect.setAttribute('y', j * 60);
                    rect.setAttribute('width', 60);
                    rect.setAttribute('height', 60);
                    rect.setAttribute('fill', (i + j) % 2
                            === 0 ? 'red' : 'yellow');
```

```
                    checkerboard.appendChild(rect);
            }
        }
    </script>
  </g>
</svg>

</body>
</html>
```

Explanation of the Code

SVG Container:
An <svg> element sets up an SVG container with a width and height sufficient to hold an 8x8 grid of 60x60 rectangles.

Drop Shadow Filter:
The <defs> element defines reusable components, here a filter with the ID dropShadow.
<feGaussianBlur>, <feOffset>, and <feMerge> elements create the drop shadow effect.

Checkerboard Pattern:
A <g> (group) element with the filter attribute applies the drop shadow to all its child elements.
The <script> tag contains JavaScript to dynamically create the checkerboard pattern. It loops through rows and columns, creating <rect> elements with alternating colors (red and yellow).
The setAttribute method positions each rectangle (x, y) and sets its size (width, height) and fill color.

JavaScript for Checkerboard Creation:
The JavaScript code dynamically generates the checkerboard pattern. It creates rectangles in an 8x8 grid, alternating the colors based on the sum of the row and column indices.
When this HTML page is rendered in a browser, it displays an 8x8 checkerboard pattern of red and yellow squares, each with a drop shadow effect, showcasing how SVG and JavaScript can be combined to create complex graphical patterns.

Now launch the Web page gpt4_svg_checkerboard1.html by navigating to the directory that contains this HTML Web page and then typing the following command:

```
open gpt4_svg_checkerboard1.html
```

After a few moments you will see the image in Figure 7.16 that displays an SVG-based checkerboard.

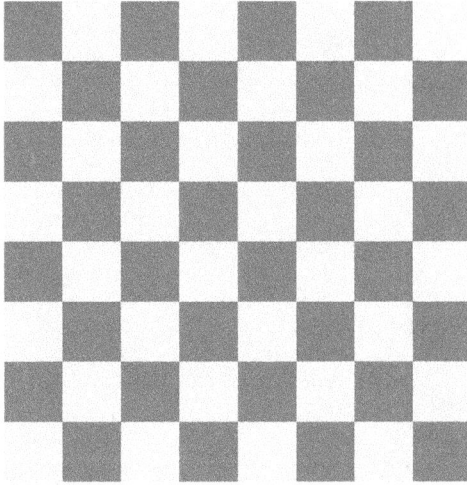

FIGURE 7.16. An SVG-based checkerboard.

AN SVG CHECKERBOARD PATTERN WITH FILTER EFFECTS

The following prompt was supplied to GPT-4 in order to generate SVG-based 2D transformation effects:

Please generate an HTML Web page that contains an 8x8 checkerboard pattern of red and yellow rectangles whose width is 60 and whose height is 60 that are rendered with an SVG blur filter and an SVG drop shadow, along with an explanation of the code.

ChatGPT:

To create an 8x8 checkerboard pattern using SVG with red and yellow rectangles, each having a width and height of 60 units and rendered with a drop shadow, you can use the following HTML and SVG code. This code will create a checkerboard by alternating the colors of the rectangles in an 8x8 grid and applying an SVG filter and an SVG drop shadow to alternating rectangles.

Listing 7.18 displays the contents of gpt4_svg_checkerboard_filter.html that contains GPT-4-generated SVG code that displays an SVG-based checkerboard with an SVG filter.

LISTING 7.18: *gpt4_svg_checkerboard_filter.html*

```
<!DOCTYPE html>
<head>
    <meta charset="UTF-8">
    <title>SVG Checkerboard with Blur and Drop
                                    Shadow</title>
```

```
    </head>
    <body>

    <svg width="480" height="480"
                        xmlns="http://www.w3.org/2000/svg">
        <!-- Define a drop shadow filter -->
        <defs>
            <filter id="dropShadow" x="-20%" y="-20%"
                                width="140%" height="140%">
                <feGaussianBlur in="SourceAlpha"
                                        stdDeviation="3" />
                <feOffset dx="2" dy="2" />
                <feMerge>
                    <feMergeNode />
                    <feMergeNode in="SourceGraphic" />
                </feMerge>
            </filter>
            <filter id="blurFilter">
                <feGaussianBlur in="SourceGraphic"
                                            stdDeviation="2" />
            </filter>
        </defs>

        <!-- Create checkerboard pattern -->
        <g filter="url(#dropShadow)">
            <!-- JavaScript to generate SVG elements is a
                        placeholder for actual SVG elements -->
            <script>
                const svgNS = "http://www.w3.org/2000/svg";
                let checkerboard = document.querySelector
                                                    ('svg g');

                for (let i = 0; i < 8; i++) {
                    for (let j = 0; j < 8; j++) {
                        let rect = document.
                                createElementNS(svgNS, 'rect');
                        rect.setAttribute('x', i * 60);
                        rect.setAttribute('y', j * 60);
                        rect.setAttribute('width', 60);
                        rect.setAttribute('height', 60);
                        rect.setAttribute('fill', (i + j) % 2
                                    === 0 ? 'red' : 'yellow');
                        rect.setAttribute('filter',
                                        'url(#blurFilter)');
                        checkerboard.appendChild(rect);
                    }
                }
            </script>
        </g>
    </svg>

    </body>
    </html>
```

Explanation of the Code

SVG Container:
An <svg> element sets up an SVG container with a width and height sufficient to hold an 8x8 grid of 60x60 rectangles.

Drop Shadow and Blur Filters:
Inside the <defs> element, two filters are defined: dropShadow and blurFilter.
The dropShadow filter uses <feGaussianBlur>, <feOffset>, and <feMerge> elements to create a drop shadow effect.
The blurFilter uses <feGaussianBlur> with a stdDeviation of 2 to create a blur effect.

Checkerboard Pattern:

A <g> (group) element applies the drop shadow to all its child elements.
The <script> tag contains JavaScript to dynamically create the checkerboard pattern. It loops through rows and columns, creating <rect> elements with alternating colors (red and yellow).
Each rectangle is assigned the blurFilter to apply the blur effect.

JavaScript for Checkerboard Creation:
The JavaScript code generates the checkerboard pattern dynamically. It creates rectangles in an 8x8 grid, alternating the colors based on the sum of the row and column indices.
Each rectangle is given a filter attribute linking it to the blurFilter for the blur effect.

When this HTML page is rendered in a browser, it displays an 8x8 checkerboard pattern of red and yellow squares, each with a drop shadow and a blur effect, demonstrating how SVG filters can be used to create visually appealing graphics.

Now launch the Web page gpt4_svg_checkerboard_filter.html by navigating to the directory that contains this HTML Web page and then typing the following command:

```
open gpt4_svg_checkerboard_filter.html
```

After a few moments you will see the image in Figure 7.17 that displays an SVG-based checkerboard pattern with an SVG filter.

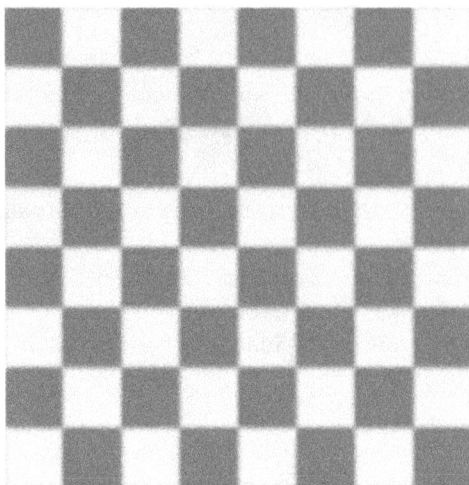

FIGURE 7.17. An SVG-based checkerboard with an SVG filter.

A MASTER-DETAIL HTML WEB PAGE

The following prompt was supplied to GPT-4 in order to create an HTML Web page that provides master-detail functionality for a list of people (based on simulated data):

Please generate an HTML Web page that displays a drop-down list of people based on simulated data, and when users click on one of the people in the drop-down list, the Web page displays the details of that user, which also involves simulated data.

ChatGPT:

Sure, I can help you with that. We'll create a simple HTML Web page with JavaScript to handle the interactive elements. Here's the general plan:
HTML: The structure will include a dropdown (select element) and a section to display user details.
JavaScript: We'll create a simulated dataset of people with details.
When a user is selected from the dropdown, a function will be triggered to display that user's details.
CSS (optional): For basic styling.

LISTING 7.19: index.html

```
<!DOCTYPE html>
<html lang="en">
<head>
```

```
        <meta charset="UTF-8">
        <title>User Details</title>
        <style>
            /* Basic Styling */
            body {
                font-family: Arial, sans-serif;
            }
            .user-details {
                margin-top: 20px;
                border: 1px solid #ddd;
                padding: 10px;
            }
        </style>
    </head>

    <body>

        <h2>Select a User</h2>
        <select id="userSelect" onchange="showUserDetails()">
            <!-- Options will be populated here -->
        </select>

        <div class="user-details" id="userDetails">
            <!-- User details will be displayed here -->
        </div>

        <script>
            // JavaScript will go here
        </script>
    </body>
    </html>
```

The following JavaScript code contains simulated data for several people, which will be placed within the <script> tags in the HTML file.

```
// Sample data
const users = [
 { id: 1, name: "Alice", age: 30, occupation: "Engineer" },
 { id: 2, name: "Bob", age: 24, occupation: "Designer" },
 { id: 3, name: "Charlie", age: 35, occupation: "Teacher" }
 // Add more users as needed
];
// Function to populate the dropdown with user names
function populateUserSelect() {
    const select = document.getElementById('userSelect');
    users.forEach(user => {
        let option = document.createElement('option');
        option.value = user.Id;
        option.textContent = user.name;
        select.appendChild(option);
    });
}

// Function to show user details
function showUserDetails() {
    const userId = document.getElementById('userSelect').value;
    const userDetails = users.find(user => user.id == userId);
```

```
        const detailsDiv = document.getElementById('userDetails');

    if (userDetails) {
        detailsDiv.innerHTML = '
            <h3>${userDetails.name}</h3>
            <p>Age: ${userDetails.age}</p>
            <p>Occupation: ${userDetails.occupation}</p>
        ';
    } else {
        detailsDiv.innerHTML = 'Select a user to see details.';
    }
}

// Initialize the dropdown on page load
window.onload = populateUserSelect;
```

Explanation
HTML provides the basic structure.
The JavaScript creates a simulated dataset of users.
When the page loads, it populates the dropdown with
usernames.
When a user is selected, their details are displayed in
the userDetails div.

This is a basic implementation. You can expand upon it by adding more details to the user dataset, improving the styling with CSS, or adding more interactive JavaScript features.

NOTE *The HTML Web page* master_detail.html *(in the companion files) contains all the necessary code that GPT-4 generated for this task.*

Now launch the Web page master_detail.html by navigating to the directory that contains this HTML Web page and then typing the following command:

```
open master_detail.html
```

After a few moments you will see the image in Figure 7.18 that displays the output that you will see when you select one of the people in the drop-down list.

Select a User

Charlie

Charlie

Age: 35

Occupation: Teacher

FIGURE 7.18. A master-detail Web page.

SUMMARY

This chapter started with a description of the strengths and weaknesses of SVG, followed by SVG use cases, SVG accessibility, and potential security issues with SVG. Then you saw examples of GPT=4 generating linear gradients, radial gradients, and various SVG 2D shapes and gradients.

Next, you learned how to render quadratic Bezier curves and cubic Bezier curves, as well as how to add animation effects for Bezier curves. In addition, you saw a comparison of SVG and CSS3 as well as a comparison of SVG and PNGs.

Then you learned how to work with SVG filters, such as blur filters and turbulence filters. You also saw code samples that combine SVG and CSS3 in an HTML Web page, as well we combine SVG and JavaScript in an HTML Web page.

Finally, you saw how to create other effects that involve JavaScript and SVG, such as rendering elliptic arts, checkerboard patterns, and also a master-detail HTML Web page that involves SVG.

Index